Education for Responsible Living

LONDON: GEOFFREY CUMBERLEGE
OXFORD UNIVERSITY PRESS

EDUCATION FOR RESPONSIBLE LIVING

---

*The Opportunity for
Liberal-Arts Colleges*

By

WALLACE BRETT DONHAM, LL.D., L.H.D.

*George Fisher Baker Professor of Administration
Graduate School of Business Administration
Harvard University*

HARVARD UNIVERSITY PRESS

Cambridge, Massachusetts

1946

COPYRIGHT, 1944
BY THE PRESIDENT AND FELLOWS OF HARVARD COLLEGE

Third Printing

PRINTED IN THE UNITED STATES OF AMERICA

*We sail a changeful sea through halcyon days and storm,
and when the ship laboreth, our stedfast purpose
trembles like as the compass in a binnacle.
Our stability is but balance, and wisdom lies
in masterful administration of the unforeseen.*

Robert Bridges, THE TESTAMENT OF BEAUTY

Contents

INTRODUCTION 3
    Forty years' experience with liberal-arts and engineering-school graduates raises questions about these institutions and their education for life.

Part I

An Appraisal

I   THE LIBERAL ARTS FACE A CHALLENGE   11
    Present liberal-arts education suffers by comparison with the concrete effectiveness of scientific and engineering training.

II   ENGINEERING TRAINING AND LIBERAL EDUCATION   17
    The narrow effectiveness of scientific and engineering training and its serious limitations magnify the opportunity and increase the need for effective liberal-arts general education.

III   THE DUAL FUNCTIONS OF THE LIBERAL-ARTS COLLEGE   27
    Specialization and general education. Confusion of purpose. General education suffers.

IV   SOURCES OF WEAKNESS IN GENERAL EDUCATION   37
    Graduate schools of arts and sciences. The elective system. Concentration and distribution. Prerequisite courses. Accrediting agencies. Specialization.

V   SCIENCE, SOCIAL SCIENCE, AND THE PRACTICAL WORLD   55
    The great dividing line of human life and experience between the practical certainties of the material world as studied by science and the rapid

change, uncertainty, human interactions which dominate social and humanistic fields and even the applications of science. Science and technology functionally related to the material world. Breakdown between social sciences and life.

VI THE UNCERTAIN WORLD IN WHICH MEN LIVE 70

The growth of spontaneous organizations adapted to deal with problems surrounded by uncertainty in practical life compared with the specialized academic approach through social sciences. Judgment and skills *vs.* principles and theory.

VII SPECIALIZATION IN PRACTICAL LIFE 82

Specialization universal in the world of affairs. Resulting dangers of narrowness. Need and opportunity for a program of general education which is redefined in terms of life's problems as men face them.

VIII ABOUT SPECIALIZATION IN THE SOCIAL SCIENCES 90

Insecure foundations for the logics of specialization. Economics and economic history as examples. Confusion between the expert and the policy maker. Place of foresight and adjustment where certainty is impossible. Necessity of dealing with concrete situations as a whole, regardless of social-science subdivisions. Dangers of academic detachment from problems as they arise.

IX HUMAN RELATIONS 100

A neglected field for research and instruction. Theory and practice almost completely divorced. Need for many clinical studies of concrete human situations. Illustrations of such studies. Obligation of the college to assist individuals in social adjustments, and to give organized instruction in human relations. Dangers of narrow intellectualism. Importance of emotions and sentiments.

THE HUMANITIES, RELIGION, AND PURPOSE 110
    Need for national purpose after the war, for greater loyalties and a higher sense of responsibility. Distinction between planning and purpose. Present necessities and distant ideals. Tasks ahead for the humanities and religion. Individual and group responsibility. The art of living together.

Part II
An Attempt to Be Specific

GENERAL EDUCATION: THE OBJECTIVES AND ORGANIZATION OF THE CURRICULUM 153
    Necessary to reconcile specialization with general education. Unity, interest, and self-discipline. Inspired teaching and effective methods. A general discussion of the curriculum.

THE FOUR-YEAR CURRICULUM IN GENERAL EDUCATION 164
    The required core of the curriculum. Mathematics. General science. Contemporary civilization. History, including art and literature. Human relations. Economics. Policy. Place of elective work. Suggestions for a transition period.

THE INDIVIDUAL—THE UNIT OF EDUCATION 214
    Group education is essential, but the individual's background, capacity, and interests should dominate the process from high school through graduate school. Better adjustment between college and graduate schools to meet individual needs is required. Admission problems, ways of fitting the college course to individual abilities, a two-year self-respecting stopping point, freer transfers among institutions, stricter selection at the end of two years, easier acceleration for able men—all these are needed.

x   CONTENTS

xiv   CONTINUOUS OPERATION   225
            Both a student and a faculty problem. Psychological need for fallow periods as an element in intellectual integration. Faculty and students need free time.

xv   VOCATIONAL TRAINING AND GENERAL
            EDUCATION   229
            Division of labor among types of institution desirable. Transfers of students. Tests for vocational subjects. Dangers and aids to general education from vocational training. Antidote to drifting.

xvi   LANGUAGES AND INTERNATIONAL UNDERSTANDING   236
            Iconoclastic suggestions for reappraisal of language study. Relationship to international understanding. Need for evening up the attention paid to civilizations now becoming vital to our future in comparison with Europe.

xvii   SUPERFICIALITY AND GENERAL EDUCATION   246
            The bogey of superficiality in general education. Inherent impossibility of avoiding superficiality. Narrow specialization as superficial as shallower breadth. Imposing difficulties of acquiring the background habits and skills necessary to grasp things in relationship with sound judgment. Relative ease of mathematical and scientific specialization.

xviii TRAINING MEN TO HANDLE PROBLEMS RESPONSIBLY   254
            Breadth of background, trained imagination, and habits and skills acquired by long and responsible practice are necessary objectives. New methods and closer touch with reality is essential. Case system one tried and successful method. Danger of carrying responsibility beyond men's

capacity. Case material. Pedagogy. Importance of the present.

XIX SCIENCE, SOCIAL SCIENCE, HUMAN RELATIONS AND THE HUMANITIES—THEIR INTERDEPENDENCE 271

Mutual dependence depends on mutual adjustments. Science long in watertight compartment; growing social difficulties resulting from its accomplishments. Need of coöperation with other fields—not by controlling their methods. Other fields need better understanding of science and its consequences. Mechanisms of contact and joint study of many problems needed. Examples.

XX ACADEMIC AUTHORITY, LEADERSHIP, AND RESPONSIBILITY 285

Can the academic world adapt itself to social change? Place and limitations of the authority of trustees and administrative officers. Faculty functions and the self-imposed limitations on faculty and administrative leadership through the development of powerful departments. Not authority but leadership must be commensurate with responsibility.

XXI IS GENERAL EDUCATION POSSIBLE? 297

Yes, but experimentation is necessary. Widespread importance and essential similarity of problems faced by leaders in great variety.

Unevenness in results. Science helps some fields like medicine. It both helps and complicates other fields like industry and government. Education varies in effectiveness in different fields. Professional schools have breadth lacking in liberal-arts colleges if appraised from student viewpoint, but they suffer from the lack of effective general education at the college level.

Difficulties of transition; group teamwork needed. Separate faculties for university colleges important. Research in General Education is a job for the Liberal-Arts college.

Germany used controlled education to support the Fascist state. Can we do less with a free educational system? Effective general education is essential to effective leadership and coöperative effort in a free democracy.

Education for Responsible Living

Introduction

THE CONSTANTLY INCREASING speed of life is the keynote to most problems now oppressing the civilized world. This is of course a collateral result of the conquests of science in the material world. Individual human beings have learned through their long evolutionary history to respond quickly to sudden changes in their physical environment. Their social responses and their social organizations have, however, been dominated through prehistory and most of history by custom and tradition. Now the same forces which speed up change in their physical environment, and the material changes themselves, bring a long train of social consequences. A scientific engineering and business triumph like the modern automobile radically changes the mode of life and social surroundings of multitudes.

Neither individual men nor their most cherished institutions are prepared by their social evolution to cope with social change on the new scale and at the new pace. They respond haltingly. Liberal democracy, for example, is well adapted to discussion, to compromise, and to setting rules of the game which control the individual so that he may be free. It is as yet badly adapted to the quick decisions and action required to deal effectively not with occasional new problems but with constant change. Totalitarianism is not solely the result of lust for power. It often appears under the mantle of democracy. It gets its opportunity sometimes in a revolution against established privilege, that is, against change that is too slow; sometimes as a method of securing a larger participation in the material progress of the world. Sometimes it is a reaction against slow and intolerably inefficient processes in a democracy. This last reaction may be a sort of creeping paralysis. It is our danger. To preserve our democracy we must improve it.

Education at collegiate levels is, through science, a powerful accelerator of social change. But, like other social institutions with a great past, it is itself bound to a large degree by its history, its customs, and its traditions. It adjusts itself slowly to the challenging problem of equipping men and our democracy to live responsibly and effectively in a rapidly changing world. If it is to do its part in developing men with the essential capacities of individual and social adaptation without which freedom must be lost in centralized controls, far-reaching changes in its own processes are necessary.

A bold educational job must be done. It should start with a fresh look at scientific and liberal-arts education in search for a better integration and balance between the two, and for methods which will, so far as may be, bring our general education to a pitch comparable in effectiveness with scientific and engineering training. Business is the main instrumentality by which science brings social changes. Since many more college graduates find careers in business and affairs, public and private, than in all other fields, and an increasing number of engineering-school graduates become business administrators rather than engineers, I have long been interested in this topic. Business, too, must learn how to adapt itself to constant shifts in its environment. It needs more help from education. Obviously, in a democracy based on mass education, the secondary schools as well as the colleges, engineering schools, and universities are involved in the educational adjustment which is required. I shall not consider the school problem, both because I lack the habitual intuitive grasp of facts which is needed and because I think improvement in the schools necessarily waits mainly on the colleges. My emphasis is on the liberal-arts college. I believe it is the key to the situation. I shall necessarily consider the engineering schools and to a minor extent the university graduate and professional schools.

The subject is not new. For some years now an active ferment has been working in many colleges looking toward diagnosis and clinical treatment of the diseases of liberal-arts general education. Many experiments have been tried and many more talked about. The mention of Chicago, St. John's, Antioch, and Bennington includes only institutions which have struggled with radical solutions of the problem. Today it is a rare college which lacks a committee actively studying it. I hope that my combined experience in business and educational administration may have some significance.

I am disturbed by the failure of all types of collegiate institutions to prepare their graduates for the inevitable but unpredictable novelty of the problems they must face in life, or to take an understanding part in meeting the needs of our democracy. I have no idea that any single statement can do much more than define the educational approach which is necessary if men are to be fitted to their environment. To find really satisfactory educational solutions, important research areas must be explored and much experience gained by trial and error. I believe, however, that real progress is possible now. My views are based on long-continued reflections about the characteristics of Western civilization and on concrete experience over a period of more than forty years with graduates of colleges and engineering schools.

Before I became Dean of the Harvard Graduate School of Business Administration, I had been in administrative charge of many liberal-arts graduates and considerable numbers of engineering-school graduates. As Dean of the Business School for the twenty-three years preceding July 1942, I had exceptional opportunity to observe, both directly and indirectly through the comments of a closely knit professional faculty, some twelve thousand graduates of about five hundred undergraduate colleges and technical schools—large and small, independent and connected with universities, privately endowed and state-supported. I followed also the careers of many such men after their graduation from the Business School and contrasted them with the careers of men I knew who entered the world of affairs direct from liberal-arts colleges.

During these twenty-three years the Business School was evolving the essential specialized training needed narrowly by the business administrator. More important, however, it was studying the functions of the business administrator, public or private, in his wider relation to the national life, and working out ways of relating its training to such functions. Business administration in a technical and immediate sense is often peculiarly efficient. It is relatively weak in its overall public relations and in its handling of human problems. The primary objective of the Harvard Business School became not so much training specialists as developing the student's capacity to examine as many of the constantly changing facts and forces surrounding administrative situations in business as he can bring effectively into his thinking, and to use these facts imaginatively in determining current policies and action. This capacity is an essential condition to socially sound performance of the administrator's most important functions. The same capacities are needed by large numbers of college graduates as citizens in a democracy. Breadth of background and the capacity to integrate many viewpoints at the point of action are, both to administrators and to citizens as such, more important than specialization. Administrators and men responsible for policy should be able to handle problems as they arise with understanding not only of their intellectual and logical aspects, but of the emotional nature of human and social reactions to the action they take. Obviously these objectives are difficult to attain. The time customarily allotted in the School, a maximum of two years, is short. What can be accomplished depends largely on the maturity and previous training of students.

There was a great variety in the undergraduate training of men who came to the School, but they fell into general classifications. College men who did not specialize in science formed the largest group. Another large fraction was made up of graduates of schools of technology. To them I add college graduates who specialized in natural science. I class this latter group of college graduates with graduates of technical schools because in their assets and limitations they have more resemblance to graduates of technical schools than they have to other liberal-arts graduates. In recent years technical school graduates and liberal-arts graduates who specialized in science made up about 20 per cent of the student body of the Business School and other graduates of liberal-arts colleges about 50 per cent. The rest were mainly graduates of undergraduate business schools who had taken two years of liberal-arts training along with or before their undergraduate business training. I am here concerned primarily with the first two of these three groups.

Inevitably I appraised the strengths and weaknesses resulting from each type of training and formulated certain general conclusions about the institutions themselves both as preparation for work in the Business School and as final stages in the organized educational process of fitting men to live in contemporary society. I am of course aware of the wide diversity in these institutions. Exceptions will be found to all general statements. Moreover, I intend no criticism of individuals teaching in any of them. I am interested in the patterns into which education at collegiate levels falls—patterns so fixed in their outline that the individual is almost powerless except as he fits into them. My thesis is a plea for a new pattern in general education.

Part I

An Appraisal

CHAPTER I

The Liberal Arts Face a Challenge

LONG BEFORE the present emergency there was clear evidence that the liberal-arts colleges were out of step with changing social conditions. Many had begun to raise serious question. Parents and thoughtful students alike complained of four years spent in not-too-hard intellectual effort, "bull sessions," organized athletics and social events, play as a major objective, long summer vacations—all valuable but leading nowhere; and all at the age when New England boys of a century ago were officers of ships that scoured the seven seas and when other young Americans were opening new country to the westward. Students themselves are not so contented as they used to be. They are full of questions about things formerly taken on faith. They feel too much detached from real things. Frequently they are at loose ends. Uncertainty, loneliness, discontent, obsessive thinking, and neuroses afflict large numbers, particularly in the big city colleges. These difficulties are far more frequent than they were when I entered college nearly fifty years ago from a small town and a small-town high school. Many graduates feel that the four years, often four happy years, they spent in college led nowhere.

Nevertheless it took the war, the Army Specialized Training Program, and the Navy V-12 Program to bring the whole structure and objectives of liberal education under active reconsideration in most colleges. That part of the educational world primarily interested in the social sciences and the humanities was severely shocked by these programs. Professors themselves had no difficulty in understanding why competent mature research men in chemistry, physics, and mathematics are especially useful in war. Victory or defeat may well be determined by the effectiveness of scientific research and its applications. Obviously, long training and experience are essential before men can do such research effectively.

It is quite another thing that the Services intent on the sole problem of winning the war—and to this end, in part at least, on selecting candidates with a capacity for leadership —required men to take almost exclusively subject matter customary in the early stages of engineering training and showed little or no interest in the rest of the liberal-arts curriculum. Many observers question whether elementary scientific training carries men to the point where they can make effective use of the subject matter. They know that neither physics, chemistry, nor mathematics, to say nothing of thermodynamics or the theory of electricity, is understood by the multitude of American youths who not only operate but keep in condition automobiles and other mechanical devices. They know that American industry utilizes a multitude of men who operate and maintain complex machines and control functions and processes in factories through scientific instruments. If the notion was that for all men the instruction must be immediately practical, I personally would see more reason for courses aimed to develop manual dexterity and skills in operating and maintaining complex machinery—that is, for "know how" courses —than I do for the basic requirement of elementary instruction in subjects like mathematics, physics, and chemistry.

I suspect that the narrow emphasis came not because the Services think elementary science essential as part of the training of all officers, but because they see little value for their purposes in the training through which liberal-arts colleges put men who do not specialize in science. On the other hand, they are convinced of the value of engineering training.

Most engineering-school students seem to work harder and acquire a greater sense of personal accomplishment than the general run of college students. Their work is concrete, definite, and seems to offer a satisfactory way of life. Realization of limitations, if it comes at all, usually comes later. Even when the Services used liberal-arts colleges, these facts superficially justified emphasis on subjects appropriate in the first year of engineering schools. Yet qualities of human leadership, of trained imagination in dealing with the unexpected emergency, of elasticity of mind and of judgment, are perhaps least effectively developed, whether in the liberal-arts college or in the engineering school, by studying the certainties of elementary science and mathematics.

Regardless of results, and it is too early to appraise these, the Army and Navy programs have done a great service by arousing interest in self-examination by the colleges. The war has focused our attention on the plain question whether existing liberal-arts training fails in comparison with the concrete effectiveness of scientific and engineering training as preparation for life in an age which science seems to dominate. This question should be settled on a long look ahead, not on a war basis. Does scientific and engineering training meet the needs of contemporary civilization? And if not, what are its limitations? What is the place of liberal-arts general education, and does it occupy this place? Are men graduating from liberal-arts colleges and entering active life well equipped to deal with the problems they will meet in life? In the present situation vested interests are weaker than in normal times. Many are in a mood to explore new avenues toward educating youth. As military-training courses disappear, which they are rapidly doing, teachers will have time to work on building new teaching material and new courses. This is in fact a unique opportunity to make a fresh start. But where shall we go?

The answers to such questions involve some analysis of the present state of civilization, and the tasks which modern youth must face in our democracy. Surely, high among the aims of education is the training of men to take a significant part directly or indirectly in the purposeful activities of their times. Indeed, this is its primary function. It is especially important in a democracy. The search for knowledge and understanding for their own sakes is a high objective which, happily, attracts a small proportion of our finest minds; but most men need understanding which they can use in meeting life's everyday problems. The difference between the pure scientist seeking to expand our knowledge of nature, without thought so far as he is concerned for the usefulness of his discoveries, and the hermit meditating in solitude on the nature of God, lies in the fact that the discoveries of the scientist are often made useful in unpredictable ways by lesser or more practical-minded men. "If knowledge is not useful, what is it?" To be useful, it must contribute to inner contentment or to purposeful activity related to contemporary problems of Western civilization. Otherwise it is sheer pedantry. Ideally the college should make both types of contribution. In its scientific work it does this. To make a contribution in social and humanistic fields comparable in effectiveness with its scientific training and that of the engineering schools, it must fit its work not only to the accomplishments but to the limitations of specialized training in pure and applied science, and in a broad sense to the accomplishments and limitations of science and engineering themselves. It must relate its liberal-arts work aggressively to present-day and even future problems by redefining and ordering its own job in ways which give students seeking a general education an understanding not only of science and engineering but of the limitations on these subjects. In other fields it must equip them better for life. If it meets these objectives effectively, it will accomplish great results. But college education does not do this now, and I believe cannot without radical changes.

Our democracy is strong in specialized progress and weak both in general direction and in the ability to work together. To some extent this is the necessary cost of individual freedom and initiative. But clearly we have lost balance. Too many things are done shortsightedly—not viciously, as the devil-hunters would have us believe, but because men do not understand or stop to consider the longer-time social implications of their activities. Too many reforms are instituted by government to meet immediate problems with no conception of the stresses and strains the reforms will inevitably bring and no watchfulness to offset their unforeseen consequences. We are too slow in adapting ourselves socially to the emergencies which arise in a rapidly changing world.

Countless illustrations could be given. I select a few so serious in their implications that they threaten the whole structure of our democracy. We desire peace, but our whole social structure has been shaken by two wars—world wars of a new kind based on science. In spite of our scientific and technological proficiency we were almost completely unprepared. We prided ourselves on being an asylum for all comers, but we admitted multitudes faster than we could assimilate them, and racial tensions were never so acute. We have the fewest class distinctions of any great nation, but group hatreds have been inspired and utilized for political purposes. Our industries are the envy of the world, but in our triumphant use of technology we have too often forgotten human beings. We have devised gadgets to meet most material wants and desires of men, but we do not give enough thought to their effect on the family and the neighborhood. All such problems require skilled coördinated thinking and an understanding of human behavior. If our general direction is to improve, we require generally educated men to offset the dangers of specialized progress and particularly the pace of change which results from scientific accomplishments.

CHAPTER II

Engineering Training and Liberal Education

IN MY EXPERIENCE, engineering-school graduates and college men who specialize in natural science have one side of their training carried to the point where its very strength creates serious limitations. Other graduates of liberal-arts colleges usually lack the clear-cut assets of the scientific and technically trained men but are freer from their particular limitations. Of course, I am speaking of typical men, or to be more accurate, I am generalizing from forty years of direct experience and uncounted conversations with and about men trained in each way.

Engineering Training

The graduate trained on the scientific side in either college or technical school has a better capacity than other liberal-arts graduates to examine facts in his field, and he has the habit of looking at them. His mind seems better disciplined. His difficulty is the narrowness of his point of view. For him, the material world is abstracted from human life. The fact that interests him is the fact that stays put, that recurs, that can be weighed and measured. He is at home with scientific methods which in the material world give assured results from assured measurements, logics, and mathematics. On the other hand, he is disturbed by the confusion of facts as they occur in other aspects of life. He resents, often explicitly, the necessity of formulating judgments in important situations when many significant facts are not only unknown but perhaps unknowable and few can be weighed or measured. A new professor in the Business School once ended his first hour of teaching with a summary statement of his own views on a problem, but went on to say that the senior professor who was in charge of another section completely disagreed with him. A student in the back row hastily gathered his papers together and when class was adjourned rushed to the desk, saying, "I object. I came here to learn business and the very first hour I am told that two professors disagree. I object." In less dramatic form the point of view is widespread. The student's capacity for thinking outside mathematical and scientific categories has been stunted rather than developed. He has not learned how to look at life except within blinders and he is oversure in the use of his conclusions. He is inclined to take it for granted that a conclusion logically reached on an adequate technological basis should *ipso facto* be ordered into effect. He rarely stops to consider that both his own and his friends' behavior is to a large extent unpredictable and that the technical situation which he sees so clearly is surrounded by uncertainty. Even when he recognizes that his engineering methods cover only part of the situation, he generally assumes that this part of the whole will dominate and that human behavior and other factors will adjust themselves to the technological objectives. His training goes a long way toward unfitting him to bring into his thinking the human or social facets of life, or to deal wisely with uncertainties.

There is little realization of the confusion and ineptitude in dealing with social questions which result from the all but complete elimination of liberal-arts general training from engineering education. This, of course, comes about from the pressure of strictly engineering knowledge which is immediately useful to the graduate. With the great development of applied science this pressure increases constantly. Even when other work is offered, it seems to the student secondary to the concrete knowledge he gets in his engineering courses. In the past, some accrediting agencies have opposed broadening the base of engineering training, as professional groups have sometimes opposed broadening the base of professional training. Yet, although technical engineering is the career for which most engineering courses directly fit men, outstanding success in life is not usually attained through this approach. Success more often comes either through distinguished research work or through a transition to industrial management. Men in both these types of careers need breadth of vision not given by the present curricula of engineering schools.

Three separate groups are therefore the end-products of engineering training—technical engineers, research scientists, and industrial managers. A large percentage of graduates make factory management a career and, conversely, as President Compton has pointed out, a heavy percentage of our leading industrial managers are graduates of engineering schools. The problem of adjusting to these diverse objectives is difficult because the school cannot in most cases know in advance the direction toward which men will develop. The worth-while things which can be taught in science and engineering make minute specialization a present danger. I am told that some schools train over one hundred different kinds of engineers. Nevertheless, present methods and distribution of time in engineering schools give excellent technological results. This makes sufficient change at once hard to accomplish and more necessary. The very success of technological training presents its greatest danger.

As one encouraging fact, engineering administration has recently become recognized as a distinct field because so many graduates enter factory management. Such a program, though necessarily less thorough on the technical side, can be made broader, more effective, and less limiting for the engineer intending to go into administrative work. It should be possible to make men more aware of the limitations on the engineering point of view and to break down, at least partially, their rigid modes of thought. It will be hard, however, to make them tolerant of novel human and social points of view which should modify engineering conclusions. Yet in human affairs 2 plus 2 is 3 or 5 more often than it is 4. The improvement of the social situation in a factory may be far more important than a new machine or even inconsistent with it. The social consequences of near-sighted factory policies are far reaching. There is danger, of course, that such programs in engineering administration may attract the weaker men under the false assumption, easily justified by the way things may be taught, that the new field is easier. The chief advantage of coöperative programs combining academic and factory work as developed by Dean Schneider at Cincinnati seems to be that the practical half of the work tempers the certainties of the subject matter taught and at least introduces human factors which must be taken into account. Schools of technology are conscious of these problems, and some progress is being made toward programs of wider scope. When all is said and done, however, engineering training still remains specialized training. Perhaps in the nature of things it must be too narrowly technical with too short a base line to meet the need if we are to restore balance. The training now given may easily hamper men if their interests and abilities carry them out of technical engineering into other fields. Four years is too short a time to prepare for all three types of careers. In spite of current efforts to broaden the curricula in some schools for some men, I fear that engineering schools will continue to do more to weaken than they do to strengthen general direction.

The job of a graduate school of business administration in dealing with engineering graduates who choose to go into industrial management is to destroy their sense of certainty, to force them to think of relationships, to make them form judgments where no one can be sure. It must illustrate by a wide variety of actual instances or cases, which they must face responsibly, the range and importance of activities where men must act on such judgments. Indeed, these men must learn that most problems in life require responsible judgments. Before such men are equipped to deal with any but narrow technical problems they must appreciate the limitations on the scientific approach, and, by a slow process involving long practice, acquire skill and experience in making commonsense judgments leading to decision and action in novel situations where a great variety of imponderables must be considered. They must come to realize the importance of human relations and the necessity of guarding their judgments and action against the unknown and the unknowable while constantly adjusting their plans and their action to changing conditions. The ideal is approached when they can keep their habit of looking at facts but learn to bring into their judgments greatly increased numbers and types of facts and factors—certain and uncertain, known and unknown—including human beings and their behavior.

In practice, of course, many men trained in engineering direct their activities toward industrial management without taking organized administrative training either in the engineering school or in a graduate school. When such men reach positions of authority without overcoming the limitations of their engineering training, their narrowness may have serious consequences. The overwhelming emphasis on material process in their training intensifies some of the most imposing social problems we face, e.g. the labor problem. If technical training is not broadened so that men realize the limits of scientific methodologies and so that they acquire, with less instinctive opposition, habits and skills based on more generalized points of view; if they do not come to appreciate intuitively that the engineering logic of production is only a part of the total human and social problem involved in production, the narrow training of many industrial managers will continue to be dangerous. "The folly of intelligent people, clearheaded and narrow-visioned, has precipitated many catastrophes."

The Liberal-Arts Task

Surely, and particularly in view of the present narrow efficiency of schools of technology, one of the greatest tasks and opportunities of the liberal-arts colleges is to train many men through a sound general education to breadth of background and viewpoint, wide grasp of relationships, and the habits and skills essential for sound judgments. Unfortunately, the colleges fail in nearly all cases to accomplish these things. Success depends not on defense of the liberal-arts tradition in a series of unsuccessful rear-guard actions, always aspects of retreat, but on searching self-criticism and aggressive attacks on the problem. Conceived in the largest setting, I believe the main task of the college is to see that men seeking general education rather than specialized training actually get it. This requires different methods and a different content than are now available, and it requires a clarification of the purpose of general education.

General education in the colleges needs to be so developed that teachers—and, so far as may be, students—get a better grasp of the intricacies of human behavior and human society and the difficulties presented by a changing world.

Students need to achieve a sense of power in the constructive and responsible use of their capacities as they meet novel problems. They do not get this sense of power from absorbing the most brilliant lectures. When these things are achieved we shall have less of the irresponsible cynical criticism so general in the colleges between the two wars, and more sympathy with mistakes of judgment. There will be better realization of the difference between easy appraisal by hindsight and the difficult choice among alternative policies which is necessary when, in spite of inadequate knowledge of past and present, men compelled to prophesy must project action into the uncertain future. We must make clear the dangers involved in applying present tests to past performances. The process of general education must require value judgments about current problems from both student and teacher, and give practice in bringing the experience of the past to bear on them. Of course, past experience cannot settle present problems, for the conditions are never identical; but it can illuminate thought and judgment both by its similarities and by its contrasts. In discussions designed to help formulate such judgments, men should be expected to use their other college work and their personal experience and background. No effort should be made to restrict discussion to those facts which chance to fall within some arbitrarily selected academic field or book. Life is not that way. We must remember that the only time men act responsibly is in the present, but that tomorrow's present will be different. The invaluable part of our training will lie in the development of background and imaginative habits and skills which men can use to face new problems as they meet them in the future.

We have not learned to use machinery wisely, nor do we understand how to deal with the lessened hold of religion or the growth of materialistic concepts. These facts constantly present new problems. Regardless of the stage on which men play their parts, be it large or small, such problems require skilled general thinking based on constant study of the flux in pertinent facts seen in wide perspective. Men must come to realize the importance of preserving the essentials of orderly social organization and the capacity to co-operate not only in a national or institutional sense but in the smaller parts of the whole where most of us are involved —the family, the town, or the factory. Social order on all scales must be conceived as a moving equilibrium. Since flux and uncertainty are inevitable, men can secure the necessary understanding only if they feel confident that many things can be treated as persistent factors and concentrate their attention on appraising the impact of changing elements. The current national interest in security, even at the expense of adventure, without which security in our democracy is in the long run impossible, clearly indicates that we have lost balance between the things which are sure and the things which are uncertain.

The problem of equilibrium in society is similar to that presented by Dr. Cannon in *The Wisdom of the Body*.[1] He discusses many ways in which the body mechanisms serve to keep the processes essential to human life varying within almost fixed limits. If—either because of too great changes in the external environment, or through disease, i.e. changes in the internal environment—these limits are passed, death, i.e. chaos, quickly follows. Social changes that are too rapid or too extreme similarly threaten civilization and bring about revolutionary changes toward autocracy as a way of avoiding chaos. We have too few social mechanisms of adjustment to changing conditions. Freedom may be a self-limiting process unless we maintain an essential degree of equilibrium. The

[1] Walter B. Cannon, *The Wisdom of the Body* (W. W. Norton & Company, 1932).

liberal-arts college should develop the capacity for understanding and adaptation to change and give to it order and objectives. In the study of relationships, neither objectives nor conclusions can be determined by fixed principles. Generalizations must change with changing facts, and facts are in constant flux. At best, therefore, most generalizations are only "currently useful" as guides to conduct. The college will accomplish most if it inculcates habits of thought and so thoroughly develops skills in searching out and handling facts that these habits and skills last through life as a basis for understanding new situations. Now, for most men, liberal education stops on Commencement Day.

Every advance made by science brings a greater need for men capable of keen incisive action with reference to successive novel situations. Every such advance of science presents a more important need, a more obvious opportunity for liberal-arts colleges. Their contribution must be powerful enough to balance the convincing demonstration seen all around us that science and scientific training, conceived as narrowly as they conceive themselves, accomplish much in important and obvious but material ways. They must show students the catastrophic consequences of the resulting overemphasis on material progress. It is too bad that, instead of thoughtful analysis leading to such affirmative demonstration of useful values, the liberal-arts colleges have so generally taken the easy attitude of disclaiming any intent or desire to be useful—truly a pathetic defeatist attitude for the custodians of the highest values and those most critically needed in the whole range of education and civilization.

I believe general education is the most important opportunity open to the liberal-arts college. It is the job of training men so that they have and use effectively in everyday affairs the qualities of leadership and the influence which educated men should possess. It is a large part of the job of making our democracy work. The liberal-arts college is the place for it. It alone reaches many selected men. It is the terminal point in the training of many and the source from which the professional and graduate schools draw nearly all their students. Can the liberal-arts college modify itself and develop new methods and approaches to meet this challenge? I believe it can.

CHAPTER III

The Dual Functions of the Liberal-Arts College

OUR COLLEGES, universities, and engineering schools serve scientific and other specialties well. But in the important aspects of social life where men of general education are needed, not only the engineering schools—where it might have been expected—but the colleges fail us. In their liberal-arts work the colleges have substituted unrelated specialties for general training instead of making general education the core of their work. They have specialized on specialization in a multitude of subjects instead of using specialties to aid general education. The opportunity of choosing a few courses out of a thousand does not assure the student a general education. Rather, in the ignorance which he entered college to reduce, it adds to his confusion and makes almost impossible a selection of courses out of which he can attain the grasp of relationships vital in his later life.

It is easy to see sources of confusion. One lies in the dual functions, both important, undertaken by the liberal-arts college. In one of its functions it uses about half of its four years giving future specialists a long head-start on vocational work which is to be completed in the schools of medicine or in the graduate schools of arts and sciences. In this two-year period, it also prepares students for undergraduate professional schools. Of course all these men need as good a foundation of general education as their limited time will allow, but they rarely get it. Such education should stimulate them to think of things outside their special fields in relation to their chosen specialties and thereby lessen the dangers of narrowness. In its other aspect, the college has the function of giving effective general education to men who wish to use the whole college course for this purpose rather than to use a large part for vocational specialization. Four years is not too long to accomplish this task.

This duality has introduced great confusion of purpose, aim and method into the college curriculum, as a result of which general education suffers. Specialization has almost completely driven out integrated general education. This is serious. The modern world has attained great success through effective specialization, particularly in pure and applied science and mathematics. Unfortunately, a similar proportion of the retreat toward chaos in Western civilization is the result of failure to balance by breadth and understanding the uneven results produced by specialization and especially by the uncertain and materialistic effects of scientific progress.

Most college specialization is just as vocational as engineering training. Indeed the sharp contrast between liberal education and vocational education so much emphasized by many colleges is historically and contemporaneously untrue. Our liberal-arts colleges have always been largely, if not mainly, vocational schools. I use the word vocational, I think properly, to include all training for carving out a career and making a living. I therefore include those vocations usually referred to as professions. All except the independently wealthy have a basic motivation which is directly related to these objectives. My own alma mater, Harvard, in its early days not only trained men for the ministry but provided a severe intellectual discipline which, under the simpler conditions of those days, qualified men to enter apprenticeships in the counting house, at the bar, in medicine, and in politics. During the intervening years Harvard College was a training school for teachers and gave an effective background for apprenticeship in affairs. Today it trains many secondary-school teachers, takes most men who become college or university professors through the first part of their specialized training for teaching and research in our universities and colleges, gives premedical training, and in all major sciences gets men well started toward jobs in industry. All such students think of their work in vocational terms. They are a large fraction of the student body. Yet, except as it emphasizes preparation for medicine and for college teaching, Harvard University pays less attention to vocational objectives than almost all other universities and a large percentage of liberal-arts colleges. The trend toward more vocational work is strong nearly everywhere. The state universities, city universities, and many colleges train for a great variety of vocations outside those long included in the liberal-arts tradition. The only large group of men in our colleges who are not now being trained vocationally are those seeking a general education but getting instead a diffuse and uncorrelated mélange of courses, never tied together except in some special field.

When the college gives specialized training to miscellaneous groups who start vocational training as undergraduates it has a real responsibility to lessen so far as possible the dangers of narrowness for such men. It takes this responsibility lightly. It does little more to offset the dangers than the school of technology. One result is many narrowly trained college teachers. Of course, it is often necessary and desirable that the early stages of specialized training for academic vocations should be given in the college. Obviously, also, in most cases such training cannot be finished in four undergraduate years. The danger, particularly in the large endowed universities, is that the specialist may start his training so early and concentrate his interest on the special field so completely that he never understands his own self-imposed limitations or the relations of his specialty to other aspects of civilization.

Narrowness is especially dangerous in college teachers, in the professions, and for able men entering the world of affairs, public or private. One brilliant college professor of science recently lamented the current interest in vitalizing the liberal-arts curriculum in social science and the humanities and dismissed these subjects with the remark that they are a futile waste of time which might be spent in studying really useful subjects in mathematics and science. Surely this is an unfortunate viewpoint, but it emphasizes the need that liberal-arts education shall itself be more useful. In the professions, lawyers—particularly because men so generally enter politics from the law—need breadth of background and perspective which will make them aware of the dangers of fixing by law segments of complex changing situations, the necessity of constant watchfulness for unexpected results, and at the same time the dangers of government by men.

Similar dangers exist when men intending careers in the world of affairs start professional training at the end of two years, or specialize vocationally in a large part of their college work. If such dangers are to be minimized, the liberal-arts college must realize its function as the custodian of general values in our educational system and attack the necessary educational job effectively, not only for the man who intends to spend his whole college life gaining a general education, but in so far as it can in a limited time, for the man who cuts the period short to take specialized vocational training. Whenever the liberal-arts college allows competent students to undertake specialization in one aspect of the material or social world so early and so intensely that other facets of civilization are ignored or driven out of mind, to this extent it gives up its liberal birthright and becomes a technical school. It does a disservice particularly to the able student and a disservice to the nation.

The primary justification of a liberal-arts college should be, not that through some of the student's work it prepares him to make a living, but that through other parts of his work it contributes to keen, incisive and disciplined general understanding. It is doubtful whether two standard academic years of general education or its equivalent will be enough to accomplish the desirable result when it is followed in the next two years by intense vocational specialization. Every effort should, however, be made to do this as far as it is possible in two years. Otherwise, graduates who, by the accidents of fate, find themselves in positions of wide administrative responsibility in private life or in public service, or as university professors in some special field, may find it difficult to broaden their base lines and pick up neglected factors. Private administrators so trained will be slow to recognize the importance of breadth of vision. College professors who started training for their special fields with heavy undergraduate concentration will find it hard to see their narrow specialties in a philosophical setting. They may be well trained to give specialized instruction, but they will be badly equipped so far as their college work goes to take part in the general education of youth.

Unfortunately, general education as now given, even to those using the whole four years for this purpose, is not adequate. It is diffuse and as a whole uncorrelated, though men are usually required to concentrate a large part of their training in some restricted field. When a student is under high-grade teachers he may get both interest and discipline. Nevertheless, he rarely sees any unity in his college course or any real relationship to life except in his restricted field.

One able young man, a graduate of one of our fine small colleges, now on the professorial staff of Harvard University, commented to me recently that he concentrated in history in college but that not once could he remember having any aspect of history discussed in terms of its bearing on his life or on current problems. Accordingly, regardless of minimum standards at the bottom and the bait of possible collegiate honors at the top, interest is apt to be lukewarm. This statement does not apply so generally in state universities, where a long array of immediately practical courses are offered, but it applies to much of their work. Nor am I advocating a great expansion of immediately practical courses. I think we already have too many such courses in some universities and colleges. I fear a stampede to such subjects in many independent liberal-arts colleges after the war, including a stampede to science based on student recognition that science is a great factor in winning the war. Youth may fail to realize that winning the peace requires wiser leadership in other fields.

The failure of college training to inculcate useful habits and skills in generalized thinking and action is the inevitable result of its failure at any point in the student's career to pose problems so general that no specialized course or subject taught gives the basis for sound judgments. As a result, he thinks in watertight compartments and gets little concept of life's problems as processes involving many interrelated forces. If he acquires habits and skills useful in meeting complex new conditions it is usually in spite of, not because of, his training.

Specialized courses of instruction deal with intellectually separated periods or parts of the social process, with little effort to inform the student of wider relationships. The case system of instruction—where problems drawn from life, and reported with an effort to show the variety of pertinent facts, are the center of instruction—is rarely if ever used, though it has revolutionized professional education in medicine, law, and, in our experience, in business. Tutorial and preceptorial systems go part way, for they force the integration of specialized courses and reading into a wider grasp of things, but unfortunately the integration is limited to the particular field and its most obvious surroundings. Indeed, when the student is allowed or required under rules for concentration to work in more than one field, these combinations are usually allowed not because the fields are diverse but because there is close, obvious connection between them. Too often, also, particularly in universities with large graduate schools of arts and sciences, the tutor or preceptor is himself seeking a Ph.D. and therefore intensifying his own specialization. In the nature of things, such men may find it difficult to give a generalized point of view even within the field.

Many, if not most, college students take part or all of their work as preparation for making a living. Why, so long as this is true, should any college take pride that students who come seeking a general education leave without securing any education which equips them with background habits and skills useful in either living or making a living? Men seeking a four-year general education have decided to postpone vocational training in its narrow sense. It does not follow that the general education should be useless in the large fraction of a man's life spent in earning a living. Properly given, it could be of the greatest value. Progress toward wider responsibilities always involves the capacity to take new factors into account, to fit them into other factors, and to handle novel situations without being tied down by conclusions previously reached under different conditions. Sound general education should prepare men for growth. The vocational training of specialists is the special task of our schools of technology and of graduate or professional departments of our universities. In some important aspects it is the task of our state universities. Considered by the test of social importance, it is at this time in history the lesser of the dual functions undertaken by the college. The college, whether it is independent or connected with a university, should not forget or minimize general education. If it is to serve Western civilization as it can and should, it will give primary attention to this part of its work.

The job of a school of administration in dealing with liberal-arts college graduates who did not concentrate in science is to offset their diffuse training by focusing their minds on studying in relationship facts pertinent to specific problems at hand, by developing their capacity to bring in imaginative new points of view which modify old ones, and by leading them progressively to the point where more and more facts and wider relationships come within their powers. The need is dramatized by the confusion of mind, resulting from the rapid social changes of the last fifteen years, which has stultified so many college men in business.

We have learned at the Business School by experience in doing it that college graduates can be trained by practice in the habits and skills and imaginative grasp which will enable them to handle novel situations with good judgment as they meet them later in life. We unfortunately know also by experience and observation that most men come to us with no well-rounded understanding of great types of human thought and experience and no skill in bringing them usefully to bear on new situations. This is true in general, regardless of whether the courses they took in college had a scope and diversity to which one might have looked for a rounded background. They almost never see the segments of their background in any related unity. They have acquired no habits of searching out cross-bearings from subject to subject, and no skills in formulating wide judgments. Their grasp of human problems is slight. Like Solomon, they need an understanding heart, but the college has rarely given it to them. Yet we have learned from experience that effective training in human relations can be given. "They are overladen with inert ideas." In the phrase so often used by teachers in a graduate professional school, liberal-arts graduates have not learned to think.

If general education does not do these things at least reasonably well, what does it do? In my observation, the liberal-arts graduate who stops with the A.B. and enters active life in many cases faces pathetic problems. Somehow he feels his training ought to prepare him to do a better job in life but, judged by the difficulties of making a real start and the drifting process through which he frequently goes, it does not. Some colleges seem to glory in this fact. It is frequently stated that liberal-arts training gives cultural values, trains men for life; not to make a living. But cultural values fly out the window when men can't get and hold jobs, and little self-respect remains if they can't make a living. The gaps now left are too wide even for the ablest men. The ability to apprehend facts in their constantly shifting relationships without education directed toward this objective comes slowly if it comes at all. None of the essential skills can be acquired except by practice.

I do not advocate emphasis on vocational training for men of quality who seek a general education. Quite the reverse. For practically all other men, college education is in large part directly vocational. Certainly in view of its basic objectives, general education should stay general, but I repeat that this does not mean it should be useless or even that it should include no work of direct vocational value. I am asking recognition of the fact that diffuse training, tempered in part by narrow specialization, is badly designed to give men the control of their own minds which they need,—for responsible living in the constantly changing world, for lasting cultural values, for making a living, or even for the continuance of self-education. Is it strange that for most liberal-arts men, education, so conceived, stops on Commencement Day? Why continue a process which has such thin values? Yet many engineers continue to study their fields. This is because they use their education. In view of the rapid advance of science, such men realize that if their education is to continue useful they must keep it up to date. Similarly, able lawyers, doctors, and professors continue to study their fields. In contrast, few men who choose the so-called general education ever use it effectively in the activities of life. This should not be so. General education in liberal-arts colleges should lead many to seek—and use—breadth so long as they live. If general education were well carried out, many men would keep the habit of searching for a general grasp of things in spite of continuous change. They would find that it made them more effective. They would keep the skills they acquired in college and develop them further. Their educations would be functionally related to their lives. Such men would contribute much toward bringing our general direction up to the quality of accomplishments in special fields. Liberal-arts colleges and liberal-arts graduates that can make such contributions are critically needed.

CHAPTER IV

Sources of Weakness in General Education

IN CONTRAST with the useful but narrow training of schools of technology and with the success of many professional schools in finding methods of integrating wide fields, we find in the liberal arts and humanities methodologies and specialties badly related to general education; confused thinking, floods of ideals not related to practical conditions, emphasis on logics and principles in spite of constant change and uncertainty in facts, neglect of human problems. Clearly the liberal-arts college fails in its job of general education unless it increases the capacity of men to live together co-operatively, improves their ability to see shifting facts in wide relationships, and enables them to implement their ideals and attain their objectives more effectively as they go about the business of life.

In the last fifty years, in spite of great progress in special fields, I suspect that the colleges have done a less satisfactory job of general education than at earlier periods. The most important single reason is the growing complexity of problems arising out of the increasing speed of change. However, several developments inside the universities and colleges have weakened general education, not only in relation to the need, but absolutely. All lead to narrow efficiency. First is the development in the universities of powerful and highly successful graduate schools of arts and sciences with almost exclusive emphasis on specialization. Second, the general adoption by the colleges of the elective system in some form. Before the war, in spite of varied limitations, a large choice of student electives was almost universally offered. Third, the requirement of fields of concentration as a mode of offsetting the unfortunate impact of the wide open elective system. Fourth, the development of more and more departments, each responsible for smaller and smaller specialized fields. Fifth, prerequisite courses. Outside accrediting agencies of many types add to the difficulties created by these internal developments. All intensify the trend toward specialization.

The Influence of the Graduate Schools

In the last half-century or more, the liberal-arts colleges have been greatly influenced if not dominated by university graduate schools of liberal arts. In this respect they differ radically from schools of technology, though it will be interesting to observe the long-time effects on its undergraduate work of the great graduate research institute of the Massachusetts Institute of Technology. A graduate school of arts and sciences with a well-organized plan of operation was founded at Johns Hopkins in 1876. Similar advanced studies were superimposed on Harvard College beginning in 1872. These studies were not formally organized into the Graduate School of Arts and Sciences until 1890. The same faculty controlled both the College and the Graduate School. Prior to 1872–76, American scholars who sought highly specialized training went to the German universities which had already developed intense specialization. Most of the older professors, however, had a less specialized background. Within comparatively few years after 1876, many American universities expanded the college faculties and started graduate training, mainly on the German university pattern.

More and more college teachers were trained at home. Specialties proliferated in these graduate schools, not only in the natural sciences but also in other fields. Standards improved in special fields, but general education was completely lost in the processes of subdivision. In some universities the interest of the best-trained and most distinguished members of the faculty, all of them specialists, focused on the graduate school rather than in the college. Indeed the dividing lines between the college and the graduate schools —except in discipline and athletics—became more and more blurred, to the disadvantage of the college. Many courses designed for specialized graduate students were opened to undergraduates, who were thus tempted to early specialization. A like tendency has appeared at the Massachusetts Institute of Technology.

Except for philosophy, which as now taught is too highbrow and involves generalizations too vast for most undergraduates, the graduate schools of liberal arts pay little real attention to general thinking, and none to general education. Under the impact of specialization in the graduate schools new specialties and new beginning courses multiply in the colleges. In the multiplication they become narrower in scope and less adapted to the needs of men seeking general understanding. Such courses are well designed to fit the need of graduate departments for college courses which prepare students to specialize in their separate fields. They are badly adapted to give a cultural introduction to the special field as it is related to the desperate problems of civilization. Often, particularly in universities conducting great graduate schools, the needs of graduate students for part-time work and the desirability of teaching experience as part of their training fit into the desire of the older professors to reduce the burdens incident to teaching big classes and to get more time for research. College teaching may be turned over in large part to young men seeking doctors' degrees. Particularly in the university colleges, teaching is often subordinated to research, to productive scholarship, and to publication. Young faculty men, rightly or wrongly—and in many cases rightly—believe they are judged primarily by research and publication. They look on teaching jobs as ways of supporting themselves while they earn their doctor's degrees. A similar development is taking place at the Massachusetts Institute of Technology, which is, however, making an effort to minimize the dangers.

In the sciences, laboratory work designed for the future specialist displaces an imaginative presentation to the layman of the beauties, the importance, and the significance of science as it affects life. Science is rarely taught as a liberal-arts subject. Yet men seeking general training can acquire a grasp of things needed to understand the place and importance of science without laboratory work, and laboratory work *per se* will never give it. Shaler's Geology 4 was a magnificent illustration. By making me an avid reader of science it inspired one great segment of my thinking for forty-five years. The usual introductory laboratory courses given in special sciences like chemistry and botany are badly adapted to give the sweep of things to students who are not to be scientists. Nor do they leave them with any philosophical grasp of science, any appreciation of its direct importance, its limitations, and its potentialities for good and evil. Little effort is made in any specialized field of science to adapt pedagogical methods and content to the objectives of general education.

To a lesser degree, because of limitations imposed by smaller size and limited resources, the independent colleges are subject to the same influences. The fetish developed that the Ph.D. is a necessary preliminary to college as well as graduate teaching. Colleges came to be rated by outside accrediting agencies in large part according to the percentage of Ph.D.'s on their faculties. It even became true that accrediting agencies expect the teacher to have acquired his Ph.D. in the field he is teaching. A historian is not deemed a proper person to teach sociology. The values to be obtained from teachers whose wisdom results from wide practical experience in life are ignored. The small college by calling such men may jeopardize its standing. Many colleges must take these accrediting agencies seriously, yet they tend to freeze education as it now exists.

The doctor's degree in the graduate schools is universally designed as a specialized research degree requiring an imposing thesis based on original research. This is usually in a narrow field. As a result, nearly all teachers in all colleges are specialists trained in the university graduate schools more as research men than as teachers. Such men take proper pride as college teachers when their students do good graduate work in their own or some other institution and when their preparation for graduate specialization is commended by graduate school specialists. They design their courses accordingly. The colleges tend to copy the university in the courses they offer. Such pressures are powerful. Men trained in subdivisions of the university graduate schools, and through these the graduate schools themselves, consciously or unconsciously exert great influence on the policies of undergraduate colleges. Since no graduate school of arts and sciences gives effective attention either to general education or to the necessary background for such education, it is not strange that almost no college gives it. In fact, within the limits imposed by the Ph.D. fetish there is no university source from which men equipped by their own training to offer general education to students can be obtained. Men trained as specialists are timid outside their special fields, and indeed may lose caste with their colleagues if they indulge in excursions into even adjoining areas. The net effect of the great success of graduate schools and their vast influence is to strengthen college specialization but to weaken general education.

The Elective System

The elective system is a logical outcome of German universities and of graduate schools as now organized. It led to better scholarship but it had other less fortunate results.

The revolt in the latter half of the last century against the insistence on an almost fixed traditional curriculum in the colleges and the resulting wide acceptance of the elective system has been analyzed many times. Reform was certainly essential. The base line was too short to meet the needs of modern civilization. Students justifiably wished more opportunity to develop their own interests, particularly in the natural and social sciences. Nevertheless, the old fixed requirements did bring order, and in the early days at least were fairly well related to the nation's needs. They had the great advantage that educated men had a common background. The reform destroyed this order and introduced chaos into the programs chosen by large numbers of students. Here again the schools of technology have suffered less than the colleges. At least in the earlier years, engineering cannot be taught without order. Liberal education, on the other hand, looked as if it could be worked out under a wide-open elective system. This is not a general truth. One evil was overspecialization, which, often through a vocational appeal, tempted many to sacrifice background; another was much scattering in elementary courses without enough severe intellectual discipline. It is hard to say whether the student who through early specialization narrowed himself for life suffered more or less than the student who drifted without order or plan through numerous elementary courses content with gentlemen's C's, while he sought, and often got, what he really wanted through social life. Certainly both routes were far from ideal ways of attaining a general education. In the small college it was, of course, true that men could, if they would, select well-balanced programs, but practically this required guidance which they rarely received. In the big universities courses became so numerous and so narrow in scope that it was often literally impossible to choose well-balanced programs. This I have found to my sorrow in attempting to advise students. Even when courses were wisely chosen, their integration was left to the student with no help from organized instruction. Everywhere, now, limitations are imposed on the elective system. These limitations are likely to increase after the war.

Concentration and Distribution

Most institutions attempt to cure the diseases of the liberal-arts curriculum by rules which in some form require concentration and distribution. Coördination within fields of major concentration is sought in some colleges by general examinations covering the specialized field. Such general examinations may or may not be backed up by tutorial or preceptorial systems. But over-all integration is still lacking.

The basic theory of concentration is that, for a man to be really educated, he must carry his studies of some subject or field beyond its elementary stages. Otherwise, he may get from college only a useless smattering of elementary courses without real intellectual discipline. The rules for distribution are designed to prevent overspecialization. There are, I believe, several errors here. It is perfectly true that many students, under a wide-open elective system, did not get an effective education because they scattered their work incoherently. This was particularly so of men who lacked any real interest in their work and of those struggling to get a general education against the limitations imposed by narrowly specialized courses.

For the first of these groups the mistake lay partly in too little effort to arouse interest by showing the importance of the things studied and how they tie together in life. Rules of concentration did much to cure one aspect of this problem, but insistence only on concentration in some field, chosen often without regard to the student's interest or his plan for life, is not enough. As a matter of fact, after the graduate gets out into the world his field of concentration is frequently wholly unrelated to his life. Even if his principal undergraduate concentration was in a social-science field, a little experience often convinces him that the atmosphere of certainty which surrounded his specialized instruction was far distant from reality. Generally, he finds by trial and error that the principles he learned do not help in the confused problems he must meet.

Some twenty years ago I compared notes with an able contemporary who, like myself, had taken a good deal of economics as an undergraduate in Harvard College. He stated that he had never been able to use his economics, that it never applied. I had frequently been able to use mine. After much thought, I concluded that the difference was that he became a manufacturer while I went into banking. Economics forty-five years ago was a long way from being realistic for the manufacturer but pretty close to the major problems of banking. It is to me an interesting fact that the excursions of government into banking and its regulation have left high and dry on the shoals of social change most of the economics of banking I learned in college and used for twenty years.

The graduate rarely sees that the difficulty in using special training lies in part in the fact that the special field was not close enough to life, in part in that it could not be isolated from the rest of life. It could therefore settle nothing.

On the other hand, in complying with rules for distribution the typical program rambles over several elementary subjects without the student's getting any grasp of their relationship to each other or to his special field. As a whole, his liberal-arts training gives little aid in understanding either his own ·problems or the great problems of society, and he is badly prepared to meet novel situations and novel opportunities which must be faced in their entirety.

For the group seeking a general education, the error lay in insisting that men elect much of their work in some one academic field instead of offering them organized interrelated instruction in a variety of subjects which would really give them a general education having unity of purpose and a functional relationship to their lives.

A considerable degree of concentration in his chosen field is logically sound for the man who decides with good reason to use the latter part of his college course in vocational specialization. Such men would concentrate anyway. The customary rules give order and set standards for such concentration. Unfortunately they pay little attention to organizing the general education which should be the background of the specialty. Except for men going into industrial science or medicine, and for those whose objectives are teaching or research, the old fields of concentration in independent colleges and in private universities have little actual vocational or general value in their lives. Unfortunately, students with their obvious lack of experience may be fooled into thinking they have such value. In the state universities and increasingly in the colleges many new fields of concentration are directly vocational.

When men seek a four-year general education, the rules in all types of institutions fail to fit their needs, for they prevent an over-all look at life. Rules of concentration intensify the problem faced by the budding specialist who needs a general background, without giving those who seek a general education any way to get it. They often prevent men who intend to follow their four years of general education with professional training from taking a wise selection of courses. Yet such professional training necessarily involves concentration in one field and needs breadth as a foundation. It is hard to defend two successive periods of intense specialization. This was a serious difficulty at the Business School, even in its relations with Harvard College.

The whole subject of concentration needs reëxamination. Too many fields of concentration are offered. Except for groups of men who in fact intend to use the work vocationally, there is little reason for including in an undergraduate curriculum many fields of concentration which now consume anywhere from one quarter to three quarters of the student's time. Often his choice is made because he must comply with the rules without reference to his native capacities or to his general aims in life, and without any effort having been made to show him how this large fraction of his college work can help him either to a more effective or a happier life. In one extreme case, I saw the college record of a man intending to go into business who concentrated over 90 per cent of his work in one field of foreign languages and literature. The only unusual aspect of his record was the percentage. I see no excuse for an undergraduate field of concentration in Fine Arts unless the college is content when it adds to the aesthetic appreciation of a student by concentrating in this one field most of his work in the humanities and a large part of his whole four years. On the other hand, I see compelling reasons for including the Fine Arts as well as literature and other aspects of the humanities in a curriculum of general education. I could give many other examples. The legitimate and important existence of a specialist group in a university is not in itself adequate reason for listing the specialty as an undergraduate field of concentration. Of course students in university colleges with great graduate schools are more apt to make such mistakes than those in small independent colleges where specialization is not carried so far, or in state universities with their great emphasis on vocational training and therefore on vocational fields of concentration.

Another important development which arose out of the discovery that concentration leads to narrowness takes the form of efforts in many colleges to secure a foundation for general education through survey courses covering great types of human knowledge and experience. This attack on the problem has considerable promise and justifies continued experiment. I question whether, standing alone, it can solve the problem. Experiments with survey courses of which I have some acquaintance seem for a variety of reasons to attain limited and not too satisfactory results. One type of survey course fails because it is not internally integrated. Biology, for example, may be surveyed by a brief treatment of one field like zoology, followed by a similar treatment perhaps of botany and thereafter by similar treatment of one after another specialized field. Human biology and social biology may be completely omitted. Each subject taught is in fact important to an understanding of man's environment, but each tends to be presented as an introduction to a specialty rather than as an aspect of life. Often the teacher is a specialist borrowed for the purpose from his real job. In such case the survey easily turns into series of lectures lacking both focus and integration or into a textbook which formalizes the subject matter at an elementary, didactic, and informatory level. Even where the individual course is well integrated within itself, the relationship of its general field to those covered in other survey courses is left vague. After such a course is completed, unless the subject is followed up, its content is quickly packed away by the student and forgotten rather than used.

To make such courses effective, every effort should be made by appropriate teaching methods and materials to evoke student initiative in using them. As the four years progress, and as students under present conditions specialize in other fields, they should constantly face problems which transcend the range of any one course or subject. Many graduates must, and all of them who succeed in special fields should, constantly bring into their thinking points of view which are outside the limitations not only of particular subdivisions of human experience as these are organized in the colleges but also outside the limitations imposed by the immediate environment in which they live. They will not do this imaginatively without practice. Any survey course which lasts a half year or a year, and is thereafter never used, will be crowded out of consideration by the constantly increasing specialization of the student both in his college program and in life. Knowledge to be useful must be used. Otherwise it ceases to have value either because it is forgotten or because the individual has no capacity to bring it into the forefront of his mind when it is in fact needed.

In a considerable number of colleges, coördination is sought in more general terms, sometimes by courses in contemporary civilization, sometimes by sacrificing direct efforts to secure general understanding of the present and substituting systematic study and interpretation of the best books of the past without much effort to relate the past to the present. While all these methods have some value, none with which I am familiar gets at the heart of the problem—the need for an integrated over-all unity, related to the present and to the future. The difficulty lies partly in vested interests, partly in confusion of purpose.

The Departmental System

These reasons for the weakness of general education are accentuated by the departmental system, based on specialties, which is intricate and powerful in all universities and most colleges. The problem is particularly serious where the graduate-school interest predominates in a faculty controlling both the graduate school and the college. Ethical dilemmas for the teacher are created constantly by the diversity of interest between students seeking general education in the college and those specializing in the graduate school. They are similar to the ethical dilemmas involved when a trustee mingles his beneficiary's funds with his own. Such dilemmas are resolved by law for the trustee but not for the college teacher. They should be resolved in the college in favor of the college student, not for the convenience or interest of the teacher or his graduate students. Just so the law settles the trustee's dilemma in favor of the beneficiary. The existence of such dilemmas, while clearly recognized by some teachers, is, I fear, not realized by most. Intellectual confusion and administrative futility are easily possible under such circumstances. Powerful departments primarily interested in graduate training often allow the interest of the poor devil of an undergraduate who wants a general education to be crowded out. Departmental jealousies affect policy and prevent coördination in undergraduate work. In my judgment the major reasons why the faculty of the Harvard Business School has been for many years a coöperative unit with a minimum of vested interests lie in the fact that it has not been formally organized into departments and that we have the habit of asking young teachers as part of their training to offer sections from time to time in courses which are outside their own major fields.

I am far from wishing to see the control of college faculties over their educational work lessened. I believe, however, that to make such control effective, departments must be weakened. More educational problems should be settled by the faculties as a whole, after study and recommendations by properly constituted committees appointed by the President in consultation with the Dean to represent varied interests and to cut across academic specialties. In this way the control would be in the faculty. On the other hand, the administrative leaders of the college, who have the function of looking at the whole situation undistracted by specialized viewpoints, and who alone have the necessary information to make an over-all look possible, would have the aid of interdepartmental organizations well adapted to working out integrated views and translating them into action. Now such a process easily arouses the self-centered opposition of well organized and powerful departments. This prevents many wise policies from being adopted. The faculty as a whole easily loses control. Of course, here too the big university suffers more than the small college. A faculty with strong departments primarily interested in graduate work will find it difficult to integrate the college. The college faculty should in my judgment always be a separate faculty with its own responsible dean who should combine the functions of leader of the faculty and assistant to the president. He should not be in any way subordinate to the dean of the graduate school or of a combined faculty. The college has a special job to do. It should be separated from the graduate school if it is to do this job well. In my judgment, the graduate school would benefit as well as the college. Other graduate faculties certainly benefit from being independent of the college.

I do not, of course, mean that I would discourage men interested in a special field from getting together to talk over common problems, but I would wherever possible, and it is certainly possible in nearly all separate colleges, have no formal organization of departments under separate chairmen. I would see to it also that there were many formal and informal meetings of groups composed of men with varied interests and backgrounds.

Prerequisite Courses

The widespread existence of introductory courses which are prerequisite before men are allowed to take so-called advanced work is, when combined with other pressures for specialization, a further source of difficulty. Men must, let us say, study medieval history before they are allowed to study United States or English history. Why? There is no logical or practical reason like the reasons which exist for understanding the elements of chemistry before studying qualitative analysis. Yet the result is that the man who under present conditions can give only a limited amount of time to history may be prevented from studying his own country.

Accrediting Agencies

A source of trouble which should be grouped with these arises from the growing number of accrediting agencies, both within and without the educational system—professional associations and the like which reach back into the college curriculum, as the medical schools are forced to do, and rate both colleges and students according to whether they give and take a certain number of courses in subjects in which the particular agency or society is interested. These agencies are almost necessarily both highly specialized and narrow in their point of view. Their limitations appear in their decisions. They are apt to care more for the immediate usefulness of graduates than for their later capacity for leadership. On the favorable side they are influential in raising minimum standards. On the unfavorable side, by discouraging educational experiments and by stressing narrow specialization, they contribute to mediocrity in education.

Effect of Specialization

The proliferation of specialties in the universities and colleges and the unfortunate influences introduced by the elective system by rules for concentration and by departmentalization make it easy to get from college a scattered, uncoördinated training combined with some start on specialization, but almost impossible to get a general education. Too many subjects are offered in college, each too narrowly limited. This is particularly true of the university college, as anyone who has tried to help students pick out orderly curricula of breadth will at once agree. Each special university group must have its place in the sun with its own introductory course leading into its specialty. The great divisions of human knowledge from which subspecialties have developed over the last seventy-five years get less and less attention. Moral philosophy gives birth to political economy and political economy becomes economics. Moral philosophy dies. We have departed a long way from Professor Charles F. Dunbar's aphorism to me in 1898: "The trouble with Professor ——— is that he likes to lay down what he calls correct rules of finance. Now in my judgment there is but one correct rule of finance and that is, do the best thing you can under *all* the circumstances." General science disappears and a great crop of specialized sciences take its place. Customarily no course is offered which attempts to give any useful grasp of science and its implications seen in the large. Little effort is made to show how or why special subjects may, in part or in whole, be useful as preparation for life, or what makes them worth studying. The student too easily but quite properly assumes that if he meets college requirements well he will get a general education. In fact, however, most colleges make no pretense of seeing that the individual undergraduate takes training which he can integrate, and few indeed make any effort to develop understanding and skills or pedagogical devices by which the student is helped to reduce *his* curriculum to useful unity.

General education under present conditions has no content and involves no accepted training. Yet our democracy critically needs men who can integrate wide ranges of facts and factors, form large sound judgments not only on general problems but on the smaller individual situations they must face in life, and turn these judgments into effective action. It critically needs an educated group with a common stock of ideas and of habits and skills in formulating judgments. The graduate schools of arts and sciences could, of course, pay more attention to integration and so supply a new and greatly needed type of teacher to the colleges. Graduate professional schools can do more than they are now doing, but they reach fewer men. To make their own work productive to the maximum such schools need men more widely trained when they enter. Moreover, each professional school is itself specialized, though the scope of the fields differs greatly.

As things are now, the liberal-arts college alone can give many men the background necessary if they are to bring to bear on the present not only the experience of the past but some real understanding of the great forces at work in the present. It has a unique chance to train men in the habit of seeking constantly for overlooked facts and forces of the widest range and bringing them into thought and action. But, to accomplish this result in ways which add to men's equipment for life, it must relate its work to the functions they will be called on to perform in life. This is now done successfully in scientific fields but, except for vocational training, not in other aspects of the college's work. I am well aware that many able and devoted teachers are doing everything they can under present conditions to make college education vital to youth. The basic difficulty lies in the system.

CHAPTER V

Science, Social Science and the Practical World

WE MUST RECOGNIZE that one of the great dividing lines of human knowledge and experience is passed when we leave the certainties of natural science and enter social and humanistic fields where rapid change, uncertainty, the unknown and the unknowable and, above all, human interactions, become dominant factors. Yet in spite of this the academic world continues to be influenced too much in its methods, in its thinking, and in the organization of subject matter by the example of science. Not enough attention is paid to the inherent differences.

The functional relationships which exist between the academic world of science and the world in which men live are not perfect, but within the limits set by their subject matter they are the closest and most satisfactory which the universities and colleges attain anywhere. Theory and practice are, in fact, closely allied. Scientific accomplishments are sure, rapid, and lasting. They quickly affect life, not only in its material aspects but by their collateral consequences in a great variety of social ways.

There are several reasons for this close functional relationship. In the first place, the natural sciences, particularly astronomy, physics, chemistry, and physiology, have developed a powerful methodology for studying the material world. They make their principal progress by assuming a mechanistic and deterministic order of nature. They assume certainty as the basis of behavior in the material world. These are the sciences which have most influenced our thinking and our material and social environment. In physics and chemistry, and with greater difficulty in physiology, repeated experimentation under controlled conditions is possible. The experimenter can predict with confidence that, if the conditions are repeated, an experiment made last year will produce identical results next year. In a great variety of cases, he can isolate, purify, weigh, measure, and combine foundation stones out of which the material world is built, and control conditions surrounding the resulting processes. The elements with which he deals are fixed and certain in their characteristics and behavior. Mathematics becomes an efficient tool. Mathematics, dealing with sheer abstractions, and natural science, with this basic assumption of a mechanistic order of nature, have developed methods of securing material results which work not only in the hands of men of genius but at the behest of numerous competent men of lesser ability. They have led to the discovery of a multitude of ways in which things useful to or desired by men can be created. Social forces translate these discoveries into action. Thus they have controlled the ways millions of people make their living and subjected them to constantly changing physical and social environment.

There is an important difference between the physical sciences, physics and chemistry, and other natural sciences such as physiology and biology. When life enters, severe limitations are at once imposed. Nevertheless, agricultural science, controlled breeding, and medicine all prove the widespread opportunities which lie before the ingenious experimenter who patiently seeks uniformities not only in the behavior of physical and chemical properties of the living tissue but in the mysterious congeries which constitute the living organism. Even in dealing with medicine and similar subjects related to living organisms, the assumption of mechanism gives results of high importance. Indeed, these results are so important that our great medical schools tend to minimize or ignore the emotional and social problems of all but the insane. Of course, many sides of biology, like most parts of such important and fascinating fields as geology and geography, present problems involving the chance working-out of numerous variables similar in many ways to the uncertainties of human problems. But these natural sciences are not the ones which have accelerated change in the environment of men, or, except by accentuating the vast expanse of space and time and of their evolutionary processes, dominated the behavior and thought of men. The dominant fields are physics, chemistry, and physiology, particularly those aspects of physiology where mechanistic assumptions work; but many other specialized sciences have grown up to study segments of the material world. This specialization is logically defensible and practically useful.

The necessary subdivision of science is unfortunate, not because it leads to conflicts in premises and conclusions but because of the limitations it imposes on the knowledge of acquaintance with both the premises and the conclusions of other scientists. This is a limitation on use, not a conflict. In the last analysis all material facts and forces are the premises of every natural science. Science can elaborate logics because it can simplify facts by segregation and control, and because under the order of nature it can make material results recur. The motive behind a piece of research in either pure or applied science may be men's desire to accomplish some specific objective, like the manufacture of synthetic rubber possessing certain qualities. The mode of attack is through the laboratory, where it is often possible to extend knowledge of nature's laws by experiments, the scope of which is suggested by existing knowledge, and thus to attain the desired result.

True, in theory the dogmatic certainty which dominated science for two hundred and fifty years after the work of Newton has been sadly shaken. Under the principle of uncertainty and other recent developments of physical theory, many basic natural laws governing the behavior of minute entities turn out to be true only as statistical probabilities. Langmuir, in a fascinating article in *Science*, suggests that these developments have destroyed almost completely the dogma of causality and substituted statistical probability in most fields where scientists work. "The net result of the modern principles of physics has been to wipe out almost completely the dogma of causality." [1] No one can foresee the extent of the change this principle of uncertainty may introduce into science itself, nor the degree of success science may achieve in exploring problems where the errant behavior of minority groups of electrons or atoms—very small things which fail to follow the usual statistical pattern—may produce startlingly novel results. This last type of problem, particularly, is all but wholly unexplored by science; it is only now that the methods of approach are being worked out. As Langmuir suggests, scientists searching for laws have naturally explored regions where the statistical probabilities are overwhelming. Yet it is similar logically and practically to the problem presented by the intrusion of a Hitler into the social situation. Nor can we predict the extent to which the behavior of large or small fractions of apparently homogeneous elementary substances may be so changed by controlling their environment that novel or subordinate statistical probabilities are evolved. The whole field of electronics and of radar offer examples.

[1] Dr. Irving Langmuir, "Science, Common Sense and Decency," *Science*, January 1, 1943.

It seems obvious, however, that since the objective of science, within its most generalized objective of understanding nature, has been for many years the search for uniformities, and since the training of scientists has been directed to this end, most of them will continue this search, even when they leave fields where overwhelming statistical probabilities determine results. Within the principle of uncertainty they will search for natural laws governing the behavior of minorities. The assumption of determinism will continue to work in great areas which deal with material things. The chemist's work is unlikely to stress uncertainties. The impact of science on civilization will still come to the man on the street in deterministic and mechanistic terms. The emphasis of science is materialistic in fact if not in intent. Nearly all progress affecting human beings which has been made by science up to the present time has resulted from the assumption that material things properly controlled and isolated always behave in the same way under the same conditions. Because these assumptions have produced results for a long period and have thereby acquired almost a religious status, they will continue to dominate the work of all but the rare scientist.

Closely related functional organizations adapted to making natural science useful to men have grown up spontaneously. They include pure and applied science in the colleges and universities, technology in the engineering schools and laboratories, pilot plants and methods of production on a commercial scale in industry. Methods of mass control of industrial processes are worked out so that they can be operated by engineers of lesser or different abilities than the research workers, or even by intelligent men without scientific training. Men in universities and engineering schools help these processes by consulting work. Throughout the whole scheme of things, as it has developed naturally, an effective integration exists between the academic scientist and his work, on the one hand, and powerful industries on the other hand. Everyone is happy and effective except the small company which finds it harder and harder to keep step with scientific and technological progress. The results of science are extended by industry through methods of financing and marketing the resulting products. The relationship of the academic world of pure and applied science to the world of affairs where men seek to get material things done practically is functional, and it gets results.

A similarly close functional relationship exists between science and medicine. Here the medical schools and research laboratories and hospitals play a vital part. Science gives great help to medicine in solving pathological problems of individuals. Such a relationship exists through schools of public health, where problems of preventive medicine or conditions surrounding community health are concerned. In medicine, as in technology, a purposeful process tying science to affairs is at work. Similar functional relationship is, however, almost completely lacking when the normal man living his daily life is involved and the individual conditions and social surroundings which determine his effectiveness or lack of effectiveness. Because he is not sick, he is neglected by both medicine and science.

Where the functional relationship exists, it is two-way. Science fertilizes industry and medicine. Industry and medicine influence the direction and accomplishments of science. The whole process constantly accelerates changes in our environment which are beyond the control of science.

The present functional alliance between science, engineering, and industry is comparatively recent. For a considerable period the mainsprings of the new technology were ingenious inventors and practical men rather than university scientists. Rensselaer Polytechnic Institute was founded in 1824 as a school of practical science. It was the first of many. To meet the needs of the time, it heavily emphasized civil engineering. The Massachusetts Institute of Technology was chartered as a school of applied science in 1861 and opened its doors in 1865. In the last quarter of a century it has become also a distinguished pure-science research institution. The General Electric Research Laboratory was started in 1900. From the beginning it emphasized pure as well as applied science. Many other industrial laboratories followed. The alliance once formed was both natural and productive: natural, because the customary basic assumptions of science, mechanism and determinism, worked with equal and parallel success both in science and on the material side in technology and each contributed to the success of the other; productive, as shown by material results.

Engineering, the phase of science which directly affects our material environment, was thought of as applied science and not as a force bringing constant change in human and social behavior. As a result, both engineers and engineering schools give wholly insufficient weight to human behavior and to shifting social situations. The human consequences of engineering are less direct and less apparent, though quite as serious as the early abuses of the factory system. Within two or three generations, the whole social order has been subjected to rapid changes in physical environment which result from applied science. Great new sources of power are placed in our hands, and we are surrounded by an inexhaustible variety of new material accomplishments.

The world becomes one neighborhood. Neighborhood rows become world war. Our capacity to produce new and potentially destructive instruments of power outruns our capacity to control and direct them for constructive community ends. The widespread changes resulting from applications of science to industry bring on an explosive human situation at home. These things are not surprising. We forget the limitations on human beings. The strength of the emotions and the sentiments which control men as they live together in communities does not change in any such moment of time as one hundred years. These emotions and sentiments are badly adapted to one world or to constant change. The growing instability of American and European society disturbed thoughtful observers long before the present crisis.

As might have been expected from their emphasis on certainty and material things, science and technology turn out to be amoral forces. Constantly they open new possibilities of material welfare. Constantly, but in unpredictable ways, they intensify the difficulties of dealing with the indeterminate and uncertain problems met by men in their social and political surroundings. Of course, the environment of men has always been changing; but before science, technology, and industry combined forces, the basic social surroundings altered in most ways almost imperceptibly from generation to generation. For the first time in history, men leave worlds radically changed from those they entered.

Along with material progress, these changes involve widespread discontent, personal isolation, and the collapse of spiritual values. Now through social and political confusion, labor problems, and wars involving the whole new neighborhood, it is widely realized that materialism, mechanism, and gadgets are alike in failing to meet the ethical aspirations, the purposeful desires, and the basic religious needs of men. Men cannot through science find ways of handling their lives and their social affairs.

Nor does scientific progress lessen with the passage of time. Scientific research backed up by industry continues to accelerate change in all aspects of our environment. Great sums are spent every year in such research and in turning its results to practical use: witness the confident predictions on all sides of revolutionary new gadgets which are to come with peace. In the material world results continue to flow from the assumption of determinism. In contrast, as the war and our confusion of thoughts about the postwar period illustrate, our methods of dealing with social change are inefficient and often dangerous.

Unfortunately, very small sums are devoted to studying the human and social consequences of the changes scientific research creates. Since results of such research are less tangible, business provides little financial support. Hundreds of millions of dollars to accelerate change, a million or two in studying the effects of change on human beings! Our general direction suffers. Can modern industry, modern democracy, and even free science itself stand this relative scale of expenditures? The great bulk of scientists continue to work in parts of the material universe where the assumptions of Newtonian physics are adequate as the basis for both research and technology. Manufacturers continue to improve their technological processes and to devise new products useful to men in a material sense without giving enough consideration to human problems in the factory, or to the social consequences of their activities. The behavior of men as they adapt themselves to the complexities of modern living is ignored or treated superficially. Controversy displaces coöperation. As one result, new processes frequently fail to produce the expected increase in production.

Right now the present structure of science is under attack in spite of the clear fact that we would have lost the war without the efficiency with which scientists in government service, in universities and colleges, and in industrial laboratories were mobilized, and without their even more extraordinary accomplishments. A powerfully supported bill in the United States Senate seeks to put all science under government control. Another pending bill seeks not only to authorize great government research laboratories for the benefit of small corporations but also to dominate the private laboratories, both university and industrial. In its present form it would be possible to define as a small corporation any company which is not the dominant company in an industry and to give it exclusive rights under government-owned patents. The powers under the bill could be used to supplement the prohibitions of the Sherman and Clayton Acts by giving affirmative aid to competitors big and small both through financial assistance and through exclusive rights under government patents. It almost reads as if private patents also were included. Coupled with these bills should be the decision of Judge Thurman Arnold in the case of *Potts et al. v. Coe*,[2] redefining invention to exclude from patentable inventions many, if not most, inventions originating from industrial laboratories because they are based on teamwork and not on "the spark of genius." It would be difficult to devise surer paths to the loss of our present strength in science. At a time when we shall soon need the aid of science in giving employment to millions of our people, and when most of us are convinced not only that our military strength is in a critical sense due to the strength of science but that we must not again be defenseless, it is extraordinary, to say the least, that the social relationships both of industries founded on science and of science itself are so bad that such measures should be seriously considered. Incidentally, small business would suffer severely from such attacks on scientific progress. It is easy to forget that a host of small companies live because big companies succeed. Science itself needs well-developed general education.

As Dr. Isaiah Bowman says,

> I do not believe that future science is going to help humanity solve its basic problems when it merely sub-

[2] Com'r of Patents, 140 F. 2d 470.

stitutes aluminum for steel or magnesium for aluminum, or plastics for metals. Neither do I believe that humanity will get much farther ahead in associative plans by reducing the death rate from a given disease by 5 or 25 per cent. Both these objects are highly desirable. But neither one enlarges the already accepted ends of life or points a way toward better cooperative living.[3]

It is frequently suggested that science, in spite of the fact that it adds constantly to the uncertainties in fields whose most significant characteristics are already uncertainty and flux, should extend its peculiar and, for its own purpose of studying the material world, proper, methodologies over the whole range of human experience. Already a senseless force which has through its sheer material accomplishments made the whole structure of civilization dangerously unstable, its success in such an effort would surely finish the job. The understanding of men and the uncertainties of social life require a wider integration and a different conceptual scheme. We can to advantage emulate their spirit of inquiry, but not their methods. Curiosity is a deepseated human characteristic, not monopolized by science. The alchemists had a spirit of inquiry. In the pure sciences, and in many aspects of technology, men can if they wish perform their function in almost complete isolation from the community around them. On the other hand, when they choose to descend into the turmoil of unpredictable human and social situations, the very narrowness of their training, modes of thought, and experience limits their capacity and often leads them to absurdities. Yet there is widespread insistence by scientists that science and its methodology for exploring mysteries are somehow on a higher plane than other activities, a viewpoint originating curiously enough through its sheer *material* results.

[3] A.A.A.S. *Bulletin*, July 1943, p. 50.

As a question of scientific methodology there can be no doubt that the scientists have been right. But we have to discriminate between the weight to be given to scientific opinion in the selection of its methods, and its trustworthiness in formulating judgments of the understanding. The slightest scrutiny of the history of natural science shows that current scientific opinion is nearly infallible in the former case, and is invariably wrong in the latter case. The man with a method good for purposes of his dominant interests, is a pathological case in respect to his wider judgment on the coordination of this method with a more complete experience. Priests and scientists, statesmen and men of business, philosophers and mathematicians, are all alike in this respect. We all start by being empiricists. But our empiricism is confined within our immediate interests. The more clearly we grasp the intellectual analysis of a way regulating procedure for the sake of those interests, the more decidedly we reject the inclusion of evidence which refuses to be immediately harmonized with the method before us. Some of the major disasters of mankind have been produced by the narrowness of men with a good methodology.[4]

The man on the street, struggling with all the complexity and uncertainties surrounding human life and experience, is less impressed by the awe and majesty of the order of nature and its evident but incomprehensible purpose unfolded through science than by his automobile, his washing machine, his unhappy life in the factory, his fear of unemployment, his doubts as to the future of his small business, and the scientific horrors of the war.

The basic working hypotheses of science are inapplicable

[4] Alfred North Whitehead, *The Function of Reason* (Princeton University Press, 1929), p. 8.

in social situations. Of course, human affairs are largely controlled by what Whitehead calls the "senseless forces" of material nature and also by cultural *mores*, but all human experience contradicts the adequacy of mechanism as a description of human action and human affairs, and of materialism as the solution of life's problems. We shall never convince mankind that Hitler and Napoleon, Roosevelt and Churchill, Washington, Lincoln, Jefferson, and Hamilton made no free-will contributions affecting this western civilization in ways qualitatively different from the existence and behavior of iron and water. Such differences require differences in method and assumptions.

In general, except in science and technology, little functional relationship exists between the liberal-arts faculty and the lives men live outside. There is in all fields except science a real functional breakdown between the lives graduates lead and their education. Men in the academic world studying social science and the humanities in general have no working hypothesis for dealing with the world of uncertainty where we all live and interact that is comparable in usefulness with the scientists' assumption of a fixed order of nature.

Whenever the interrelationships of men are concerned or whenever the capacity for experiment breaks down because the necessary facts cannot be isolated, weighed, measured, or even known, the control of process is impossible. Science, therefore, in spite of its vast influence on social problems, offers no method of dealing with the uncertain and the unpredictable. Under social conditions, long-time laws which control the future and determine human behavior cannot be worked out, and few lasting principles can be stated.

Machines can be designed in conformity with deterministic scientific laws. But even the design involves human purpose, and the machines cannot be built or operated without human beings. Nor does certainty dominate the use of machines or of their products. Always, in human and social situations, when scientific results are translated into technologies and into gadgets of infinite variety, unknown and unknowable variables are inextricably combined with known factors. Even when scientific laws are certain, the ensuing process involves other factors which are almost always uncertain. The certainties resulting from science are mixed with the uncertainties resulting from human sentiments and from the inability of the human mind to reduce the unknown and the unknowable to order. The combined result is always uncertainty. $A + Y$ and AY are uncertain quantities. These facts still have too little attention in the intellectual organization of the colleges and universities. Instead of being sure as the scientists are that the things they are studying will behave tomorrow as they do today, the social scientist can in fact only be sure that things are in flux and that the future in all complex situations is unpredictable.

In the social sciences most specialties rest on an insecure logical foundation. They are isolated artificially from the sum-total of the social structure by omitting from consideration all but selected aspects of situations which are studied and by making explicit or implicit assumptions about the omitted factors. Social science specialists rarely grapple with human and social problems in their full concrete complexity.

The humanities also have developed specialization to an extent comparable with the natural sciences. As in science, much of such specialization is sound and inevitable, but the over-all look is too much neglected.

In the world of affairs men can depend on scientific and engineering specialists to solve their strictly technical problems. As a result, a great variety of industries based on specialized techniques have come into existence. Since, however, social-science specialists omit many things which practical men in business and government must consider in making their decisions, no similar aid can be gained from such specialists, as specialists, in solving their social problems. Social science specialists are, of course, useful as experts, but neither men in private life nor in government service can safely let them settle problems. Some outstanding specialists in liberal-arts faculties have come in close enough touch with concrete problems as they actually arise to fit their thinking into realistic needs. Some professional faculties do the same. But these are exceptions.

No real functional relationship between social science and practical life can exist so long as social scientists continue to search for lasting principles and theory in spite of constant change and uncertainty, and so long as social-science specialists fail to integrate problems by starting with an over-all look at them as they arise in life. Until these things are done, men forced by their environment to struggle with constant change and uncertainty have to get along somehow without much help from the academic world. Men trained in our colleges will continue to find their education poor preparation for life.

CHAPTER VI

The Uncertain World in Which Men Live

MOST of the activities of men are carried on in the world of uncertainty. This fact has controlled the evolution of social organizations in the world around the universities and colleges, but it has not controlled the fields studied, the methods used, or the objectives in the academic world.

In so far as they can, practical men in private life must from day to day face their problems in their full generality. Unlike the cloistered academic specialist, they ignore or make assumptions at their peril about social facts which arise within or surrounding their industries. Industrialists are forced to consider the uncertain human and social results which flow from their technological processes. They must struggle with their constantly changing problems in spite of the necessity and the danger of prophesying the uncertain future. The same statements apply to leaders in public life. Both must have organized methods of dealing with such problems which are basically straightforward and functional. The weakness of our general direction is, however, an index of the inadequacy with which these methods are applied. Practical men are on the right track but they struggle under great handicaps. Practice inevitably suffers from narrowness. The immediate environment of man is always narrowing. Practice needs imaginative inspiration and help from scholars, but the scholars' work is not so organized that it can be related to actual problems as the practitioner must face them. It does not therefore offset the weakness of the man on the firing line by helping him to deal with problems in a larger setting. There is a sharp divergence between the organizations which have grown up spontaneously because men seeking to accomplish well-understood objectives in practical life must struggle with uncertainty and change, and the organization of knowledge in the universities and colleges for the study of nonscientific subjects. The first group faced by practical necessities constructed organizations functionally related to their objective of getting things done under all the concrete but changing circumstances they face. Academic social science, on the other hand, failed to study the reasons which controlled the spontaneous development of these organizations and to relate its work also to problems as they arise in their generality and change with time. Not enough attention was paid to the contrasts with science which are introduced by uncertainty. Social scientists tried to define laws or principles and to develop theory in special fields in spite of the fact that circumstances never recur in their full complexity and that new and unexpected facts inevitably vitiate one long-time generalization after another. They still seek to minimize these difficulties and to get a basis for their logics, sometimes by excluding parts of the social situation, sometimes by assumptions not based on study of the facts, sometimes by adopting slogans like "by and large" and "in the long run" and "other things being equal."

Yet social assumptions even about the past or the present are difficult to verify. In some cases this is because necessary information cannot be obtained, in others because it cannot be obtained in time for use. About the future the only safe prediction is that no complex social situation will work out "by and large and in the long run" as it is forecast or planned now. As for "other things being equal," let us say in considering economic problems, they never are equal over a period of time. Social change is a persistent fact. Moreover, even if non-economic things could be stabilized, it would not, because of this fact, be safe to leave them out and consider economic aspects of a situation in isolation. Stability is not enough. Values must be assigned, which is just what the assumption of stability was intended to make unnecessary. Whatever value is placed on them will affect the economic factors. Indeed different values assigned by different economists may even change the whole impact of an economic factor. Suppose, for example, in considering such a situation, one of the important things, included in other things and therefore assumed as constants, is the vague mass psychology of business men usually summed up by the word confidence. In all sorts of situations, the economic factors are radically affected both in their strength and in the direction in which they operate by the difference between a psychology of optimism and a psychology of fear.

Thus not only is theory separated in fact from practice but there is no possible controlling relationship between theory based only on some specialized part of the total situation and practice where men must act with reference to all the concrete flux of circumstance. In the main, the academic world has ignored practice and even looked down on it. As a result, the functional relationship between the social scientist and practical life which could so easily be worked out has not in fact been worked out except in a few professional schools and by a few individuals. Academic accomplishments, in spite of great expenditures of time and effort by able men, fall far short of the influence they should have in the world of affairs. Neither Social Science nor the Humanities take the place they might. Indeed, the social sciences often fool practical men who assume, partly from the name Social Science, that the colleges must be performing a function which will fit their needs in social fields as they know the universities and colleges fit their needs in natural science.

In consequence, they make serious mistakes by using academic conclusions as the basis for action without realizing the partial viewpoint and premises from which they are drawn.

The most numerous functional organizations which have grown up in private life to determine policy and to get things done are the business corporations. Nothing is allowed to come into these corporations unless it is or is thought to be related to their objectives. All parts of the organization are designed to contribute to the job which always faces men, the job of adopting and putting into effect the best policies they can in the concrete present situation which must be faced. The design may be imperfect. The objectives are usually too narrowly defined. The policy adopted may be shortsighted or mistaken. Just as the success of scientific methodologies led the academic world down side roads in social situations, they lead most industrial organizations to a relative overemphasis on technological efficiency. In a narrow sense this gets results. Unfortunately it also leads to an underestimate of the importance of human interactions and of long-run social relations. Nevertheless, whatever its deficiencies, the whole organization is functionally related to the job which must be done as this job is understood by those in charge.

In government, the situation is similar but less clear. It requires recognition of the theory on which our government was set up. Our ancestors feared government and wished to restrict it to essentials and to minimize its interference with private initiative. So in the constitution they created a wide range of checks, balances, and divisions of power. Policy in particular was split up. They thought of government primarily as a regulating device, a way of fixing the rules of the game, not as a method of getting things done. It was assumed that in the main private initiative would be responsible for getting things done. The major exceptions to this statement were the Army and Navy. Both are necessarily centralized in times of emergency because this is essential to national self-defense. Their organizations are functional in the same sense that business organizations are functional and follow similar patterns. They both determine policy and carry it out.

On the whole, our Federal government worked well under the theory of divided responsibility so long as it kept to the regulation concept. As the years pass the tendency toward centralization becomes stronger, and with this tendency the Federal government takes on more and more direct as distinguished from regulatory activities. It is badly designed to carry out such functions. It is not strange therefore that in the last two national administrations, when the Federal government under Mr. Hoover and particularly under Mr. Roosevelt greatly expanded its direct activities, it added to its old forms functional organizations adapted to getting things done. It borrowed the corporate form from business and organized a large number of government-owned but inadequately controlled corporations.

Our municipal governments have never done a good job. Local governments in the nature of things have to do many things themselves. The party system has developed in such a way that this function of doing things has been subordinate to the part played by local communities in State and National politics. This gives an opportunity for local governments to become boss-ridden side shows and inhibits the development of organizations adapted to doing the necessary concrete jobs. It is an interesting fact that the leading effort at reform in local government seeks to break this tie with Federal and State politics and through the device of city managers to build up local organizations functionally adapted to determining local needs and meeting them.

Similar functional relationships exist in nearly all organizations which have grown up spontaneously where men work together to get those things done which they think important. So the administrative and teaching organizations of university colleges and schools, the organizations of churches, of political parties, and of countless formal and informal social groups are all more or less perfectly adapted to carry out the functions of the institution or group in question; that is, to its objectives as these objectives are understood and to its activities in attaining these objectives. Inevitably changes in organization lag behind changes in environment so that in many cases the functional relationships are far from perfect, but no organization can persist in any vital sense if it serves no function, and no function can be performed effectively except by methods of determining purpose, objectives, policy, and action. All these I group under the term administration.

I shall examine briefly some common characteristics of such spontaneous organizations in an effort to see where the colleges can be effective. Just as in science, the universities and colleges make no effort to do the whole job including industrial applications of science, so the colleges cannot train men in the whole job of administration as it arises in the complex patterns of life. They can pick out those aspects of the spontaneous organization which are both most general and least effectively done and train men so that they will do a better job than they are likely to do without training.

In spite of the wide range of particular orientation in which such organizations are active, all in their administrative activities involve the same logical and practical limitations. All depend on background, habits, skills, and judgment, and on policy and action about shifting problems in their concrete complexity. This is fortunate for otherwise it would be practically impossible to develop academic research and instruction on an adequate scale.

The function of defining purpose and objectives and converting them into policy and action related to immediate problems as they arise often in unpredictable form is carried out in all of them by leaders at various levels who administer them. This function is a necessary part of all such organizations. Men in a great variety of occupations and with varying degrees of responsibility have this as their main job in life.

Explicitly or implicitly in all these spontaneous groups, purpose and objectives are defined and redefined as facts change. Policy is determined with reference to the situation as it exists, and action is taken to carry it out. At every stage human strengths and weaknesses affect both the policy adopted and the way it is carried out.

The colleges can stress and help men to define purpose. This is perhaps the most important single aspect of policy. A sense of direction can come only from well-understood purpose. As a matter of fact, it is at this point that policy is weakest in practice. The narrowness of the practical environment leads men to neglect subjects of great social significance and to formulate short-time and immediate definitions of purpose which in many ways ignore long-time objectives of the highest significance both to their organizations and to society. Nothing in the previous background of the typical policymaker fits him for this task by breadth of knowledge, experience, and understanding. His academic education rarely assists him. He is a specialist dealing with questions for which his specialized experience gives him little equipment. Yet he must in fact implicitly or explicitly deal with this question of purpose. The colleges have a great opportunity here.

In a more immediate sense policy includes definition of the concrete problem under consideration; the selection, imaginatively and with a broad base line, of the significant facts and forces which are involved, regardless, of course, of limitations arising out of academic specialization; and the formulation of judgments as to the action required. In this stage, also, good policy involves definition of immediate objectives, both general in the light of long-time purpose and specific, as related to action. It involves consideration and weighing of both current facts and past experience. Here, too, policy suffers severely in practice from the narrowness of the immediate environment. The college could give both breadth of background and essential practice in using this background. Foresight can be based only on past experience and present understanding. The specialized policymaker needs a breadth of experience which goes beyond his individual environment. The college could give this.

In a changing world understanding is necessarily partial and each situation is new. Foresight breaks down frequently from chance, from changed conditions, from lack of knowledge or understanding, or from limitations of human intellect which make it impossible even with the best of background to cope with the diverse facts of particularly complex situations.

Since foresight fails in many cases, the good policymaker considers possible alternative developments and, so far as possible, preserves flexibility and freedom of action to change his policies and move in other directions. This is analogous to the military necessity of keeping open lines of retreat. In this way only can the administrator or the general be in a position to reformulate policies speedily when he is called upon to deal with the unexpected. Often the skilled policymaker, like the skilled general, can change defeat into victory. The specific breakdown of foresight is often caused by some combination of circumstances which was quite beyond detailed prediction. Nevertheless the skillful policymaker can in many cases foresee in general terms the alternative possibilities which may occur. His foresight about alternative possibilities should usually be specific enough to guard against the worst effects of the unexpected happening. A nice balance between timidity and foolhardiness is required. The college can train men so that these things are clear. Now in the hurly-burly of practice men tend to deal with problems on the basis of disorganized experience and resulting intuition rather than on the basis of systematic efforts to classify experience and reduce it to order.

Human factors arise constantly out of the social and technological situation surrounding the problem under discussion and are affected by any policy carried into effect. These factors are both external and internal. They are grievously neglected by most men taking responsibility for leadership in the world of affairs as well as by universities, colleges, and engineering schools. Men can be trained in college to be more alert to see such questions and to deal with them more wisely

To summarize, our leaders of all grades must make policy decisions and get things done not only where the certainties of science are involved but in the world of uncertainty and change. Men have learned from experience to build types of organizations adapted functionally to this necessity. Unfortunately such organizations are limited in their outlook and as a result our general direction suffers. Our liberal arts colleges do little to counteract this. There is a sharp contrast between the functional relationship to the life of men of their scientific work and their detachment from other aspects of human life and experience. Where the certainties of the material world are concerned the universities and colleges have an appropriate relationship. Theory and practice, science and technology, are tied closely together and aid each other. Where uncertainty dominates the problems men face, the liberal arts faculties are not so organized that they can play a natural and useful part. Outside of science and technology, and except in some professional schools, there is a serious functional breakdown between the world of affairs and the academic world.

Systematic methods of adjusting to change are vitally needed. Individually we are in high degree adaptable to changes in our immediate environment. Socially we have for countless generations depended on customs and habits as the basis for stability. We have yet to work out methods of supplementing our weakening habits and customs in ways which keep our social institutions adjusted to our shifting technology and its unforeseeable consequences. This is a problem for policymakers but the academic world in its detachment does little to offset the limitations of the policymaker or administrator and to give him the equipment he needs to deal with it.

We are not adjusted to a machine age. Sigrid Schultz in *Germany Will Try It Again* quotes Hitler as he soliloquized at an automobile show:

> Strange that these machines and all the thousands of other machines in our factories should be changing the human character. But they are. The man who drives his car at top speed has developed a totally new set of reflexes. He does not think any more before he makes a move—there is no time to think. For his own safety he must react with lightninglike speed. Therefore he must act automatically, almost like a machine. A good part of his energy goes into automatic reflexes instead of into thought. That is why in our day and age the number of people who think for themselves is dwindling.[1]

Hitler may well be right in his appraisal of the effect of machines on individuals. Does the liberal-arts college do

[1] Sigrid L. Schultz, *Germany Will Try It Again*, Reynal & Hitchcock, N. Y., 1944, p. 181.

all it might to build up the number of people who not only think for themselves when thought is appropriate, but develop useful conditioned reflexes and understand the place of sentiments and emotions? Does it do all it might to study the problem of adaptation to the machine and the social changes it brings and to define helpful policies to accomplish this? The real problem is whether we can secure enough understanding of the structure of society and of the nature of human beings as they respond to rapid change in their environment so that the intelligent effort of widely educated men can re-create a new moving equilibrium before it is too late. The war by vastly increasing both the magnitude and the velocity of change intensifies the problem. This is primarily the job of education, but of education closely related to practice.

Obviously such questions call for greatly increased understanding of concrete human and social situations. This requires breadth of background, research in human relations, and skilled general thinking about concrete problems. The type of research needed involves field work in direct contact with men as they live and move. Libraries, important as they are, are not enough. Nor, though they may help us to appraise the shifting scene, will statistical compilations of economic and social data alone serve the purpose. We must come closer to life in all its complex and changing manifestations. Scientific methodologies have little pertinence. Obviously, also, we must give greater emphasis to the present as it is illuminated by the past. Where every situation is new, the past alone can rarely solve the problems involved. Above all, we must recognize that in a world of change few principles persist through time.

But in spite of the fact that few lasting principles can be defined, we know from observation that experience counts heavily in practical life. In every field of human activity where experience counts, it can be broken down into its component parts and important aspects of it can be acquired sometimes more thoroughly and always more quickly through organized educational processes than by the disorderly accidents of day-to-day practice. Among the aspects of experience which make men stand out in practical life are background and the ability to use it, judgment, the capacity to make decisions and carry them out, and skill and understanding in dealing with human problems. All these capacities can be developed by educational processes well within the power of liberal arts colleges. Most of them depend on habits and skills on which a good start can be made in college. When by definition lasting rules and precepts fail, or change with time, the educational objectives should be to develop and improve the basis for experience and to quicken the process of acquiring experience in ways which will offset the limitations of the practical environment in which men find themselves later.

CHAPTER VII

Specialization in Practical Life

THE HABIT and indeed the necessity of specialization is characteristic of the world of affairs as well as the academic world. Workmen have specialized skills and specialized environment. So do musicians, artists, lawyers, and clergy. All men in private life who have the responsibility for getting things done, including both employers and labor leaders, are specialists. So are men in public life. Both policy and action are determined and carried into effect from the specialized environment of the responsible leader at whatever level he works. In nearly all cases this environment is narrowing in its effects. It tends to restrict the imagination of men within ruts and to deter them from bringing into their decisions the variety and breadth of viewpoint which is really called for if decisions are to be wise. Much of the present confusion in the domestic situation arises from inconsistent and uncoördinated policies put into effect in Washington by politicians and businessmen. They, like academic specialists, deal with narrow segments of the domestic scene without considering the widespread effects of their policies, the interactions of these policies with policies established by other specialists from other narrow viewpoints, and without watchfulness to observe and adjust their policies to the unforeseen consequences of these activities. Indeed they often oppose such adjustments. Similarly, the manufacturer, impressed by the clean-cut logics essential to his particular technology and his production processes, too often forgets to look at the human consequences of these processes and to fit the two together. The success of sit-down strikes started by small groups in mass production industries is directly related to the contrast between the intense technological integration of such industries and the social confusion within and surrounding them.

Fresh general examination of shifting facts and forces is far more difficult than thinking within the specialized narrow range of daily environment. It is easier to develop logical implications of selected premises than it is to look at new facts, bring in new premises, and then think situations out. It is easier to handle problems by rote than it is to take changes into account. Men face no harder intellectual task than is required to jump the fences which controlled their youthful training, early maturity, and present environment, and to pick up and integrate new forces which often destroy conclusions arrived at thoughtfully and laboriously. They tend to fight against the necessity of considering new facts and even develop blindness which prevents seeing them. For example, collective bargaining in some form is here to stay, yet many businessmen hesitate to accept this. Business must learn to adjust itself to the new condition and to work out methods leading to better human relations and more continuous production before it is too late. These methods must go below the level of controversy into causes of discontent and into ways of making work pleasanter and more purposeful to the individual because its social organization is improved. Willing collaboration would increase production more than many new machines.

Specialization in the world of affairs is dangerous. The major problems of industry and government are not technological or even economic questions which arise out of the immediate environment. Their origin is social. They are concerned with human relations, the relations of business and government, international relations, public opinion, and widespread discontent; with the breakdown of the capacity to coöperate; with the maladjustments of human beings to changes which affect seriously the lives of most of our city folk and all of our farmers. Many of these problems are ignored when the individual situation is narrowly considered, yet they are pertinent in the larger sense to the decisions made. In spite of their specialized environment, men who are responsible leaders need breadth and trained imagination as the basis of the most important task they face—the choice of those things which they are to consider and weigh in making their policy decisions. The immediate organization of industry, labor, and government is in each case badly adapted to developing men who can handle such problems well.

General education could fit functionally into this need. Specialization in particular orientations, technologies, and practices should be left to professional or vocational schools or to experience in life. Such specialization is of course an essential part of the job of getting things done in the infinitely varied careers life offers but it is not a proper part of general education. On the other hand, general education could give men a wide background and train them to use it. It could stimulate and broaden the scope of imagination. It could by practice develop habits and skills which would make men bring into their decisions many factors now missing as they constantly face new situations. As things are now, he is a rare college graduate in business or government who habitually seeks out such factors and adjusts his thinking to them. If this defect is to be remedied, a new attitude toward and a new content in general education is essential. It is the job of the liberal-arts education to develop more rare men.

But to do these things general education must relate itself functionally and effectively to the processes which our leaders, public and private, and indeed our citizens as such, go through. It must train men so that their education supplements the narrowness of their later environment and counteracts its limitations. Education must pay more attention to the things which are common aspects of this job of getting things done. The first and most important which must be taken into account, outside science and engineering, is the fact that in complex situations the future is always uncertain and never predictable in detail. Men of affairs must prophesy not once but constantly. Their present decisions and action are always projected into the uncertain future. The past is important in dealing with this uncertain future for patterns recur in general terms as human beings react to similar conditions. Unlike, however, the predictable recurrence of material phenomena under controlled conditions, social situations can never be controlled and never recur in all their detail. In attempting to read the lessons of history it is at least as important to stress differences as it is to stress uniformities.

The true relationship in social situations is one of mutually dependent variables so numerous and so uncertain that it is impossible to forecast the interaction of the variables with assurance. As a result, assured foresight is impossible in all social problems defined with any breadth and in most activities of business and politics. Judgments are involved inevitably and just as inevitably must in most cases be based on insufficient premises. They are therefore always subject to change as facts and social forces change. Consistency in applying principles regardless of differences in the conditions surrounding the problem under attack or changes in facts which take place with the lapse of time is often a logical and practical absurdity. The British policy of muddling through is logically sound, but it requires skilled and farsighted administrators. This used to be our policy also. In our own case we called it being practical. In later years, influenced I believe by social science, we have come to glorify what we call principles. This is logically and practically unsound.

Current facts are difficult to determine, if, indeed, they can be determined at all. Because of the crudity of the raw data on which they are based, quantities in social situations are hard to fix, even with approximate accuracy. Mathematics and even logic are less useful tools. In fact mathematics and statistics readily fool even the unwary specialist. The mere use of figures or graphs gives a concreteness and an illusion of accuracy wholly unjustified by the facts. Mathematical and statistical processes are so neat and artistic that there is great temptation to use refined methods in analyzing crude material—to cut down trees with razors. Illusions of accuracy produced by the use of figures and graphs are very widespread. Accountants and income tax authorities come to believe their figures in spite of great areas of uncertainty concealed by the concrete symbols on which they rely. It is easy to assume unconsciously that figures tell the whole story or are the resultant of all the forces at work and, therefore, accurately measure these forces. It is particularly easy to assume that quantities smooth out the variety of human behavior, even while recognizing that emotions and sentiments cannot be reduced to quantities, and in spite of the fact that they are more important than reason in controlling both individual and social behavior. In quantitative studies of social facts, as in industrial technology, the ability to be concrete in one aspect of a situation tends to make men minimize the importance and uncertainty of other things which cannot be measured or predetermined. This accounts for the failure of statistical forecasting services.

Since our leaders and our people through their emphasis on materialism have formed the habit of stressing economic interpretations to the exclusion of many other sides of human experience, the present narrowness of the economic base line becomes especially dangerous. Interpretation and policy are often based on narrow and unbalanced appraisals. Of course quantitative economic studies, including studies of trends in many economic fields, are important aids not only in efforts at foresight but when adjustments become necessary to meet unforeseen conditions. Economic quantities and trends are of great importance where it is possible to measure them and their changes and rates of change. When in an absolute sense anything approaching accurate measurements is impossible, relative values as they change with time are significant. Alterations in the rate of change are particularly important. A blow in the face at slow speed is one thing. It is quite another if delivered fast. So, too, the slow loss of an export market for some farm crop may allow time for an agricultural readjustment in which many farmers must be induced to join, while a sudden loss of the market can easily impoverish a region. Such fact-gathering and interpretative work is necessary as part of the basis for judgments involving policy and action just as similar accounting and statistical information is essential in the conduct of private business. But though imperfect and partial information may be a significant fraction of the material used in formulating judgments, it is easy in using such information to forget its imperfections and limitations.

Whenever relations among human beings are involved, neither human sentiments as men adapt themselves to new situations, nor other noneconomic factors, can safely be left out of consideration. No rules or precepts will settle the unknown problems of the future as they change with time.

Under such conditions even the capacity to look at facts is severely limited. The unknown and the unknowable are not to the man of affairs, as they are generally to the natural scientist, things to be studied if he so desires at some future convenient time. They are present facts which he can rarely know in time for use in current problems. He must, therefore, consider and provide against alternative possibilities. Because facts change constantly they are hard to follow, and many facts which it would be useful to know, like for example Mr. Stalin's present objectives, or our own future attitudes toward Europe, are both unknown and unknowable. This is especially true today because the time elements and the magnitude of change affecting the environment and therefore the behavior of men have shortened dramatically. Unfortunately the difficulty in finding and facing facts in a constantly changing situation tends to destroy the habit of looking at facts realistically, and leads men to make assumptions and develop logics which control action but disregard the concrete situation and its alternative possibilities. Conflicts of logics displace coöperative effort to solve problems and tend to obscure the fact that problems are always in process of change. The temptation to substitute intellectual conclusions really based on wishful thinking for the study of facts is great.

> Times and men and circumstances change about your changing character, with a speed of which no earthly hurricane affords an image. What was the best yesterday, is it still the best in this changed theatre of a to-morrow? Will your own Past truly guide you in your own violent and unexpected Future? [1]

It does not follow that nothing can be done. In spite of the limitations under which they work many men acquire great skill in formulating judgments and acting in novel situations which they face. But there are not enough such men.

Unless more men can acquire the skills necessary to sound judgments about uncertain human affairs and unless the

[1] Robert Louis Stevenson, *Lay Morals* (New York, Charles Scribner's Sons, 1921), p. 12.

present widespread idealistic forces in the world can be made both more effective and more realistic, the narrowness of men's specialized environment, constant rapid change, free will, deep emotions, social disorder, and the overwhelming uncertainty in which men live may easily bring about social chaos. Centralized authority is the inevitable reaction to chaos. There is an educational job to be done. Perhaps the too little we have been doing makes it already too late to bring our general direction up to the necessary pitch, but as an associate puts it, "the Vermont way is to fight." The liberal-arts college is in the key position to make such a fight, but new strategy and tactics are required. Science can aid in the fight, but it must not dominate the methods used outside its own field. If our social sciences are to balance both the one-sided consequences of the startling success of natural science, and the narrowness of the surroundings of men of affairs, the whole conceptual scheme of the social sciences and their objectives need to be restudied and redefined in terms of life as men must face it.

CHAPTER VIII

More about Specialization in the Social Sciences

PRESENT INSTRUCTION in social science specialties has little relationship to the problems faced and the functions performed by organizations which have grown up spontaneously in practical life as ways of getting things done. It gives little emphasis to the over-all characteristics of problems faced by these organizations and does little to help by emphasizing the complex variety of social forces which they should consider as part of their premises. It pays little attention to causes of weaknesses and narrowness. In contrast it often suggests conclusions based only on restricted parts of their problems and urges the use of these conclusions as if they settled problems regardless of other facts and forces. Specialized theories and principles are taught to undergraduates in spite of the dominance of change and uncertainty. The introductory course in economics is almost always economic principles. The emphasis is on logics. It is the end of economics courses for most men. Problems such as men will meet in their novelty and full complexity are almost never considered. Judgments and imagination in handling new situations are not stressed. Human behavior is customarily assumed either explicitly, as in the case of the recently deceased but still influential economic man, or implicitly by omission, or as something which cannot be understood but will somehow work out. I find many arguments with economists ending in a refusal by me to accept dollar tests as final. Customarily only the things vaguely defined by custom as being pertinent to the particular specialty are brought into the reasoning.

By one or all of these methods economic principles and theory have secured the basis for the most imposing body of theory which exists in social science. But they have lost touch with reality. Applied economics comes closer to life than economic principles and theory, but relatively few men working even in applied economics understand their fields in their full social complexity by first-hand contact and experience with practical problems. They are still restricted to economic interpretations. They tend to stress public points of view without realization of practical difficulties faced by the individual or the variety of noneconomic elements which need consideration. On the other hand, teachers of business administration often give too little attention to public viewpoints. Both are necessary to understanding.

Economic history may be used as an example to illustrate the difficulty of specialization in social science. Even in highly developed business and industrial nations economic motives and forces cannot be separated from other motives and forces which surround men.

> How do these facts affect the function of the economic historian? Largely interpreted, the subject of his study is the economic condition of mankind at large through the recorded past. But, over a great part of the earth, and during a still greater portion of the past, he finds he has to deal with men who have not reached that clear separation of the economic motive from the other social motives, so that, even if they are actuated unconsciously by economic motives, those motives have to act through the resisting medium of non-economic ideas. This is still the case

if he confines himself to the past history of a country like Great Britain or America, where the fluidity of capital and labour and the comparative absence of restrictive laws and customs give at the present time a large scope for the calculations of the economic theorist. As soon as the economic historian takes a single step into the past, he finds the economic situation more largely influenced, if not dominated, by forces and ideas which are non-economic—the authority of the State, the power of custom and of voluntary associations, the force of nationalist sentiment or of ethical conviction.[1]

If it was true in 1908 when Unwin wrote this, that not even a single step into the past could be made without confusion between economic and noneconomic forces, it is even more clearly so now. It is far more strikingly true than it was in 1908 that the world is dominated by forces and ideas which are noneconomic, including particularly the authority of the State. It is rare that economic motives are clearly separate from other social motives. But surely if economic history cannot disentangle economic factors and motives from other forces, neither can an economic interpretation of the present give a true picture. Even less can economic theory assume that things will work out in set patterns.

The present confusion of thought which afflicts economists and the violent controversies it engenders as we struggle with the dynamic forces surrounding us only illustrate the insuperable difficulties which stand in the way of purely economic interpretations of social situations. Many current economic theses ignore the human characteristics of the electorate. As a result their economic conclusions may be used by less scrupulous men to justify action which in fact

[1] *Studies in Economic History: The Collected Papers of George Unwin* (London, 1927), p. 22. By permission, Macmillan & Co., Ltd.

tends to debauch the electorate by playing on human weakness. Economics can illuminate many but can settle very few problems. The important thing is not specialized economic theory or specialized economic interpretation but general policy based on judgment. Policy must be determined with reference to present facts not conceived as an aggregation of specialties but selected for their current significance and interpreted in their relationships. Policy must always be thought out in the light of human sentiments, desires, and purposes, as well as in terms of the senseless and often unpredictable forces affecting civilization. Human sentiments are facts to be examined currently, not to be assumed or covered by vague general terms.

The dangers of social science specialization and the search for principles are intensified because of emotional reactions. The natural scientist preserves objectivity in his work and minimizes the influence of his own emotions. The social scientist is himself a part of the social organism and is inevitably influenced by his emotions. This is true even when he consciously makes an effort to preserve a strictly intellectual and detached viewpoint. Obviously when the social scientist is seeking understanding, he must do all that he can to submerge his emotions and sentiments, even though at best few can do this with complete success. By such efforts, he can at least avoid many errors from creeping in because he unconsciously rationalizes conclusions actually reached emotionally. But his purpose is rarely limited to the purpose of the pure scientist: the objective understanding of phenomena. One of his objectives is generally reform. He is emotionally interested in converting his understanding of the past and present into programs of action. Here emotions and sentiments are inevitably and properly involved but, certainly if he is in a university, his bias should be fully disclosed. If he realizes the self-imposed limitations on the premises he uses in his specialized approach, the partial nature of things he takes into account, and even more important, the wide range of things he decides not to consider; if he thinks of himself as an expert who can aid in understanding part of the situation rather than as a policymaker; if he makes clear to others that in parts of his work where he seeks understanding he claims objectivity, but that by contrast in other parts of his work he is impelled by his particular and candidly defined purposes of reform; his attitude creates no danger.

Unfortunately the failure to keep in mind the limitations imposed by arbitrary restriction of premises has caused confusion between the function of the expert and the function of the policymaker and doer. The distinction between objective understanding and purposeful reform is rarely made clear. As a result we find many academic specialists in Washington making policy decisions on the basis of the limited facts they are in the habit of considering, and carrying into effect specialized theories without enough attempt to relate other facts and factors to their own customary data and to modify their conclusions accordingly. Nor in recommending policy decisions are they generally explicit as to their purposes. Such limitations are often understood in business which has suffered too often from its experts to forget their limitations; rarely in universities where, in general, professors are not in a position to turn theories into practice, and are therefore not obliged to face responsibly unforeseen practical consequences of their theories; almost never in democratic government where, because no effective method exists for looking at things generally, serious consequences often follow delegating policy formulation and action to narrow specialists or to men who are assumed to be objective when in fact they may be dominated by undisclosed desires for reform. On the other hand, the real value of specialists as experts is frequently overlooked in all three places.

To make social studies useful to citizens and men of affairs in the points where they are weak, there must be a constant search for and study of relationships within and outside the social sciences, always including human relationships concretely studied rather than assumed, and these studies must be functionally related to present problems. There must be constant effort to weigh factors, old and new, which by the flux of events acquire importance. History at its best does just these things, but it faces back. In general, history is apt to minimize or fail to state both the similarities and the differences between the period under study and current situations. Men must act in the present. Their acts affect the future. They must look forward.

Background, methods of attack, habits, skills, and intuitions, necessary for sizing up novel situations and formulating judgments about them, must become major educational objectives. The theoretical and practical limits and bases of foresight in human affairs must be worked out. Ways of adjustment to the unforeseen and unforeseeable must be explored.

> We must not expect too much of social science. We could not regulate the weather even if we could forecast it a season ahead; all we could do would be to adjust our actions to it. There is always hope that if we knew the economic and social future we could do something and would do something about it, other than adjust ourselves to it; but be that as it may, we can at least so educate ourselves as to adjust better to whatever may develop and that is in itself worth while, it is in line with being governed by intelligence.[2]

Specialization is the enemy of this type of approach for it always excludes by express or implied limitation many factors

---

[2] Dr. Edwin B. Wilson, *Science*, February 19, 1943, p. 172.

which should be brought into relationship with the specialist's factors, and the very perfection of his logic tends to impose his conceptual schemes on the unwary. Yet specialization is carried into as atomistic detail in social science as it is in the natural sciences where it is appropriate and successful. We have paid too little attention to the logical differences. Specialization is, I believe, the most troublesome problem facing the social sciences. It will make it difficult for them to make their appropriate contributions to the general education so critically needed by men who are to enter the practical world. In that world the hardest and most important thing to be accomplished is the imaginative selective process of determining as wisely as possible what factors to consider in the situation under the scalpel. This process requires trained alert imagination. The limitations to factors customarily considered in some special field are disastrous.

The harmonious relations which exist among natural scientists when differences of opinion exist or new facts must be fitted into theory rarely exist among social scientists in different specialized fields. When such differences of opinion arise as to social situations, instead of examining premises in an effort to agree on them, most discussions take the form of arguments, often with high emotions, about irreconcilable conclusions drawn from overlapping but different partial premises. Economics may say *A*, and political science, in part from other premises, say *not A*. Without any agreement on premises, arguments end in compromise or in new conclusions reached logically by treating the conclusions of the two specialists as premises in the same way that scientists use each other's conclusions as premises. When this happens the fallacy is as clear as the fallacy of averaging averages.

Such conflicts are inevitable until it is recognized that the real problems are present human and social situations seen and handled in their widest implications.

This does not mean that the social sciences and particularly specialized social sciences must be unproductive. In spite of the suspicion that, through failure to give adequate attention to these limitations, social sciences have done more harm than good since intense subdivided specialization developed, I reach no such dismal conclusion. Careful examination by competent scholars of selected parts of the total social situation, and logical analyses of the interaction of such parts, as they would behave if in fact they could be isolated, can be very productive. Their value, however, lies in modes of attack. They illuminate dangers, suggest constructive possibilities, arouse thought and guide analysis, create partial understanding of the complexity of all social and human problems. The specialized scholar can give expert assistance on aspects of problems, rarely on the problem seen in the large. Sometimes indeed for a time the forces studied in isolation may be powerful enough to dominate a situation. Then his understanding may contribute greatly to efforts to guide the future. Right now, for example, the historical and theoretical study of past inflations may well point the way to methods of avoiding an explosion of our currency and price structure. Even here the general social situation will control action, but an explosive inflation does control social behavior. Except where special factors take such a dominant place, the specialist can rarely be trusted to formulate overall policy.

A strong effort is being made by many social scientists to get closer to life, and the war has contributed a great deal to accomplishing this. But the handicaps are serious. There is far too great dependence on books, periodicals, and statistical material and far too implicit faith in logics. There is too little stress on firsthand contact with men who are struggling with current problems and with the facts surrounding them. The courses men offer are still specialized to the patterns of the established curricula. The teaching methods used are typically either readings, discussions of texts, lectures, or all three. Printed material usually not based on field contacts is almost always the main basis. Problems as they arise, if used at all, are so large and general that they have to be limited in scope. The easy and natural way to limit them is to stick to the type of material customarily included in the specialty. In considering problem material the point of view of the man or group who must decide and act under the burden of responsibility is rarely taken. As a result there is a widespread belief that administration cannot be taught. Indeed it cannot be taught except under this burden of responsibility to select and weigh premises, and to determine action.

Many men, particularly young men, are in revolt against the historic situation, but in liberal-arts faculties as now organized it is almost impossible for the individual to take an over-all point of view. To get promotion he must convince his associates that he knows his specialty and even the subdivision which is his special field. If he wanders far off the ranch he may lose standing and be rated as superficial. Even when he takes the chances involved he lacks the financial resources to acquire firsthand experience with facts. As a result he is apt in his ignorance of many aspects of problems to indulge in large generalizations from the limited materials which are accessible to him. These are mainly within his special field. When he rebels, in his detachment from concrete reality he frequently becomes an ideological radical, as any young man tends to in face of the evils in the world when he is not close enough to problems to realize the difficulties which stand in the way of change and the dangers which may result from reform. The present situation, because it is well established throughout the social sciences in practically all academic institutions, binds the hands of the individual.

Specialization in social science is the inevitable reaction to the growth in volume of printed records, the increased knowledge of history, rapid communication, contacts with the great variety of races and tongues which has resulted from rapid communication, the definition of great research areas and the sheer impossibility that any one person or group can cover the whole field. The objection is not to subdivision of the field. It is to the serious lack of methods and organizations apt to bring about close coöperative effort of many types of specialists in studying the critical problems of society. Moreover, from the viewpoint of the college undergraduate, social sciences, even when he studies several, usually come to him not with unity but as disassociated specialties with no effort at integration. They should be so presented that the student sees their vital relationship to each other and to his life.

> The solution which I am urging, is to eradicate the fatal disconnection of subjects which kills the vitality of our modern curriculum. There is only one subject matter for education, and that is Life in all its manifestations. Instead of this single unity, we offer children—Algebra, from which nothing follows; Geometry, from which nothing follows; Science, from which nothing follows; History, from which nothing follows; a couple of Languages, never mastered; and lastly, most dreary of all, Literature, represented by plays of Shakespeare, with philological notes and short analyses of plot and character to be in substance committed to memory. Can such a list be said to represent Life, as it is known in the midst of the living of it? The best that can be said of it is, that it is a rapid table of contents which a deity might run over in his mind while he was thinking of creating a world, and had not yet determined how to put it together.[3]

[3] Alfred North Whitehead: *Aims of Education* (New York, 1929), p. 10. By permission, The Macmillan Company.

CHAPTER IX

Human Relations

THE MOST IMPORTANT aspect of human knowledge and experience is human relations. It is critically important in connection with the clash between certainty and flux, between the mechanistic successes of science and the confused social situation which is our basic problem. All our civic and private leaders and, indeed, all of us must struggle constantly with human interactions. Curiously, the behavior of ordinary men as they go about the business of life individually and in social groups still lacks the systematic attention both from men of affairs and from universities and colleges which is, I believe, essential to the preservation of western democracy.

Unfortunately, leaders of men, successful practitioners in fields which depend vitally on human behavior, in the main rely on their individual experience and intuitions. This kind of experience is inadequately reported, analyzed, and passed on from individual to individual and generation to generation. Politicians and men of affairs who possess the necessary skills are little interested in reducing their experiences to writing for the benefit of others and are badly equipped to do so. They rarely understand the reasons why they behave as they do. Yet it is such men who have the experience. It is not easy for men in practical life to separate human behavior from other parts of the job to be done and focus attention on understanding human relations or the part they play in the whole situation. In industry attention is apt to be on the logical structure of technology and production. Yet human relations are closely tied in with the working of this structure and vitally affect what is accomplished. Human problems cannot be straightened out if the technological situation is chaotic, nor will ideal technology work well if human relations are bad. Witness the human difficulties of mass production industries. Men working under pressure and fully aware of the importance of technological order in their plants often neglect the more subtle unsystematic human situations and rarely give them explicit attention.

The help of academic groups is essential; yet there are few academic studies of human relations except in labor problems and these usually deal with controversies rather than with the basic human reasons for discontent. Unfortunately, academic theories covering human behavior, individual and social, have in the main been built up, often after isolating men in laboratories, by men little acquainted with such behavior through experience in practical life. Thus practical men develop few generalizations about their experience, and theoretical men have little practical experience. Except in medicine, theory has been separated from practice, and most medical research is concerned with pathological situations. In the universities and colleges adequate attention to human interactions calls for help from a variety of sciences, from social science, and from the humanities, in making concrete studies which will end in an intimate knowledge of acquaintance with men as they live in their ordinary surroundings. Such research is essential to the furtherance of our understanding. In the interest of both theory and practice we need to break down the fences which divide the academic world from the practical world where nearly all the experience in dealing with human interactions exists.

It is difficult to exaggerate the importance of the subject. Allyn Young, perhaps as distinguished intellectually as any economist this country has produced in recent years, summarized a conference with me in January, 1929, on his last trip to this country before he died in England, by saying, "If human behavior turns out to be something radically different from what we economists have been assuming it to be, the extent to which economics and economic theory must be rewritten is almost beyond belief." Yet the behavior of men, individual and social, as they live their ordinary lives continues to be one of the most neglected of studies, mainly because academic people are detached from practice. When serious open-minded study is given to concrete human situations, they almost always turn out to be different from preconceived notions. Since our social equilibrium depends so much on human relations and since rapid change and general uncertainty are constantly complicating all human interactions, there is the greatest need for systematic realistic research carried on in both industry and government by university and college men in close contact with practical men. There is a growing recognition of the need. Men of affairs are being forced by the social confusion which surrounds their activities to pay more attention to these human problems. As a beginning, personnel departments are assuming greater importance both in business and in government. The academic world is beginning to pay more systematic attention to the problem. The time is ripe for real steps forward. Nevertheless the separation of theory and practice still persists in most cases, and even where men wish to break this separation down the resources which would make it possible for men in academic life to acquire firsthand experience with human interactions as they actually arise in life are rarely forthcoming.

I have been associated at the Business School with one research group which had for a number of years both the desire to do clinical research in this field and the resources necessary for the purpose. The human relations group at the School, made up of a small number of men of very diverse background under the leadership of Professor Elton Mayo, has been engaged for over fifteen years in coöperative research based on field work in efforts to get a better understanding of the ways men behave as they work in industry. This work was mainly financed by generous temporary grants from the Rockefeller Foundation. It had extensive industrial coöperation. During the latter part of this period the Grant study under Doctor Bock's Department of Hygiene has engaged in similar research. We have gone far enough to know that many points of attack are needed, all relative to the concrete reality of everyday life, and that such research produces important results. Anthropology gives an essential background with, so far, too nearly exclusive attention to primitive or slowly changing societies and too little consideration of modern societies which are struggling with rapid change and the necessity of adapting to it. This limitation is gradually being removed. Psychology, not of the laboratory type, but closely allied to the kind of sociology which studies men in their everyday social surroundings, plays an important part. As we know from the work of the Fatigue Laboratory, established as a part of this research, physiology has much to offer in peace and in war. Men experienced in administration of human affairs both need help and can give it. At this time an elaborate structure of theory is not the objective. This would be pure metaphysics. We need intimate objective studies of specific human situations—studies carried to the point where men attain an intuitive familiarity with the ways men interact, and come to possess a useful method of looking at them. Theory must follow familiarity with facts and be based on it. This familiarity must be illuminated by insight gained from the sciences referred to above, from recurring social phenomena, and from previous workers who have studied firsthand concrete factual situations involving human beings. I would add also the insight of great writers who based their writings on firsthand experience. It is my judgment and observation that such work skillfully pursued by scientists, by social scientists, including administrators, and by humanitarians, working coöperatively because they want to do it, can contribute greatly to our general understanding.

The research work done at the Business School has been carried into the training of students in ways which improve their grasp of practical situations. Not only by specialized instruction but by constant use in many courses not labeled courses in human relations it has become an important part of instruction. It has proved equally interesting in the adult training of business executives of long experience. But the largest job of education in human relations ever undertaken is not at the Business School. It is the Job Relations Training conducted by the Training Within Industry Service of the War Manpower Commission. In its origins it goes back to a request by the Advisory Commission of the Council of National Defense in January, 1941, addressed to the National Academy of Science, asking the Academy to answer the question "What can be done to increase knowledge and improve understanding of supervision at the work level?" The need was particularly acute because the war expansion had compelled industry to use great numbers of new and relatively inexperienced foremen. This request was referred to the Committee of the Council on Work in Industry of the Academy of which Dr. L. J. Henderson, then Director of the Fatigue Laboratory referred to above, was Chairman. This committee recommended that training be undertaken toward improving the method of handling human situations; in other words, it recommended foreman training in human relations. The Training Within Industry Service undertook to organize such training. The group in charge included men of long and important experience in industry. After months of preliminary work, in which members of the research staff studying human problems in industry at the Business School collaborated, and after thorough field trials a short course was worked out and adopted. The teaching methods adopted rely heavily on realistic cases presented both by the trainer and by foremen themselves out of their own experience. Public announcement of the program was made in February, 1943. The early results were so satisfactory that the training expanded rapidly. Two hundred twenty thousand foremen were given this training in the first year. There is convincing evidence that as a result of this necessarily brief training many foremen improved their human relations and therefore the quality of their supervision.

If effective instruction in human relations can be given successfully in a comparatively narrow field to industrial foremen and more broadly both to regular students in the Business School, and to special groups in the School which are made up of men with long executive experience ranging in age from thirty-five to over fifty years, such instruction can be given successfully to college students.

In this field of human relations I am suggesting the intensive development of another specialty closely related to the lives men live, and indeed such a specialty is needed. It should, however, be noted again, not only that the necessary research work requires coöperative effort of men with varied backgrounds, but also that human relations are ubiquitous in their implications. Outside the pure sciences, they are generally among the important controlling factors which determine judgment and action. This specialty should, therefore, be related to and used in almost all other special fields. Theory and practice should be closely related.

The college has a real opportunity to start men on this process both by organized instruction and by greater attention to their social life. Such instruction is rarely given.

By contrast much of the success of the American college in attracting youth to prolong their education beyond high school has come through recognition of the values gained from the social life offered by the college. For generations this socializing process was both spontaneous and exceedingly effective. It still works well with many students but more heterogeneous groups with more diversified social backgrounds are coming to college. Though they live in close association, the emotional gaps between men are deeper. The complexity of the social situation in the nation has increased. The growing heterogeneity of the modern student body and in many cases the increased size of the college have lessened the results obtained from the old laissez-faire methods. Men start further apart in their background and traditions than they did formerly. It is harder, yet more important, to bring them together in satisfying social organization. For many the problem of adjustment to a new social environment is greater than it was for their predecessors.

If it is to prepare men for life, the college can no longer leave human understanding and social experience to the accident of college environment. These subjects should be taken into the curriculum as part of the educational process. Nor can it leave individual personal adjustments to the social life of the group to extra curricular activities, the dormitory, the fraternity, and the athletic field. These are all valuable, but they are not enough. It is not that the college is doing less with reference to problems of personal adjustment; on the contrary, it is doing more, but the need is greater.

Similarly, three generations ago the social organization of the factory was usually good and labor difficulties relatively few. When factories were all small and men lived in compact well-integrated communities, competent employers knew their workers. The growth and disorganization of industrial communities, the increased heterogeneity in factory workers, and the greater size of factory units make concrete organized attention necessary if, under present conditions, employers are to attain any understanding of the worker's point of view and are to compensate for the new human difficulties in factory management introduced by size and by constant changes in technology. The thread of human adjustment and coöperation should run through much college training and experience, and temper the present emphasis on individual intellectual work. We should remember that man is primarily a social animal; that the intellect does not displace and rarely controls emotions and sentiments. Educated men have many heavy responsibilities, but one of the greatest is to understand themselves and other men. The present effect of college training unfits too many for coöperative effort by emphasis on the individual's intellectual life while it ignores his social life and his basic emotional characteristics. Emotions and sentiments are even looked down upon as intrinsically objectionable characteristics to be completely submerged in the intellectual life. For example, President Hutchins, in what seems to me a modern example of medieval scholasticism, says, "An education which is liberal should free man from the mammal within." And again, "The noblest achievements of mankind, the highest aspirations of the human spirit, these are the essence of our education designed to suppress the mammal, or the earthworm, within us and make us truly human."[1] But the development of the intellect is surely a capstone held up by the physical and emotional foundations of human life and not a substitute for everything which went before in the long history of evolution. Surely educated men do not desire to give up the joys and sorrows and the personal and social ties which depend mainly on these foundations. To me, the ideal he expresses is inhuman. Is it not one of our primary intellectual tasks to

[1] New York *Herald Tribune*, December 19, 1943.

understand and learn how to guide, so far as we can, the elemental emotional forces which so largely dominate our interests and our behavior and lend significance to life even as they complicate it? President Hutchins' thesis would lead us to despise rather than dignify life. We shall not change human nature.

The college is too narrowly intellectual in the criteria under which it trains and judges students if it desires to fit their later needs. Too great a premium is placed on memory, on verbal brilliance, on cleverness, sometimes on stolid but uninspired hard work; too little on common-sense adjustments to men and things—on those qualities which we find so hard to define but so easy to recognize—qualities summed up in such words as "teamwork" and "leadership." In choosing teachers also, personality, character, and the capacity to understand and lift men emotionally are often overlooked in favor of distinguished academic records. I suppose this neglect of human qualities occurs because colleges think of themselves as intellectual institutions and human behavior is deeply emotional. But after graduation men must live in a world where emotions and sentiments have greater power than the intellect.

Individuals live and move and have their being, if they are normal, in constant social contact with not one but with many social groups. Moreover, the individual is not an intellectual machine. He is full of habits, customs, emotions, and sentiments which affect and usually dominate his social behavior and his thinking. His activities are largely controlled by conditioned reflexes, though he often builds complicated logical structures to rationalize his action after he has reached decisions on customary or emotional grounds. When his decisions are not dominated by habit his surroundings are both complicated and uncertain, and he can ordinarily use only simple logics as the real basis for decisions. We can magnify the power of thought if we understand better the emotional mainsprings of action. More effort should be made in college to direct men's minds toward understanding the processes, intellectual, emotional, and cultural, which are involved in the behavior of men as social animals.

The need is great. Much of our labor problem results from the effort of employers to impose technological logics, which are after all essential, upon emotionally upset employees without any understanding of the roots of their discontent. Employers resent the fact that reasonable arguments on the merits of the technological system have so little effect. They oppose C.I.O. fervor with technological logics and material accomplishments instead of by more attention to making men happy. They do not understand why appeals to prejudices are so often more effective than intellectual appeals. This is why since 1929 the reasoned arguments of businessmen have been so ineffective in comparison with political attacks presented as appeals to widespread sentiments. One young man summed up his experience working for a summer as a laborer on an I.W.W. construction job by saying, "Those men don't think, they feel! Why is it?" The summer was well spent. Men should leave college understanding that in most situations men feel rather than think and that sentiments affect the thinking of all men. They should also understand that emotions are never logical and can almost never be changed by reasoned argument. Anyone who has tried to argue the logical merits of a situation with an upset wife or child, particularly when he is himself upset, should know this.

Even now in spite of the long neglect of this subject both in practical life and in the academic world, useful training directed toward better social adjustment of the individual, and greater skills in handling people can be developed. I shall outline one possible approach to organizing such instruction in discussing the Four-Year Curriculum in General Education.

CHAPTER X

The Humanities, Religion and Purpose

ONE OF THE striking things which stuck out in our national life between the two wars was the loss of a sense of purpose. True, we had no large revolutionary movement seeking to overthrow the government or to substitute other ideologies for our own. If we ignore for the minute the antisocial individual and the criminal groups, there is little dissent from this over-all statement. One thing on which the country is clearly united is opposition to and fear of totalitarianism. Labor, management, and capital are in agreement on this. So are all important political parties. The churches are in practically complete accord. No one of our great social groups likes what it sees happening to similar groups when autocracy follows chaos. So we fight hard and with substantial unity to defeat Germany and Japan. As long as we are fighting militant totalitarianism, we have accurate maps and compasses to guide and give a sense of direction and purpose to our activities. But this situation appears to be the combined result of habit, of the fact that men properly fear radical changes because no one can predict their consequences, and of external pressures.

When by focusing our activities and objectives on winning the war we have accomplished our purpose of defeating the enemy, this objective will no longer serve as a guide to the future. For the peace ahead we have as yet no adequate substitutes. When we seek a basis for the continuance of free but ordered society, and for the sense of purpose and willingness to coöperate which alone can give such a basis, we do not find any unity. There is little evidence of any burning emotional interest drawing us intelligently and with united purpose in the direction of perfecting our existing society. We have lost a sense of direction in the midst of overwhelming change. As a result, many serious observers think we are drifting toward totalitarianism.

Here again, and particularly in view of the lessened hold of religion, there is an educational job to be done. A democracy without purpose is on the way to disintegration. Unfortunately, instead of trying to stem this tide, the colleges in the same period seem to have lost their own sense of purpose. As a result they contributed to the loss of purpose in the national life.

I have of course no thought that everyone should agree on all subjects and thereby obtain a well-understood national purpose. A large part of the zest in life and most progress come from disagreement. Nevertheless equilibrium in a changing society depends on the society's capacity to adapt itself to change. That capacity in turn depends on its preserving a large measure of stability and basic similarity in many of the habits, customs, and traditions of the people. Otherwise rapid change leads the society in the direction of chaos. Human intelligence can do little to prevent this for if there are too few stable habits, customs, and traditions, the foundations of judgment are lacking. So it is with national purpose. There must be common ground on which most of the people are in agreement without argument. The general structure of the society and the major things it exists to accomplish must be supported almost automatically as starting points from which disagreements as to the best ways of perfecting the national purpose and attaining its objectives arise. Otherwise orderly evolution of the society is impossible. The heterogeneous characteristics and background of our people, in many ways a source of strength to the nation, in this respect present a problem. Neither the habits, customs, traditions nor the underlying purpose of the nation have had time to shake down into a common basic pattern which is accepted by the principal groups in the nation. Until this is accomplished the nation is in dangerous state. There is an educational job to be done under the lead of the colleges if we are to consolidate the nation in this fundamental sense.

When methods have been devised which prepare men to face complex situations responsibly and to create habits and skills useful in forming judgments on changing facts; when we have learned how to train men to better their understanding of human relations and correspondingly to accomplish things practically through better human relations, this whole field of purpose still remains. Policy depends on purpose. Judgments and action must be related to objectives. The colleges need a more critical definition of their own purpose in life, and students need more stimulus to the analysis of their individual and social purpose. Both need to contribute to building a more unified national purpose.

Anything less than defined purposes for the American college, thoughtfully related to contemporary civilization both to serve as guides in judgments related to short-time policies, and as ideals steadily held as long-time goals, will lead inevitably to flabby planning and to inconsistent action. Except by accident such purposeless efforts must lead to unsatisfactory educational results. Yet in spite of many reform movements, it is doubtful whether there has been since science was established in the curriculum any fresh widespread and comprehensive effort to think through the job of the American college in relation to contemporary needs. Constant patchwork changes have been made, but the main trends in the college have been controlled by the subtle intrusion of specialties until general training has all but disappeared, by the opposition of vested interests to any change, or by the influence of habit and custom on the educational process in spite of rapid changes in the surrounding social environment. I am far from advocating change just for the sake of change. We have too much of that. But all biological evolution points up the lesson that organisms and species faced by change succeed or fail by the measure of their ability or lack of ability to keep adjusted to their environment. The more rapid the changes, the greater the problem. The time has come when comprehensive reappraisals and readjustments will be the price of real usefulness for the colleges in the postwar world. The same wholehearted resiliency will be required in face of the new conditions that so many colleges have shown in adjusting themselves to war, but this time there will be less aid from outside pressure and a heavier burden on initiative from inside. This adds to both the difficulty and the opportunity. Academic people are alert to the danger that in peacetime the nation may fail to adjust itself to changed world conditions. They may be loath to face the thorough overhauling of their own institutions required to readapt these institutions to the changed needs of this century. As I conceive it, in redefining their objectives one of the starting points must be a reappraisal of function in view of the lessened hold of religion in the community and in the colleges.

In the good old days, before organized religion lost so much of its sanction, the fear of Hell and the hope of Salvation were potent forces in maintaining individual character and community standards, just as service to others was at least ideally an integral part of the religious life. Much of the purpose of the college and a large part of the behavior and purpose of individuals was dominated by a sense that this life was preparation for life in the hereafter. Men lived under a sense of responsibility to God. The fear of Hell and the hope of Salvation have less hold now, while the ideal of service has become for too many a cold ethical rather than a warm religious concept. Men have come to feel that God is not interested in them. Reverence is weakened. These changes are, of course, less marked in those colleges which still preserve strong church affiliations than they are in the colleges which have become thoroughly secularized, or in the state universities which never had church affiliations. There is no blinking their widespread significance all through the national life.

A postwar planning committee was recently appointed by the associated boards of trustees of a group of Christian colleges founded in China by Protestant missionary groups in Britain, Canada, and the United States. The planning committee included in its membership men in this country and Canada, selected from the boards of trustees of the colleges and from allied missionary boards. It had the help of several Chinese actively connected with one or another of the colleges. Although I am in no way connected with the Christian missionary movement, I was invited to join this committee as a representative of the Harvard–Yenching Institute which coöperates with several of these Christian colleges in developing Chinese cultural studies. This committee has recently presented to the colleges in China for their comment and criticism a tentative statement of purpose for Christian colleges in China. The objective is to aid the colleges in China as they face the unknown future after the war. Unlike most of the current confusing statements about American collegiate education it started spontaneously with a clear foundation for the development and fulfillment of purpose in the Christian ethic and the Christian religion. I was impressed by what followed from this start.

Of course, the statement would hardly be appropriate for colleges and universities which have no active religious affiliation. Nevertheless, it is worth noting that this Christian base led directly to a definition of the function of these colleges in terms of rounded student development—not only intellectual training, but character training, discipline, responsibility, individual and social service, and even physical well-being. Moreover, religious training and example are the vehicles which the committee proposes for use by the colleges in working toward all these important objectives. So it was in American education in earlier days. But with the weakening of religion as a community force and the collapse of religious instruction in the colleges, the vehicle used for emphasizing all except the intellectual side of education was lost. Even on the intellectual side there was no longer a unifying sense of purpose. Wholly inadequate attention was devoted to finding alternative ways of accomplishing all these important objectives. Indeed except for training in cooperative effort on the athletic field and for minimum policing of ethical standards in student work, the other objectives too often disappear almost completely in favor of purely intellectual training.

At the same time, through the progressive disruption of family life and the breakdown of neighborhood life with its steadying social pressures, the community problem becomes more difficult. In appraising men, monetary tests of success in life and the glorification of power are too easily substituted for judgments based on character and community service. Material things become controlling objectives. Materialism is often substituted for spiritual values and ideals. Cynical appraisals of other people's motives are too often a reflection of the personal standards of the critic and of his detachment from the complexities of life. These are difficult problems to handle. Must our colleges continue to put the men they train through a process which gives almost exclusive emphasis to the intellect and to the accumulation of knowledge? Must they leave not only a respect for facts and their complexity but the whole field of purpose and discipline, character, ideals, and sense of responsibility to the accident of men's disorganized environment during and after leaving college? If so, education presents a real threat to the future.

There is, of course, good reason why in a nation like ours church and state should be separated. Nor is the widespread separation of church and education subject to criticism. Nevertheless, the omission of any real emphasis in American colleges on the essentials of religion and with it the lessened emphasis on human hopes, ideals, aspirations, emotions, and sentiments is a national calamity. Surely, ways can be found to turn out men who will be interested less in material success as such and more in the satisfactions which come from service to family, neighbor, state, and country. Surely the necessity for coöperation in our democracy can have greater emphasis. But to make ideals stick in after life men must be so well prepared to make a living and the social situation must be so organized or reorganized that the opportunity to make a living, necessary to self-respect, is kept open to willing workers. When this is done this essential part of life will stop arousing constant fears, and men trained in our liberal-arts colleges will have less reason to concentrate their intellectual and emotional faculties on the material aspects of life; more chance of keeping their ideals. If, in its training, the college has not stressed ideals and standards, it falls down on its job. I am not criticizing the colleges for the relative loss of religion as a controlling force. In this respect, the college follows the community. I was, however, impressed as I observed the spontaneous evolution in this committee of a definition of purpose for colleges in China which proposed to use Christianity at every stage as the vehicle to accomplish the desired results. Our American colleges have lost this vehicle, and they have not found substitutes. I don't know that there are substitutes for all these things. I am sure that logical, unemotional courses in ethics and social philosophy are not convincing vehicles for character training, for developing a sense of responsibility toward others or for any of the other things which followed so naturally in the work of this Committee from its start with Christian ethics and Christianity.

I believe the American college can turn out men with a deeper sense of reverence for the human race and the job ahead of it. I believe the college can train men with a greater sense of responsibility and a higher sense of their obligation to the community. I am sure it can give men a better understanding of other men and their hopes and aspirations. I am sure the colleges can restate and revivify the ideals of our democracy. Methods can be devised by experiment to accomplish some of the results needed. The best thought we have ought to be devoted to exploring problems of this kind to see if fortunate answers can be found. In this way the whole national problem might be influenced.

We in this democracy ought not to have to wait for a world war to arouse loyalties. There should be less risk that at the end of this war we shall lose the peace because we think too narrowly and selfishly and because we do not think of problems from the other man's or nation's viewpoint. In peacetime we have the most widespread unloyalty, I believe, that there is anywhere in the world. I do not mean *disloyalty*. The failure to hold hard to a thoughtful responsible loyalty is widespread. Yet our forebears did so. Many groups and more individuals have that kind of loyalty and sense of responsibility now, but too many lack it.

In my judgment if such unloyalties are to be cured within a reasonable length of time, if we are to create loyalties that will survive the emotional urges of a war and last through the infinitely more difficult period of peace, there is an educational job to be done. It is a job that to some extent an individual can do for himself. He can accept responsibility, he can make his own, the kinds of loyalties, the kinds of emotional standards, the points of view of which the Christian religion is full. But how to get loyalty and a sense of purpose in the community at large except through education—that I don't know. We have no loyalty in this country in peacetime comparable with the loyalty of Nazi Germany or with the loyalty in Russia. In each case that loyalty is based on a religion which has a strong emotional appeal. Few of us like that religion. Years before this war I saw the youth of Germany marching, happy and singing. Many of our men sing in the middle of war—German boys were singing in the middle of peace. They had been tied together by a new sense of loyalty. It is very well to say we are going to free the world from all sorts of things. We cannot preserve our own democratic freedom unless in some way we get in peace as well as in war a higher degree of community loyalty and loyalty to ideals, unless we can think in terms beyond immediate livelihood and material gain, beyond the short-time objectives that have come to be the impelling motives of educated men partly because colleges have done such a one-sided and purely intellectual job and partly because the community has lost the ancient hold of religion. Intellectualism easily turns materialistic. I do not believe freedom can be preserved unless there is greater emotional interest in and love for ordered freedom as we practice it in peace as well as when we fight for it in war.

We have a chance as a result of the war and the magnificent job of American industry and American boys to restore and keep goodwill. We have a chance to preserve the loyalties which the war has brought forth, to make men minimize the immediate point of view and pay more attention to social responsibilities and obligations. But it is a chance easily lost. Twenty years ago, in the period of great prosperity around 1923–1927, I felt that this nation was one of the least stable nations on the face of the globe. I still feel that way. The only reasons instability has not overwhelmed us are our geographic location and the fact that the war gave us a common objective. In times of peace our capacity to work together, to coöperate, and our sense of long-term ideals for the nation were largely lost. Now that we have at least partially regained them, something must be done to keep them.

We must refuse to accept dollar tests as final. There are more fundamental things to be thinking about. We must think of what we do to society and not be content with the statement that we know the cheapest ways to make gadgets.

> The truly quaint materialism of our view of life disables us from pursuing any transaction to an end. You can make no one understand that his bargain is anything more than a bargain, whereas in point of fact it is a link in the policy of mankind, and either a good or an evil to the world.[1]

We should not forget, however, that to secure a basis for keeping and implementing ideals we must maintain many aspects of our social life in a moving equilibrium. Men must think in terms of ideals and long-time objectives; but they must realize that great ideals and objectives can be approached only by short steps. We require of educated men not only long-time objectives as programs of reform related to distant ideals, but the responsible planning of immediately practical next steps. Balance between the immediate present and the distant future is needed to tie ideals concretely and practically into life. Moreover, if the wise ideals

[1] Robert Louis Stevenson, *Lay Morals* (Charles Scribner's Sons, 1921), p. 19.

of the few are to influence the many, the aid of farsighted men dominated in large measure by self-interest must be enlisted. Long distance enlightened self-interest will not in general be antisocial. Indeed it is quite as important a force as practical idealism. It is when idealism and self-interest both refuse to look at facts at the same time practically, farsightedly, and imaginatively that we must fear both.

As I have pointed out, civilization is a complex of routine and stability on the one hand and change on the other. Partly as a result of the strength of science and the relative weakness in other fields, Western civilization is dangerously unstable. Under such circumstances, steps toward reform, toward long-time purposes, should be taken carefully and not too many reforms should be undertaken simultaneously. Otherwise the whole structure of civilization may be overturned by the unforeseen consequences of changes imposed from above, in spite of the fact that each change seems to the reformer a step toward higher ideals. Moreover, reforms should be scrutinized with great care to appraise and forecast so far as possible their effects on other elements in the social structure, and when they are adopted, similar care should be exercised to make adjustments necessary to meet their unforeseeable collateral consequences. The intellectual Utopia which ignores the limits of practical accomplishment in the present is in no proper sense either purpose or plan. Ideal aims giving a sense of direction must be clearly differentiated from specific Utopian blueprints. A sense of direction need not distract attention from the complex necessities arising out of current fact. A Utopian blueprint does.

In so far as humanity can accomplish long-time idealistic purpose it will be because the ideal slowly but steadily affects action, not because men successfully blueprint the future. The man or the society of idealistic purpose can be tolerant both of human frailty and of the slow nature of social progress. The Utopian reformer is always in a hurry and rarely tolerant of any frailties but his own. As a result he is apt in his attitudes toward current difficult problems to combine witch-hunting with action which brings about a destructive distortion of social equilibrium. Yet a moving equilibrium with much emphasis on routines and habits is the sole possible foundation for progress toward the basic ideals in any civilization. In contrast with the importance of distant purposes and ideals distant planning is excluded both by sheer human limitations and by the unpredictable nature of future events. There is, however, grave confusion between planning and purpose. Many things which should be stated in terms of purpose and ideals and which when so stated would be influential over a period of time in affecting conduct constructively, are in fact set down in blueprint plans for instant accomplishment. In this form they may easily become destructive. So a second European front was a clear strategic necessity if victory is to be won in this war. Prematurely undertaken, it might have caused our defeat.

Commonsense planning as distinguished from long-time idealistic purpose is necessarily short-time and practical; it is a piecemeal attack on problems, recognizing long-time ideals as ultimate objectives, but moving toward them a step at a time whenever such steps are practical. It must always face present difficulties and watch constantly to make adjustments to the unpredictable distortions which new factors introduce. We knew Japan planned war with us many years before Pearl Harbor, yet we were surprised. Our initial defeat did not alter our long-time purpose of victory. It did seriously affect interim strategy and especially all short-time plans or tactics.

Whitehead, using slavery as an illustration, has discussed in his *Adventures of Ideas* this conflict between distant ideals

—programs of reform constantly criticizing the contemporary scene—and present problems. He has shown how general ideas implicit both in Plato's philosophy and in Christian ethics served as constant critics of the fact that classical civilization was founded on slavery and later as critics of the existence of slavery in the modern world. But it took 2,000 years and the development of democracy for this program to culminate in the abolition of the British Slave Treaty (1808), the freeing of slaves by purchase in all British dominions (1833), and the violent conflict which freed slaves in this country. I cannot take the space to do justice to Whitehead's treatment of the subject. Nevertheless in these days of multifarious reforms imposed rapidly by fiat on a society already dangerously unstable as a result of the rapid changes induced by science, a few paragraphs emphasizing the nature of the impact of general ideals on shorter time problems are directly pertinent.

> So modern Democrats, in the nineteenth century, nerved themselves to face the question of Slavery, explicitly and with thoroughness. The slow working of ideas is thereby illustrated. Two thousand years had elapsed since the foundation of Plato's Academy, since the reforms of the Stoic lawyers, since the composition of the Gospels. The great program of reform bequeathed by the classical civilization was achieving another triumph.
> The slow issue of general ideas into practical consequences is not wholly due to inefficiency of human character. There is a problem to be solved, and its complexity is habitually ignored by impetuous seekers. The difficulty is just this:—It may be impossible to conceive a reorganization of society adequate for the removal of some admitted evil without destroying the social organization and the civilization which depends on it. An allied plea is that there is no known

way of removing the evil without the introduction of worse evils of some other type.

Such arguments are usually implicit. Even the wisest are unable to conceive the possibility of untried forms of social relations. Human nature is so complex that paper plans for society are to the statesman not worth even the price of the defaced paper. Successful progress creeps from point to point, testing each step. It is not difficult to frame the sort of defense that Cicero would have advanced, if challenged on the question of slavery. The Roman Government, he would have said, is the one hope for the human race. Destroy Rome; and Where will you find the firmness of the Roman Senate, the discipline of its legions, the wisdom of its lawyers, the restraints upon misgovernment, the appreciative protection of Greek learning? . . .

In fact, we do know exactly the stand taken upon this very question by the lawyers, Pagan and Christian, and by the bishops and popes, of the five centuries succeeding Cicero. Among them were statesmen with more than Cicero's practical sagacity, and his equals in moral sensibility. They introduced careful legal restraints upon the powers of the masters; they protected some of the essential rights of slaves. But they preserved the institution. Civilization, Hellenic and Roman, was preserved intact for more than seven centuries after the death of Plato. The slaves were the martyrs whose toil made progress possible. There is a famous statue of a Scythian slave sharpening a knife. His body is bent, but his glance is upward. That figure has survived the ages, a message to us of what we owe to the suffering millions in the dim past.

We may ask, Would Rome have been destroyed by a crusade for the abolition of slavery in the time of Cicero or in the time of Augustus? Throughout the whole period of classical civilization the foundations of social order could scarcely sustain the weight upon them—the wars between states, the surrounding barbarians, the political convulsions, the evils of the slave system. In the age from the birth of Cicero to the accession of Augustus to undisputed power, the whole structure almost collapsed, before it had finished its appointed task. Even earlier, it had nearly met its fate, and later by a few centuries came the final collapse. It is impossible to doubt the effect of any vigorous effort for the immediate abolition of the only social system that men knew. It may be better that the heavens should fall, but it is folly to ignore the fact that they will fall.

Suppose that, in the middle of the nineteenth century, the shock that overwhelmed the Confederate States in the American Civil War had equally overwhelmed the whole of North America and the whole of Europe. The sole hope of progressive civilization would have been lost. We may speculate about a recovery, but of that we know nothing. In the ancient world, the dangers were immeasurably greater.

The argument of the previous section can be generalized. It amounts to this:—that the final introduction of a reform does not necessarily prove the moral superiority of the reforming generation. It certainly does require that that generation exhibits reforming energy. But conditions may have changed, so that what is possible now may not have been possible then. A great idea is not to be conceived as merely waiting for enough good men to carry it into practical effect. That is a childish view of the history of ideas. The ideal in the background is promoting the gradual growth of the requisite communal customs, adequate to sustain the load of its exemplification.[2]

[2] Alfred North Whitehead: *Adventures of Ideas* (New York, 1933), p. 24. By permission, The Macmillan Company.

Unfortunately, the specialization of teachers, except in philosophy and religion, tends to make them think of and define the ideals which they try to inculcate in too narrow terms and to make them in a hurry for results. Generality of viewpoint even about ideals is too often lost in the narrow limitations imposed by the specialized subject matter each makes his own. As a result specialized Utopian programs too often take the place of virile general ideals and ideas. It is to be regretted also that philosophy, with its heavy emphasis on metaphysics, has to a large extent, at least from the viewpoint of undergraduate education, lost its hold on concrete reality, as religion has lost its "ancient hold" on both the college and society.

If general ideas and general ideals are to attain their necessary posts of influence in the modern world, our educational system must pay more attention to the processes involved in formulating immediate programs which minimize violent change while at the same time it keeps constantly in mind more distant ideals and general ideas as goals toward which we should strive. Now it does neither effectively. Yet every policymaker, every administrator, public or private, every politician, every citizen in his daily life must, in the nature of things, struggle with the first of these two problems, the necessity for immediate action. The college gives students neither a conceptual scheme under which they can work, nor habits and skills which supplement their untutored approach to such immediate problems. In the interest, on the one hand, of the stability without which civilization is impossible, and, on the other hand, of the capacity to maintain the freshness of life in response to change without which the decay of a civilization is inevitable, the second of these objectives, the critique of general ideas and ideals, while it should never submerge the first, should likewise never be far in the background. Our leaders in both public and private administration need to combine these two points of view. It is through such combinations that politicians become statesmen. The college does far too little to aid men in understanding such relationships between the immediate and the ideal, and far too little in searching out and helping men to understand and make their own, great concepts which give purpose and zest to life. For some this zest will come in ways quite apart from the immediately practical and proper necessity of making a living. For others it will come in ways which lead to a more complete harmony between the mode of making a living and the opportunity wrapped up in it for constructive social accomplishment. The desire for such accomplishment is shared by multitudes of men. One grave fault in the machine age is that for so many it separates work from social purpose realized through work.

These are difficult problems for the colleges. The detachment of academic people from the life around them and the fact that practically all are specialists who see only a fraction of the situation create a strong tendency for each to exaggerate the importance of his own segment. Yet specialized knowledge is no substitute for general understanding. The two aspects of purpose, short-time next steps closely allied to planning and long-time idealistic objectives, are rarely differentiated clearly. Moreover, the elements which need to be taken into account in planning practical next steps are often passed over lightly. The limitations necessary in the short view are even looked down upon or dismissed in favor of long-time principles or Utopian solutions; or by the easy assumption that immediate difficulties are but temporary departures from the normal.

Because of the limitation imposed by specialization, distant ideals tend to be narrowly conceived and carried in this form into immediate programs. Too often a philosophical and truly humanitarian viewpoint which brings in the past experience of the race is lacking, and high-minded sentiments ignore the difficult problems of human adaptation to change. The teacher, particularly in social fields, in his detachment from current difficulties tends to seek distant objectives or to attack specific present evils with little study of the collateral results of his attacks. He is inclined to assume that quick steps toward distant objectives could be taken successfully or that immediate remedies for evils could be put into effect if men would only listen to him. Since they do not, he tends in recent years to be impatient of the slow nature of social progress and to seek his objectives through the fiat of government. When he attains either influence or authority in government he is apt, like the totalitarians, to favor using the battle-ax of government power in frontal attacks and to ignore the carnage he is bringing about through his narrow understanding of current social and technological situations and his overweening confidence that, regardless of consequences, his particular program should be attained here and now.

Now the weakness of political idealism is that it tends to exaggerate the force of circumstances. In East London we see around us the power of circumstances over man for evil, and we conclude, not unreasonably, that under better conditions, they might exert an equal power for good. Then, as our imaginations awaken to the vast possibilities of social reform, as we "contrast the petty done with the undone vast," it seems as if, compared with the larger and fuller existence which we believe the future will bring, our present life were scarcely worth having. This is a fatal error. The future we hope for must grow, not out of the thought, but out of the life, of the present. The moral energy needed to carry our ideal to its realization can only be generated in a determined struggle to make the best of the actual. To dwell too much on the future is to dream of the golden egg while the neglected goose dies of starvation. This is the fallacy of political idealism.[3]

Only the inertia of students in classrooms prevents this tendency to be in a hurry and to ignore the force of circumstances from being a more serious danger. Active propaganda in the classroom for special reforms usually creates reaction sooner or later and is generally rather unimportant. But the habit of mind which it inculcates by example in the student is dangerous. Bad mental habits may last for life. When such propaganda is transferred from the classroom to government service the consequences may be far-reaching and destructive. Unfortunately there is a growing tendency to think that all evils can be cured by government activity.

The paucity of men of wide general background and experience on academic faculties and the failure to develop methods of educating students to think of wide present relationships are serious obstacles to reform in liberal-arts colleges. Yet if men are trained to see things in wide relationship, and if at the same time they are trained to think responsibly, they will be less apt to act overhastily on one-sided views of situations or to ignore practical difficulties preventing the immediate accomplishment of distant ideals. They will be more likely to accomplish important immediate objectives. Nor is this point of view inconsistent with maintaining ideals. Again I quote Whitehead:

> In the midst of this period of progress and decadence, Christianity arose. In its early form it was a religion of fierce enthusiasm and of impracticable moral ideals. Luckily these ideals have been preserved for us in a literature which is almost contemporary with the origin of the religion. They have constituted an unrivalled program for reform, which has been one

[3] George Unwin, *Studies in Economic History* (1927), p. 451. By permission, Macmillan & Co., Ltd.

element in the evolution of Western civilization. The progress of humanity can be defined as the process of transforming society so as to make the original Christian ideals increasingly practicable for its individual members. As society is now constituted a literal adherence to the moral precepts scattered throughout the Gospels would mean sudden death.

Christianity rapidly assimilated the Platonic doctrine of the human soul. The philosophy and the religion were very congenial to each other in their respective teachings; although, as was natural, the religious version was much more specialized than the philosophic version. We have here an example of the principle that dominates the history of ideas. There will be a general idea in the background flittingly, waveringly, realized by the few in its full generality— or perhaps never expressed in any adequate universal form with persuasive force. Such persuasive expression depends on the accidents of genius; for example, it depends on the chance that a man like Plato appears. But this general idea, whether expressed or implicitly just below the surface of consciousness, embodies itself in special expression after special expression. It condescends so as to lose the magnificence of its generality, but it gains in the force of its peculiar adaptation to the concrete circumstances of a particular age. It is a hidden driving force, haunting humanity, and ever appearing in specialized guise as compulsory on action by reason of its appeal to the uneasy conscience of the age. The force of the appeal lies in the fact that a specialized principle of immediate conduct exemplifies the grandeur of the wider truth arising from the very nature of the order of things, a truth which mankind has grown to the stature of being able to feel though perhaps as yet unable to frame in fortunate expression.[4]

[4] Alfred North Whitehead, *Adventures of Ideas* (1933), p. 18. By permission, The Macmillan Company.

Surely one of the functions of the college and the university should be to seek the explicit statement through "fortunate expression" of great ideals and general ideas, which will do their part in haunting humanity and slowly modifying immediate action through the uneasy conscience of the age. But surely, too, one of their functions is to stress the importance of the immediate present and the fact that it continuously confronts us with problems which must be solved. Nor is this immediate function of minor importance. The glory of France as of the Greeks has been their insistence on general ideas, with perhaps too little attention to the immediately important. The glory of Rome and of England has been their capacity to muddle through, with perhaps too little attention to distant ideals and general ideas. Yet the Pax Romana and the Pax Britannica alike testify to the importance of sufficiently high levels in the administration of immediate problems continued over long periods of time. It was the British who freed the slaves. It was Rome from which Christianity spread. And France collapsed, largely in a confusion of ideologies. Social progress depends on the slow process of meeting day-to-day problems with the skill which alone gives vision a chance. Training which brought such contrasts out explicitly would give the beginnings at least of a basis for both judgment and intuition with reference to changing present facts, as well as a better basis for the play of general ideas and ideals. For many it would be the foundation for wisdom in maturity. We need such wisdom to make our democracy work.

In this field of ideals I believe the humanities can make the greatest contribution. Out of the vast experience of the human race as it struggles toward a morally defensible and at the same time practically efficient organization of human society, there is a long record of human hopes and aspirations, successes and failures. To a large extent the humanities are the custodians of this record. The great arts and the great literatures, philosophy and religion, history, all should be interpreted with reference to the present as it includes the past and looks to the future. Out of such a sorting process should come a large part at least of the imaginative grasp and insight which would give emphasis to the general ideas most significant to us. The great arts and the great literatures should help us to define concretely, out of the experiences of the race, the ideals toward which we should be striving and in some measure the difficulties of attainment. But here, too, we run into atomistic specialization. The gaps are too big for the student to bridge. The way our educational paths are organized, the undergraduate never sees the forest for the trees and very few of the trees. The sweep of man's struggle through the ages is concealed from him. The study of history, for example, involves too many courses, too little high lighting, too many dead kings, rulers, and military leaders, too little discussion of the assets and liabilities of different approaches to the "endless adventure of governing men"; too little sorting out of the ideals and ideas which have influenced men; too little of the lives led by, and the hopes and aspirations of, different sorts of men in different times and circumstances, too little of the evolution of scientific thought and engineering, and its social impact. Above all, too little emphasis on the likes and differences between the periods studied and our present world with its distinctive pace of change. History could be so conceived and taught that it would include the great arts, the great literatures, philosophy and religion, science and technology and bring all to bear on the present. True, history so taught would necessarily be superficial, but would it be any more superficial than the smatterings of courses in history and the humanities now taken by the ordinary undergraduate in his disassociated mélange of courses? Except as required for pedagogical reasons, the college, when it is engaged in general training, has no proper place for small unrepresentative segments of subjects given without perspective or association with other fields.

The humanities can contribute much to the understanding of human relations. They cannot do the whole job. Both scientific and social research of a very concrete nature is necessary. Yet both literature and art include many works of genius by men who possessed peculiar insight into human problems which might both guide research and illuminate its results. Literature and art can be used as the basis for interpreting great ranges of human successes and failures. So, to me, the art and literature of the period between the world wars stands out for its chaotic quality and thereby illuminates the social conditions which existed. The disillusionment and lack of purpose in human and social life which are apparent from the art and the literature supplement economic and political interpretations in ways which give the basis for a better and deeper insight into the over-all social situation and the inadequacy of economic or political action as the solution of our long-time problems. If we had no other evidence than the graphic arts and the fiction of this period, we would know we were dealing with a disintegrate purposeless society.

Of course there are other reasons for studying the humanities. There is the sheer joy of living which they can bring and the contribution they can make to the constructive use of leisure through worth-while hobbies and the pleasures which come from trained and sensitive aesthetic appreciation. These are important objectives. Standing alone, are they all the humanities have to offer to a troubled world?

By the variety of experience the humanities offer, they can do much to prevent the sense of futility and boredom which is such an easy consequence of thinking and acting within narrow bounds and such a damper on imagination. We too easily go stale and resent the intrusion of new ways of thought or new facts into the comfortable dead level of our accustomed rounds. The hardest job we have is the imaginative grasp of new facts and factors and their integration with our established notions. The humanities can be a great stimulus to the imagination and to its breadth of background. But can they make this contribution by atomistic specialization?

If the humanities are to make major contributions to the critical needs of Western civilization, they must, as in the case of social science, come to have a functional relationship to the lives men live and to loyalties, ideals, and purposes which dominate men's activities. Now they are too completely disassociated from the lives men live. When the humanities influence men it is too often by giving them a kind of private apartment to which they can retire from the turmoil of reality—a pleasant place detached from the active lives they lead. Religion, philanthropy, and the humanities are all apt to live apart from the rest of life. The intercommunication system, if it exists at all, has grown like Topsy rather than to a unified design of living.

If this lack of functional relationship is to be remedied, objectives must be defined and pertinent areas in the humanities must be integrated. Then instruction must be so organized that its direct relationship with life is made clear to the student. How this may be accomplished, I do not know in any detail. History, stressing also art and literature, seems most likely to be the key. As the humanities are now organized, it is easy to suggest roads to interesting hobbies or to the development of aesthetic appreciation in some special field. But it is hard to advise students how to get what they properly desire when they seek a rounded education and feel that it should include substantial emphasis on the humanities.

Religion should not be ignored. In universities and colleges, and in independent institutions training for the ministry, religion should take an affirmative part not limited to theology. Many independent theological seminaries are closely related to state universities and can help toward such objectives if there is significant coöperation. Unquestionably, theology is important. Its organized study can be one of the great ways in which the essentials of religion are separated from glosses of historic error and of irrational and uninspired superstition. So is training in seminaries for preaching and for parish work important. But these schools and our colleges have another function in relation to religion. In spite of relative weakness in comparison with their standing even three generations ago, Christianity and its visible manifestation in the church, and the ancient religion of the Jews can surely contribute something to the restoration of a sense of purpose to Western civilization and to the critical problems we face because we have lost our old sense of responsibility to God and to an alarming extent our sense of the dignity and importance of the human race. In the last analysis these are individual attitudes, but they are fundamentally related to the general community attitude. I know it will be said the churches are making such contributions. But to me they have to a distressing degree lost their functional relationship to life as men meet and struggle with it. I do not believe they regain this functional relationship by frantic efforts to hold and express opinions on every current social problem, regardless of their grasp or lack of grasp of its intricacies. The social organization of religion is an important element in the church, but religious training does not equip ministers with knowledge or understanding on which they can safely make great social generalizations. Religion may easily suffer from efforts of the church to take an active part in the solution of complex current problems as it has suffered from attempts to defend error against the progress of knowledge.

It is one thing, and an essential contribution, for the clergy to point out critical evils in the structure of modern society. Persistent or intermittent unemployment of men seeking work can be used as an example. The church could have done more, while work in industry was becoming the only way of earning a living for a constantly increasing percentage of our people, to challenge laymen by stressing the insecure moral and religious foundation of an industrial society which fails to attain substantial success in solving this problem. It is quite another thing to jump at Utopian solutions couched in idealistic terms without facing the vast difficulties to be met. Industrial unemployment is a new problem in its scope and intensity. So far only two solutions have been found and proved, war, including preparation for war, and totalitarianism with its attendant loss of most of the progress toward individual freedom for which Western civilization has struggled for centuries. All important social problems in the rapidly changing modern world are inevitably complex. So it is with the peace which must follow victory. We shall not find the way to a durable peace by imposing on the world any piece of mechanism idealistically conceived in a wave of widespread popular appeal unless there is behind it the persistent purpose to make it work, shared by a multitude of people and groups of people with conflicting interests. Mutual understanding and willingness to sacrifice both resources and lives to accomplish this will both be necessary. There is grave danger that the churches will actively and uncritically support any idealistic plan in the beginning and in the end fail to do their part in preserving the essential interest and spirit of sacrifice which will be necessary when popular interest tends to fall off. In all such problems it should be the function of the church to arouse and keep aroused the moral, ethical, and religious energies of the people rather than to find the necessary successive solutions to constantly changing problems as they arise. These will always require intimate knowledge of facts and a careful appraisal of the difficulties which of necessity go with diversity of interests, limitations on human foresight, and the frailty of human nature. Faced by the sure fact that the future is both unpredictable and dangerous, we must watch and tend any machinery we set up as Holland watches her dikes.

The minister or priest can, if he has sufficient understanding, be of great help to individuals. Many people need help in integrating their own lives into a consistent unity in which ideals always play a part. He can also do much to arouse important social groups to a keener sense of group responsibility and of the significance of group attitudes in relation to the community at large or to other social groups. The field of specialized group ethics and group responsibility is inadequately stressed. Indeed, its scope and importance is hardly appreciated. This is not strange because group ethics are part of the larger subject of human relations and the whole subject is neglected. Religion in a democracy, if it is to be an effective force, must influence the behavior not only of individuals but of groups. Neither conscience nor a sense of responsibility can be created for men, but conscience may be enlightened and a sense of responsibility already existing can be stimulated and developed not only in individuals but in great social groups. Such groups can be aroused to the magnitude of the task of learning how to live together. Religion and the humanities can help bring the subject home to youth. They can add to the understanding of youth and set up guides to conscience.

No greater challenge exists, for live together the human race must. No one lives to himself. Ethics deals always with groups. As Professor Palmer has said, the smallest social and ethical group we can imagine is three, father, mother, and child; and everything that happens after birth almost inevitably broadens the group, with internal conflicts and external conflicts for each group we define. Conflicts of interest are inherent in life. The interests of the family with all its internal conflicts are diverse from those of the church, the local community, or the state. In ethics, as in life, the individual and the group must constantly appraise situations, resolve conflicts, and ultimately determine action, always with insufficient premises, and always, if the individual or the group respects itself, with final accountability to itself alone.

Through long centuries of evolution, through constant trial and error, the community at any one time lives under, or at least understands, a fairly definite set of general ethical concepts. In addition, coherent special groups tend to develop additional group concepts to govern the behavior of its individual members. At the present time, the group ethics of Politics, Business and Labor are especially important. Obviously each of these is subject to the rules of the game which apply generally, for each group is part of the community. General community ethics does not become specialized group ethics simply because a politician or a businessman or a labor leader is involved; nor should any self-respecting man ask for lowered ethical bars simply because he is in such a group. Each group must adhere to the rules of the game as played in the community or it is non-ethical under those rules. While conflicts arise which necessitate the breaking of given rules under the dictates of a higher conscience, the burden is heavy on members of any such group, as it would be on each of us as members of a family group, to justify giving precedence to our own specialized ethical viewpoints when such precedence requires overriding and trampling under foot the evolutionary ethics under which we as a community live. I am not referring here to the rules laid down by the law and the policeman but to the ethical concepts which have their roots in conscience, to infractions of the rules from which one shrinks because of one's own self-accountability.

What, then, is left for group ethics if general community ethics are both assumed and eliminated from the discussion? Twenty years ago I should have answered—nothing; for I should have said that just as business English is bad English unless it is good English, and good English is *ipso facto* good business English, so good ethics is *ipso facto* good group ethics and that ends it. I now think I should have been wrong—wrong in one of the most significant areas for human study. For two whole ethical areas still remain: the internal relations of the group, how businessmen or politicians or labor leaders are to live together each within his group; and the external relations of the group, how they are to live with the community. Both these fields are obviously included in the ethics of the group and conversely, as I conceive it, nothing else exists as a part of the special ethics of the particular group.

The art of living together within the group is here omitted from consideration, except for the statement that in many ways bad ethical standards within a group have bad repercussions on the relations of the particular group to the community at large. It is in the second part of the subject, which deals with the art by which each group may live in and with the community, that the most significant and most neglected aspects of the subject lie. It is here that the religious workers of the college can help most. The basic concepts of group ethics and group responsibility are hardly beginning to take shape in all three of the groups I have mentioned. Social evolution is only now touching upon them. At the same time they are of all ethical areas, with the exception of international relationships, the most important with which the race has to struggle.

Yet politics has been with us always and business started long centuries before the dawn of history. Men have ever earned their living by labor. Apparently, if time and the trial and error of centuries are the basis of evolution, the subject should be most highly developed. In fact, many of our general community concepts must have developed out of the slow results of many centuries of politics and of trading and working together. But politics, business, and the labor movement as we know them are new in their broadening scope, new in their social significance. In their present form they are so deeply affected by the progress of science and by the industrial revolution that the whole problem of group relationships is new for each group. No one of the group has learned how to handle these changes well. None yet recognizes the magnitude of its responsibilities for the future of civilization or that these responsibilities require restraint as well as action. The ordinary forces of evolution, tuned to the measured tread of geological and biological evolution, work too slowly for the new ethical problems which now face these groups. An intelligent race must find a quicker answer to the problem of living together in our constantly changing environment than through slow evolution by trial and error. One necessity is a far greater development of group responsibility and group ethics to fit the new need.

I am most familiar with business and business ethics. Nevertheless I think the improvement of political and labor ethics of equal importance and their present state at least equally dangerous. All the forces of the humanities and of Church and State and all the aid we can obtain from the unity given by war are needed if we are to have time to work out these problems. For without overlooking the outstanding men in each of these groups who have a sense of this overwhelming responsibility, politicians, businessmen, and labor leaders as groups fail to recognize the problem. The ethics of politics is wholly inadequate for the new functions assumed by government. Only in the last half-century has any considerable sense of group solidarity developed among businessmen. Moreover, much of existing group consciousness in business is defensive in character. Too frequently the most critical elements in codes are inserted merely to defend the existing state of things. Men feel their common need for defense far more readily than they develop a sense of constructive group responsibility, and the infinitely varied technique of modern industry tends to obscure common aims and common responsibilities. Labor is as a group militant rather than constructive. Through religion a keener sense of group responsibility in all these groups might be aroused.

But in addition the intellectual background and training of politicians, businessmen, and labor leaders is inadequate to a serious degree. This is partly because of the slow development of general education in our colleges. The lawyer who enters politics rarely has the wealth of experience necessary to realize the ramifications of his activities. There is nothing comparable, in the typical group background of the business group, to the severe intellectual training of the scientist or even of the doctor or lawyer. Labor leaders, with more excuse, are all too frequently short-sighted to the disadvantage of labor. Much must be accomplished before we shall find in the leaders in all these groups the trained capacity for considering the social consequences of their activities. Unfortunately, with the best of intent, this task of defining group ethics, of developing the art of living with the community, cannot be accomplished without trained, hard-boiled, institutional thinking—thinking, not in terms of this and next year's election, profits, or hourly wages but in terms of the permanence of institutions and groups so managed that the community wishes them to be permanent.

Of course, in developing this art, we should take advantage of the widespread idealism which exists in this country of ours, but this idealism easily turns into high-sounding phrases used to persuade men to other 'isms. No high-sounding phrases will long conceal political lust for power; no amount of support by businessmen of hospitals and charities, of fine arts and universities, will remove the stigma of materialism from our civilization; no agreement not to strike will offset the fact of strikes in wartime. Idealism must be focused by the group involved on the great task of adjusting its progress to other community interests. Moreover, the idealist will always be in the minority. In order to accomplish the desired result, we must bring to our aid in all possible ways the elemental basic instincts of our common humanity, such as fear and selfishness, as well as the desire to stand well with our peers. We must be concrete in our handling of specific cases and definite in our interpretations of situations.

Fortunately, we can bring to our aid one fundamental human characteristic. We tend in all matters to live as if we were eternal. Among the complicated hazards of modern life, we continue to plan for the future as if we were institutions instead of men. With the fly-by-night and the thug we shall make no progress, but these are a minority. More and more men are taking this institutional point of view and the institutional view brings to our aid the element of time.

With this time element we can build much on our other basic instincts. Fear may become fear for the future; selfishness, long-distance intelligent planning; and the desire to stand well with our peers may easily translate itself into pride in the progress of the institution or profession we serve. Through this type of institutional thinking, and through the conscientious and responsible use of power on sound social lines, permanency of institutions soundly evolving to meet changing human needs may be secured and constructive systems of group ethics may be achieved.

The sense of responsibility developed must be group responsibility. It is the political or business or labor group as a whole which must live with the community. Every subdivision of the group and every individual who departs from sound ethics and fails to recognize his share of this group responsibility, is antisocial, and threatens by so much the whole orderly evolution of our civilization. Yet this group recognition of group responsibility hardly exists today. The leadership imposed on these groups is still thought of as an opportunity for power or money-making rather than as a call to the most farsighted leadership.

Let me illustrate what this means by comparing the ethical code of law and medicine with the typical trade-association codes. So far as I know, no similar codes exist at all in politics or labor. The first group of codes is evolutionary in character. In other words, the compilers of these codes were attempting to reduce to writing the then-existing state of the best ethical practice in their several professions. This practice was the result of centuries of evolution. The trade-association codes, by contrast, are handmade. At their best, and in so far as they are not merely defensive, they represent the effort of forward-minded men to create and define canons by which their business should be run. This is a real advance but the differences between these and the evolutionary codes are striking. Both types of codes include certain community concepts which hardly belong in the specialized ethics of a group. Both deal with problems which arise from living together within the group. There, however, they part company. The codes of law and of medicine each include important categories of activity which from the community standpoint are ethically neutral; that is, from the outsider's standpoint they depend for their ethical coloration on the facts of the individual case, are good or bad as the facts in each case determine. Yet the codes say that the whole type of activity for the particular profession involved is bad and taboo. In every such case, the type of activity which is condemned either tends to bring the good name of the profession into disrepute, because it puts too much of a strain on human nature, or it bears even more directly on the relations of the group as a whole to the rest of the community. Practically nothing of this sort occurs in the handmade business codes unless we except their re-enactments of the Golden Rule. Group solidarity and group responsibility have not reached the point where even high-minded men see that types of activity, which on the average tend to lower the tone of the group or to hurt its relations with other groups and with the community, must be taboo irrespective of the ethical coloration of the particular situation. Mingling the funds of the client with one's own funds may be all to the advantage of the client, yet the ethics of the law forbids the whole practice, obviously because it puts too great a strain on human nature. He would be a rare businessman or labor leader who refrained from an individually sound transaction because on the average such transactions put too great a strain on human nature. The same statements apply in politics and labor. Yet such considerations are the very core of the art of living together and the substance of group ethics.

In the evolutionary development of codes we have an apparent departure from the basic principle that the test ethically is good conscience. This departure, however, is only apparent. Indeed, what we really have is an extension of the rule to make it include the group as a whole. Politics, Business and Labor must each develop and enforce a group conscience if the evolution of their ethics is to be speeded up—

a group conscience which will hold not only the individual but the whole group to both personal and group responsibility for relations with the rest of the community. When this degree of solidarity is accomplished, and when all three groups have to a reasonable extent acquired the ability to enforce their own sanctions, and not till then, will they have assumed the responsibility which has been forced on them by science.

It will be said that it is a function of the law to define these standards, for the law is made by the community, and the community should define the basis on which it wishes its economic structure to be organized and managed. Of course, the law and the policeman must define and establish those minimum standards to which the lowest must conform, and they may even in many fields determine the average of conformity. But the statement that in a world of change we should have our standards fixed by laws is open to serious question.

For illustration we may consider a few of the great economic changes of the last three hundred years and see how they have actually been dealt with: the development of the credit structure in England, the change in England and the United States to the factory system, and the development and curbing of trusts in the United States.

When our modern instrumentalities of credit were developed on a large scale in a tidy little situation in England, they at once became instrumentalities of oppression of a most serious nature. Popular legislation had not then been developed; and the common-law courts, with their doctrine of *stare decisis*, were powerless to find ways by which a deed, given as a mortgage, could be prevented from taking effect as an absolute conveyance on failure of the most technical condition. The church courts came to the rescue with penalties impinging on the conscience of the litigant. The common law gave unquestioned secular rights, but common-law rights were hard to enforce with Hell's fire and damnation and the pains of excommunication brought to bear from the other side on the ground that the transaction was unconscionable. Not everyone even then, however, respected the orthodox church, and in due course a whole system of jurisprudence—our modern courts of equity impinging with their decrees on the conscience of the individual but backed up in their authority by the secular law—was brought into existence to cope with such problems. The socializing of our credit structure was slow, but it was effective. Now we are quite unconscious of the extent to which we depend on the smooth and fair working of credit instrumentalities. In spite of the fact that the structure creaks under the weight of recent government controls, the credit structure is a great social asset.

Between the time when the equity courts developed and the rise of the factory system in England, two things occurred. The doctrine of *stare decisis*—by which principles of law once decided are binding on future similar cases—was taken over by analogy from the common-law courts into the equity courts. This was natural, for the judges in the equity courts were all lawyers trained in the common law, and the doctrine was thought of as the cornerstone upon which the common law was built. The collateral effect was, however, inevitable. Conscience, like law, became reduced to rules, and slowly the daring and the initiative of the courts of equity in dealing with new situations in new ways grew less and less, until today our equity jurisprudence is almost as ritualized as the common law.

This process was accentuated by the growth of popular government and the rise of Parliament. More and more in England the solution of unsatisfactory social conditions was sought through Acts of Parliament. While the House of Lords was still powerful and the House of Commons still predominantly agricultural in its control, the factory system grew up in England. This is not the place to discuss the social disintegration which came from the early failure of both courts and Parliament to deal properly with this startling change and to socialize it before the wounds became too deep. Nothing but our huge undeveloped hinterland, with its limitless opportunity to settlers, prevented similar consequences here. We did not entirely escape. Too many New England mill towns partook of the characteristics of old England, and the arrogance, feudalism and shortsightedness of our business barons of the last half of the nineteenth century is directly responsible for many inept legislative remedies for recognized social ills. Consider the Interstate Commerce Act, one of the by-products of which was to weaken the initiative of our railroad executives; and the Sherman Antitrust Law and its amendments, which today prevent socially sound cooperation, price-fixing, and combinations, and are largely responsible for the shocking social waste of natural resources like coal, oil, and lumber. As a result of the failure of social groups to rise to the necessary heights, the skilled function is taken away from the skilled hand till the skilled hand loses its power and the social responsibility is wholly in the State.

Our financial history is full of incidents of particular industries and companies which at certain times have had the most optimistic prospects for the future both in their mechanical developments and in their marketing prospects. In many cases these prospects have not materialized because of the failure of part or all of them to take into account public opinion. This was true of the railroads at one stage in their history. It was true of the public utilities and of the stock exchange. On the other hand, we have notable examples of companies which intelligently study their public relations and avoid blindness and arrogance in these relations.

Changes in thinking and in public attitudes are apt to be as rapid as mechanical revolutions. Only foresight and adaptability in policies and management can meet this changing situation.

The only success the English-speaking world has had in dealing with rapidly changing environment has been through the church courts and the equity courts in their period of untrammeled vitality when they impinged freely on the conscience of the individual and dealt freshly with new problems, not by fixed rules.

In the nature of the problem static legal solutions, whether defined by the courts under the doctrine of *stare decisis* or enacted by Congress or by the state legislatures, are ill adapted to a changing society. If even the best among us, with the best possible knowledge of economics and society, were members of legislative bodies solving through fixed laws our problems of living together with the community, such laws would be obsolete before they could become binding and inept almost from the start because their consequences would be unpredictable. As the difficulties of fixed laws are realized we seek to cure them by delegating authority to administrators and administrative tribunals as a modern substitute for the discretion of the church and equity courts. Unfortunately we have thereby substituted government by men and zeal for quick reform for the even-handed application of laws. In the present state of our politics these are poor substitutes for the church and conscience. The development of group ethics, the task of learning how to conduct government, business, and labor in ways that add to general security and happiness, should be undertaken primarily by men of experience whose objective should be to do the job so well that the law and the policeman are unnecessary. If business or labor fails, the law will treat it as antisocial, and inept remedies with unpredictable but surely bad social consequences will continue to add stresses and strains to the structure of civilization. If politics fails to attain the necessary standards, democracy cannot endure. The test of group ethics is good conscience, not of the individual for his own actions alone, but of the individual and the group for the group, to the end that the good name of the group may not suffer, and that its affairs shall be conducted with an aroused and trained sense of responsibility for the future. All types of group practices which under this definition put too great a strain on human nature must be considered unethical, and men in all three groups must be rated by their fellows less for their ability to appropriate political or economic power and for their success in accumulating power or dollars and more for their social imagination and institutional farsightedness. The humanities and religion in the college could do much to arouse men to this type of responsibility and to make them realize its overwhelming importance.

Just as the law is inadequate to solve the social problems of an individual civilization because it is slow to operate and static in its nature, so codes of ethics have their limitations and their dangers.

The ethics of the legal profession largely stopped its evolution with the codifications of professional standards of the last century. Today the ethical codes of the law need rethinking to fit them to a changing business and social structure. Professional and business codes have their field of usefulness. Just as the law itself as defined by legislation and the courts must needs define minimum standards to which all must adhere, so codes of ethics may well be adopted by business and professional groups to define that minimum of ethical standards without which proper relations with the community can never develop; but if we must codify, let us realize the static characteristics and limitations on codes and constantly study and revise them as our understanding progresses. The only stable thing must be the spirit with which we approach the subject—enlightened conscience. Rules must change with every significant change in environment or method. The challenge is constant and calls for the best there is in us.

I have intentionally left to the end a word as to the power of the community generally to regulate the ethics of particular group relations, aside from its power to regulate by law. Here we are dealing with perhaps the most significant element in the whole situation and one of the most dangerous.

It is the behavior of the tribe which determines the character and type of tribal leadership. If the community expects much from its leaders it will get much. If it expects and honors political appeals to prejudice or cynical money-making or if it values labor leaders who get results regardless of methods and esteems these accomplishments, it will produce this type of leadership. Many in university faculties are still inclined to look down on the whole world of affairs and to rate its activities in a lower category than the arts and sciences. This point of view ignores the intellectual, ethical, and social opportunities and the challenging responsibilities which lie in this field. Such attitudes lower the ethical standards of the community and of important social groups.

A discriminating public opinion, approving and rewarding socially sound accomplishment in politics, business, and labor, and ostracizing the socially unsound, might bring about a real contagion of health. For most of our ethical and social standards in all areas are made effective, in the last analysis, by the force of public opinion.

Both religion and the humanities in the colleges could do much to focus public opinion on such problems by making educated youth understand them.

Our religious leaders should carve out for themselves

functions which are religious or closely allied with religion and at the same time within the powers of men trained in religious work. Have not men in our universities and colleges who are engaged in religious work a function to perform, similar in some respects to that performed by pure scientists in the field of technology? Should they not do more, both to make religious ideals and ethical concepts explicit by fortunate expression and to make clearer the processes by which such ideals may be related by the individual to his life? The Golden Rule is a great ideal, but its application to concrete situations is a difficult and complex problem involving intimate knowledge of detail, real intellectual effort, and not only skilled human understanding, but human sympathy which is not easily converted into sentimentalism. Should not our religious work make it clear to students that the final stages of relating religious ideals functionally to the concrete circumstances of life are an individual and group responsibility depending for wise handling on a wealth of detailed knowledge about the concrete situation which neither the teacher nor the minister can possess. Just so it is made clear to scientific students that the final stages of applying science to life are a task for the man on the firing line who knows, in their complexity, the concrete conditions which must be met. I believe there is an important opportunity for the colleges and universities to take part in restoring strength and vitality to religion as it relates itself to life.

Part II

An Attempt to Be Specific

CHAPTER XI

General Education — The Objectives and Organization of the Curriculum

IN SPITE of my understanding that any organized curriculum in general education must be based on the coöperative effort of a diversified group of men, I shall hazard suggestions in part as long-time objectives after a faculty has had time to reorient itself and in part for immediate action starting with present conditions. I know it is dangerous to be specific, but many of my points of view have been tried out in logically identical areas, where men must deal with uncertainty and change. When this is true, the suggestions are the direct result of experience. I make no attempt to develop a complete curriculum in general education. Rather, I am picking out things which seem to need emphasis in any such program. I shall deal with languages in a separate chapter.

The life of the normal individual has a close approach to unity even though he must struggle with changing and conflicting forces. Ordinary men do not go about the world as agglomerations of different unrelated personalities. When this does happen, such men present serious problems of abnormal psychology or insanity to the psychiatrist and the psychopathic physician. Ideally our society would have similar unity underlying its conflicting crosscurrents and novel conditions. Unless it attains something like this unity, successful and durable democracy appears impossible. As I observe recent history, the first task of a revolutionary totalitarianism after it has consolidated its victory is to accomplish, ruthlessly if necessary, by the bogy of war, by youth movements, by attacks on the old religions and efforts to substitute the State as a religion, by a great variety of means, a unification of social psychology similar to the normal unification of individual personality. We know this can be accomplished for we have seen examples. Can similar basic unity be maintained by peace-loving democratic peoples? If so, it must, I am convinced, be through coördinating processes in education. If such processes are to be effective, college-educated men must share some common educational experience.

To make the vitally needed contribution to the life around us which lies within its power, general education must be functionally related to the purposeful activities of that life, and must give men training which fits them for the constant struggle with concrete but novel problems which life presents. Great variety of instruction in special fields is not enough. Such instruction neither guarantees nor even offers an opportunity for general education. Things must be tied together and in this unified form the functional relationship of general education to life be made clear.

Interest in work, student initiative, and self-discipline are especially important educational objectives. There is a stage in the education of youth where enforced discipline is a sound basis for training not only in essential subject matter but also as the foundation for self-discipline. At this stage it is not enough if interest only is aroused. Order must be introduced. The disciplined capacity to do well necessary but unpleasant work must be acquired. Many modern schools overlook these objectives. As a result of this and of other community forces working against self-discipline, too many of our youth entering college lack control of their minds.

Minimum college standards should therefore be strictly maintained at some level fixed by experience. At college age, however, education to be effective should rely as much as possible on interest and student initiative rather than on minimum requirements or even evanescent college honors. As I know from experience, men will work harder under the spur of interest than they can be forced to work. The best chance men have to acquire effective self-discipline comes from the discovery that they can satisfy their interests only by hard and responsible work, often unpleasant work, undertaken voluntarily because it is necessary for the attainment of their objectives. Some subdivision of history studied because men find it helps them understand the world in which they live will arouse far more interest and give far better training in discipline than the same subject studied because it is a required course reached in the timetable of Ploetz's Epitome.

The college is most effective when it arouses the enthusiastic interest of its students. In this the great professional schools all succeed better than the college. More attention to teaching and to teaching methods and material, and more explicit effort to relate the subject matters studied to the life and purposes of the student are necessary if the colleges are to rival the professional schools in this regard. Of course, great teachers are needed. In undergraduate work the great teacher should be esteemed above the specialized research professor or the so-called productive scholar. We shall get more great teachers if teaching is more highly thought of.

It is in personal relations with students, in their intimate understanding, and in the development of methods and teaching material which will light their minds by lighting their understanding of the world in which they must live that college teachers, particularly those concerned with general education, should find their great place. So the good coach lights the understanding and secures the interest of his team. Such problems should be the prime object of research and experimentation for college teachers. They can to the net gain of their work get most of the materials on the substantive side of the things they teach from secondary sources. Their aim should be to utilize effectively the materials furnished them by productive scholars who delve deep for details while they throw them into a wider perspective. They must transmute these materials by evoking imaginative integrations. So John Buchan wrote his *Life of Augustus* and so he made Augustus live. Without inspired teaching only uninspired results can be expected.

Of one thing I am thoroughly convinced by experience. Inspired teaching comes into being only as the result of deep interest in teaching for its own sake, and in youth—backed up by hard work. Too often now teaching comes as an interruption in what is thought of as the really important work of the professor. I rate, also, more highly than most observers, the close adaptation of teaching material and teaching methods to the objectives sought. I have seen the quality of teaching by the same professor change in successive hours for better and for worse according to the kind of materials available and the methods he used. General education particularly will call for much constructive accomplishment in these directions. Indeed the college if it is to do as good a job in general education in either two years or four as it now does in special training will need to find or develop a different kind of teaching material and a different kind of teacher than the graduate schools now train or find a place for.

The liberal-arts college must accept the fact that it has a dual function. First, a combination in some proportion of general education and specialized training. Second, general education as the objective of the whole course. The two types of education should be combined only to such an extent as turns out to be practicable without significant loss. Of the two, general education is now neglected not only as an over-all objective but even as a start on specialization. Its essentials should no longer be lost by compromise or forgotten either as the foundation for specialization or in the four-year course. If the program of general education is designed to meet the needs of civilization, four years is not too long even for the ablest men. But many men entering special fields are forced to shorten the process. Two years of general education followed in one four-year course by two years of specialized training will inevitably give inadequate time for a thorough job. Two years is all too little for men to attain an effective general education. Yet it can give a real start toward breadth of viewpoint and sound habits. The specialist needs these to offset the narrowing effect of his later training. The two remaining years are certainly not too much to conquer the important vocational specialties on which it is possible to make a beginning in the liberal-arts college. Indeed for thorough training in such fields at least two further years of specialized graduate work is usually a minimum. It is a curious anomaly that four to six years is considered a normal training period for academic specialties, while it is becoming more and more customary to stop unspecialized liberal-arts training in about two years. Yet no liberal-arts college ever attempts a serious case study of its graduates to see, not only what happens to them in life, but what limitations on their intellectual equipment and human capacities prevent them from being more successful both in their specialized careers and in their communities. I believe on the basis of my experience that any such study objectively pursued would disclose three limitations more serious as handicaps than any other which might be brought within the scope of education: their unsystematic background and, in any useful sense, its narrowness; their lack of ability to search out and relate novel facts to their customary modes of thought with good judgment; and their lack of human understanding. All these could be major objectives in general education. All are difficult and would take real time. The difficulties of designing curricula to meet these needs and of converting them into effective instruction have hardly been tackled.

Obviously a four-year curriculum of general education will not necessarily be adapted in its early stages to the needs of men who choose to start specialization in a particular field. But there are cogent reasons why the two groups of men should be kept together for the first two years of general education if this can be done without harm to either group. Few men when they enter college know enough about themselves or the alternative possibilities ahead of them to make wise long-time choices. Moreover, if they decide to start specialization in college, they will profit from two years spent in securing breadth and perspective before they begin the narrowing process inevitable in any form of specialization. If two years of a curriculum designed for men who use the whole four years in securing a general education can at the same time give the future specialist a general foundation good so far as it goes for his purposes, the resulting simplification will be important for him and the college. But four-year general education should not as now be lost in the shuffle or take second place.

I believe a combination can be worked out so that the first two years of a curriculum designed primarily for four years of general education is an effective two-year general background for specialization. We designed the first year of the two-year course in the Business School with this as its major objective. I shall make suggestions about such a curriculum in the following chapter. I believe further that even from the viewpoint of specialization, the beginning courses which introduce men to their special fields would, in many cases, attain better results if they were conceived as liberal-arts courses placing the subject, its methods, and results in the general scheme of things, rather than being conceived as specialized courses. Now too often no effort is made to disclose to the student why a subject is worth studying, what its limitations are, what it means in terms of human accomplishment, problems, and understanding. Such instruction might in many cases so fire the imagination of students that it actually cut down the time required to accomplish the specialized results now obtained in college fields of concentration.

The colleges and the undergraduate professional schools in the universities already offer the kind of specialized work needed in many fields by students who wish to use their last two years as a start on specialization. But many men pass through the college educational sieve who are not competent to take graduate work in any special field, to get satisfying results from any existing fields of concentration, to succeed in undergraduate professional schools or to benefit from four years of general education. Such men really ought not to have entered college. In most cases they need specific vocational training.

For men who elect to seek general education, a unified core should run through the four years or its equivalent. To meet this objective they should be given closely integrated training. We should unhesitatingly require work which we believe necessary. The most important electives are those men choose after leaving college and they need preparation for the choices involved in these later electives. Present requirements may give freedom later in life. The core of instruction should be required work so organized that its value and vital interest is obvious to the student. It should illuminate not only the world in which he is to live and its complex relationships but also his relationship to that world. At the same time, a limited part of general education should be left to the free but considered elective choice of the individual, a choice based on interest and a desire to explore, often growing out of his other work. These free electives should be chosen by him because they, too, or the men giving the work, stimulate his mind into activity. Present interest is not to be lightly trampled down. Inasmuch, however, as the experience required to make wise choices is lacking, every effort should be made, not to compel the choice of unpleasant electives because we think they will equip men for life, but rather to see that in choosing work students understand the reasons for studying great areas of human thought and experience which unwarned they may completely and to their later regret ignore. All electives, whatever they may be, should be integrated into the general training of each student.

The freshman year, so far as requirements are concerned, should be as complete a break with high school as possible. This is already the case in many colleges, but in many others there is little difference between the two so far as types of subjects studied and the methods and modes of thought involved are concerned. Much freshman required work can be defended best as a method of making sure the high school has done a respectable job. Yet many able youth not only successfully demonstrate their capacity in new fields regardless of defects in their prior training but also prove capable of filling in gaps in their earlier training where they undertake advanced work. We have had many such cases among mature special students admitted with no college training. So much needs to be done that the college cannot afford to use student time in unnecessary repair work. It should be assumed that men have the requisite maturity to adventure in new fields. To paraphrase one college president, when remedial work is essential to successful further accomplishment, it should be required as a penalty—not offered for credit.

Ideally, the freshman and sophomore years should start the process of general education by coördinated instruction in form and substance designed to make sure that students seeking general education are introduced imaginatively to the great areas of human achievement. This should be done through courses conceived as liberal-arts courses and not as first stages in specialization. These courses should not be kept in watertight compartments. They should be developed as related parts of one whole. The assets and the limitations of each subject in the general scheme of things should be stressed. Men seeking a general education have no time to start with one of a long series of courses in a special field which depends for its interest and vitality on the later courses in the same field. Such introductory courses may be the best start on specialization, although I doubt it, but they are not related properly to general education. Every student seeking general education needs to get from his early courses some conception of the sweep of human experience as it bears on the present and future.

The subject matter of the required work should be exciting because it is or will be important to him. Men should come to appreciate how the method of attack on intellectual problems must vary as they pass from field to field. They should understand the transition from the sheer abstractions of logic and mathematics to the basic natural sciences which deal with material things and see why and how mathematical abstractions are in these sciences effective tools leading to assured material results. But they should also understand that these subjects not only bring great material assets but in the consequent process bring unpredictable and far-reaching technological and social changes.

From these subjects they can to advantage proceed to

such subjects as geology where, so far as human understanding is concerned, chance controls the specific results of mechanistic laws even in the material world and, in contrast with experimentation, judgments based on wide observations become more and more important to understanding. They should see in this field how theories based in part on mathematics, physics, and chemistry and in part on such observations are useful in discovering many facts of great importance, like the location of oil fields. From these they might go to biology and biological evolution where the new factor of life forces essential compromises between mechanism and behavior and see how the methods employed necessarily change.

Something of the long evolutionary history of the human race should be brought in through the history of evolution and through anthropology. The early development of individual instincts, emotions, and sentiments, and of social living based on custom should be stressed. Students should come to realize that for long ages habit and custom were a necessary foundation for the evolution of effective intellectual power, but that the critical need today is for better adaptation to changes in the environment, for a better balance between custom and novelty. The relative importance of nonlogical emotional behavior in comparison with, and as a limiting factor on, the intellect and intellectual accomplishments should be illustrated and accounted for. Students should study the characteristics of human beings with their intelligent, emotional, and social nature, as they are related to the changing environment in which they must now live, exercise their free will, apply their foresight, and adapt themselves at peril to their uncertain future. History should disclose to them the influence of the past on the present. The humanities should contribute to the development of human purpose and ideals and stimulate imagination. Religion should be related to social evolution and to individual and group aspirations.

At every stage each way of using human intelligence in meeting life's problems should be illustrated and demonstrated out of the world with which the student is familiar. Successes of mathematics and science in dealing with the certainties of the material world and in transforming our material surroundings are within the everyday knowledge of every student. They should vitalize the appropriate subject matter. At the same time the disorganizing social effects of rapid change and the uncertainties resulting from the uses to which human beings put the assured results of science should be emphasized by social consequences which are within their observation in war and peace. All this work should be correlated.

CHAPTER XII

The Four-Year Curriculum in General Education

BY MAKING specific suggestions as to the four-year curriculum in general education, I do not, of course, mean that there is one way only to integrate the curriculum and relate it usefully to the lives men must lead after leaving college. I hope for many experimental approaches to the subject. My suggestions are, however, an effort to suggest a content for general education.

Mathematics

Any such curriculum should require an introduction to mathematics at a post high-school level, but mathematics may be used as an example to illustrate the kind of course I have in mind. We are not considering the mathematics needed by the trained mathematician, the physicist, or even the engineer. We are thinking of what the ordinary well-educated man needs to know about the place and limitations of mathematics in his life and environment. No one seeking a general education can afford several courses in this field though all would benefit by a well-taught introduction to the close reasoning and great basic concepts of mathematics and their application, using interesting material carefully selected for its importance to the world we live in. A course in "Mathematics for the Million" which the student takes will be important and valuable because it helps him to understand one great area of human effort with its methods and limitations and because it lights up his imagination. Understanding of limitations is important. A distinguished mathematician recently remarked to me that in practical problems involving human behavior mathematics is no substitute for looking a man in the eye. The first stage in a long hierarchy of mathematical courses, most of which the student cannot take and have time left for a general education, will completely fail to do these things. I should not make the course easy by avoiding difficulties or practice in using mathematical symbols or abstractions.

General Science

Introductory liberal-arts work in general science should be included. In such instruction I believe far more attention should be paid to general science, its evolution, scope, varying methods, accomplishments, and limitations, and less to special fields. I would rely more on great books by great scientists, on imaginative presentations by demonstrations, by correlating lectures, and by discussion, and less on laboratory work, than is now customary. I would not eliminate laboratory work but I would use it primarily to drive home an understanding of modes of attack, to give first-hand familiarity with and experience in handling materials.

The process of securing general understanding of science and its place in human affairs is slowed down by insistence on prolonged training which gives all students, whether or not they are going into science, the laboratory skills so obviously needed by men who intend to become scientific specialists. Many men acquire a strong distaste for science in this way. But I should not make general science easy. Here again, I would in all aspects of the instruction in science use things students see around them as part of their lives to excite their interest and stimulate their imaginations. There is science in great variety in the modern automobile, airplane, and telephone, and in the interesting controversy now illustrated by the contemporaneous existence of new locomotives driven by steam, by electricity, and by Diesel engines. This controversy is in part technological and in part financial. Artificial rubber, modern plastics, radio, and electronics, a host of familiar things, can be used with less logical order than existing practices secure but with far greater hope of sustained interest and understanding. Such starting points would give something like a case system of teaching science, where every case involved things the student knew to be important. Similar approaches to biological and physiological sciences are clearly possible. It is not necessary to have the knowledge and skills required to breed new plants or to perform an operation for appendicitis to understand the biological importance of the infinitely little or the possibilities bound up in patient exploration of such fields. Yet the laboratory rarely gives these things to the non-specialized student. The case approach to general science could. Written cases should, of course, be backed up by concrete material things used for illustration; e.g. by important and typical machines, and by demonstrations of processes. Too many students seeking a general education are now deterred from securing any understanding of science by unimaginative insistence that prolonged laboratory practice is the necessary approach to this objective.

Contemporary Civilization

In the freshman year there should be required work in contemporary civilization clustered around present-day social problems, taught by men chosen for their breadth and their capacity to relate together many diverse disciplines and factors in considering such problems. Every effort should be made to develop student initiative in suggesting pertinent considerations out of their other work and out of their experience in life. There should be heavy emphasis on this country in such work, but consideration should be given to problems facing the parts of the world which are exciting youth today. Russia, Japan and China, India, Latin America, lie in my mind as especially important topics, probably after the war more so than Europe to this generation. Every effort should be made to show the student that, when he seeks to understand other peoples, he must look at things from their point of view. At each stage this course should use and tie in the rest of the student's work. One of its primary objectives should be to develop pride in our national accomplishments even while it makes men think of our mistakes and of our unfinished job.

If we believe in our democracy, we shall do more in our training to make our faith explicit by paying greater attention to the constructive accomplishments of the great democracies. A course in contemporary civilization could do part of this job. It could give students a basis for loyalty to the great ideal of ordered freedom. As a nation we have lost to a distressing degree our understanding of the struggles and ideals of our forebears. If we in academic life held more faith in ourselves and exhibited more willingness to support the foundation ideals of this nation, many men would do more to strengthen our democracy.

Curiously enough while the centrifugal forces increase in strength at home, great pressures are building up for this nation to use its influence at the peace table to extend democratic government over as large a part of the world's surface as we can. So-called principles are emphasized constantly. Little attention is paid to the question whether democratic government fits the political and social background and the human activities and training of men in other specific countries. The word democracy is applied to the "four great democracies," Russia and China as well as England and America. Now if Russia is a democracy, in spite of intense admiration for her, I suggest that the word has lost all meaning. If China after the war is soon to become a democracy in any sense that I understand the word, my fears for her are great. They are based on my deep emotional interest in her future. I see no hope that China can modernize herself as, for better or for worse, the Chinese have clearly determined they shall, except under a powerful centralized and autocratic government. Nor do I see how in any other way she can rid herself of her war lords or her graft. Russia has recently demonstrated how much such a government can accomplish for a backward nation in a generation. No real democracy could have accomplished anything like so much from such a start, because no true democracy could have been so ruthless. The roots of democracy grow slowly and only in fertile soil. Widespread ability to read and write is probably one of the necessary elements. Only now a substantial fraction of the Chinese people are learning to read. We shall do well to ponder Pope's couplet even though we do not wholly agree. "For forms of government let fools contend; Whate'er is best administer'd is best"—and in so doing we might think of Rome in the Golden Age of Augustus, even while we remember that a Nero came after Augustus. Perhaps we must face the probability that real democracy reaches neither the heights nor the depths of some other solutions of the endless adventure of governing men. A course in contemporary civilization might give students a background for thinking of such points of view.

To those who dissent from the emphasis I place on our democracy at home because it seems to stress nationalism; to those who disagree with my distrust of efforts to spread the forms of democracy over the world, I suggest that the hope of the kind of freedom for men in other countries which exists here and in England lies in the virility and strength of our own democracies and our own persistent purpose in peace as well as in war. It does not lie in imposing the forms of democracy on a postwar world whether or not it is ripe for them. Peace is more of a test than war. Democracy more than other types of government needs to find "a moral equivalent for war" which shall combine discipline, coöperation, responsibility, and fervor. Perhaps this war came because our behavior convinced Hitler that we had lost belief in ourselves. General education should strengthen our belief, not by propaganda but by understanding. If we go totalitarian at home, it should be by intent, not by attrition. Social controls through rules which set standards for the anti-social will surely be required, but the habit of expecting government to do everything is peculiarly dangerous. I distrust the capacity of democratic government to direct the activities of one hundred and thirty million people of widely diversified interests and environment. I am convinced that if the effort to centralize authority continues unchecked we shall go totalitarian. Like the Nazis we shall then make vital and destructive blunders.

History

Such work in contemporary civilization would, I suggest, be the proper background for history conceived in terms of the long and generally upward struggle of Western civilization as this struggle illuminates the present. I should postpone history to the sophomore year. I know it is illogical to start studying history at the end, but history is illogical. Chronological order does not make logical sense out of China, Russia, and America. The reason for studying history lies in its value for understanding the present and to a limited extent the future. Men when they enter college have almost no acquaintance with the world around them. I believe some such acquaintance is essential before they can read the lessons of the past intelligently. The time for ancient and medieval history or even for modern history is, I think, when men already have some appreciation of the contemporary world with its complexities and problems. If they have such appreciation and have the stuff in them, they will willingly seek a better understanding of these problems out of the long struggles of civilization. For this reason history should be postponed until after instruction in contemporary civilization. When given it should be interpreted broadly to include art and literature.

In my judgment most undergraduate history should be taught selectively (history is always selective) from aspects of history imaginatively chosen not in general on a chronological or regional basis but because they throw light on present-day problems. In other words, topics of history taught to college students seeking a general education should be selected primarily by analyzing urgent problems of our contemporary situation and picking out from history material helpful to their understanding. History should start with contemporary civilization and face forward in its study of the past. So taught, history may help general grasp either because it shows how we got where we are and thus illuminates the present, or because it shows how particular types of conditions recur; how methods tried in the past for dealing with such conditions have either failed or succeeded. The past should be taught in ways which contribute to present understanding and to present policy. Such history will give only such minor emphasis to dates and kings and spot-map questions as may be necessary to give time perspective or to throw high lights on the imposing influence of physical and social geography on the problems of the modern world.

If history were always studied for its bearing on contemporary problems, defined in their wider implications, the search through the past for recurring problems and the constant emphasis not only on like earlier experiences of the race, but on the contrasts brought about by modern science and technology, or by the basic differences among cultures past and present, would lend interest and importance to its study. All this interest could be focused through student discussion in ways which trained men to make intelligent judgments with time perspective about the contemporary world. It would be part of the practice by which men would formulate imaginative intellectual conclusions about a considerable variety of complex factual situations. They would thus acquire the habits and skills they will need in life and turn these habits and skills into intuitions.

Following the study given our democracy in the course in contemporary civilization, major attention should be given to the historic development of the important problems facing us and the British democracy and to the long struggles which made our accomplishments possible. The development of this nation is a saga with which all our youth should be familiar, not because we should impose our civilization on other peoples, but because our history is important to us. If we understand our history better we shall realize that our methods do not fit all needs. Our own democracy faces many dangers from within.

Such work in history should be a substantial fraction of the curriculum throughout the last three years. It should constantly interweave the great arts and the great literatures. So given, it would, I think, be a vast improvement over our present spotty and ineffective elective approach to the subject. Readings should be used freely from carefully selected and classified lists of interesting and important books, old and new, developing those phases of the sweep of history and the humanities, most significant for our own purposes. We wish men to use the experience of the past. Would not such history lead more students to keep beyond Commencement Day an interest in the past as it bears on the present? Would not our liberally educated youth see with wider perspective and deeper understanding not only the specific problems studied in this profoundly insistent present but also new problems as they meet them later? Such reading lists (not too long) and the important books studied could be revised from time to time to include the background of problems newly appreciated as important. The books listed might well be reviewed to give continuity and reasons for the inclusion of each. The lists could be sent to graduates. We have found a strong interest in reading lists among our own graduates. They might even be a guide to men of ability and capacity for independent work who by some accident of fate are unable to carry their formally organized education beyond high school. In these ways they might become a significant part of adult education as well as in the continued education of college graduates.

I agree with St. John's College in thinking the careful study and discussion of some well selected list of the world's best books offers a fine chance to light up the understanding of men by bringing them in contact with great men at their best. Yet I am so impressed with the insistent novelty and importance of the present that I believe the books read should be selected and the discussion be so conducted that they are always tied into the problems we face now and in the discernible future.

A Suggested Problem in History

An example of how from a start in contemporary problems history might be used in general education may be useful. The particular example would certainly not do in the first year. It is better fitted for prolonged study in the senior year.

The most pressing problem of the contemporary world is the relation between the state and society. All over the world, in democracies as well as under autocratic governments, the state assumes more important functions. These centralized powers may be, but often are not, used with tolerance and restraint in administration as they were by Augustus in Rome. Sometimes the increased use of power by the state comes about because changes are so rapid and disorganization so complete that greater centralized controls are necessary to regain essential stability. This was the case with President Hoover and President Roosevelt from 1929 to 1933. At the present time the reason for new assumptions of power by the state is the war. The necessity in wartime is clear. Soon the problems will carry over into peace. The continuance for a time of many war controls in modified form will be essential to the orderly return of this country to a new normal. Now most of our energies are devoted to winning the war and half of our industry has only the government as a customer. We must return in peace to a position where many million individuals again seek fulfillment of their wants and desires. These wants and desires will again steer the productive capacities of industry and introduce great problems in marketing and distribution. Government controls must be lessened progressively to make this possible.

Sometimes as in the period between the end of 1933 and the beginning of our active program of national defense, organized reform movements are the source of centralization. The state under the guise of the New Deal dominated policy and assumed a great array of activities formerly left to society. This is superficially the easy way to get results and much good was accomplished. But it presents great dangers.

> The reformer's final resource is the State. The State is now called upon to reconstruct or replace the fam-

ily, to reconcile conflicting class interests, to break down class exclusiveness and probably to assume the conscious control and direction of all forms of social organization. But is the State equal to the great task? And how will it set about it? By what right or power, by what natural sanction, will it absorb within itself and subordinate to the control of a central will the many-sided and spontaneous activities of Society? What is the true relation of the State to the other social and economic organisms—to the Church, to the Municipality, to the Trade Union, to the family?

These are very deep and difficult questions—almost theological in their import and in their power of dividing mankind. The economic historian cannot attempt to answer them. The answers can only be slowly spelt out through the life experience of future generations. But the student of economic history is compelled to face these questions; and perhaps the chief value of his studies is that they prevent his giving shallow answers to them, that they compel him to realize the complexity of the social problems which he will be called upon as a citizen to assist in solving. In my present lecture I wish to indicate very broadly and tentatively the importance for economic history of the social factors that operate within the life of the modern nation.

The State is now the strongest instrument of social action, the final organ of social authority, and, as the life of Society has become more intense and more complicated, the need for a regulation and adjustment in the common interest involves an increasing use of that instrument and a more frequent appeal to that authority. But the life of man is not passed in a continual atmosphere of strong social action and final social authority. Nor is the State so all-powerful as the social theorists would imply. Its functions have developed immensely during the past century, but the functions of other social organisms have developed with as great, and perhaps even greater, rapidity. The power of the State has undoubtedly grown in certain directions, but it has achieved this result only by renouncing all action in other directions. We allow the State to inspect our factories because it has ceased to claim to inspect our worship. We suffer it to manage the Post Office because it has ceased to control the Press. But the truth goes deeper than this. The instrumentality of the State has been increased because it is an instrument which Society controls, not an authority which it obeys. And this social power which controls the State is no new or sudden growth. It is a continuous and silent development, which has its roots in the creative period of the Middle Ages.[1]

History from Greece contains many examples of results varying all the way from good to very bad which have come about under radically different emphases on one or another aspect of this interaction of State and Society. Of course, in all older examples there is a submerged slave class which had no share in power and no direct influence. Now we have machinery. The life histories of transition from bad to good, and from good to bad can be studied, and moral as well as intellectual judgments can be formed with reference to important instances. Being free from personal involvement in each situation, the student can the more easily see that such judgments must be related to the surrounding circumstances in which men lived. Each instance can be compared with some contemporary modern situation and contrasted with others. The different stages of technological development as they change from situation to situation can have comparative treatment. The varied implications of the ways men

[1] George Unwin, *Studies in Economic History* (1927), pp. 456–457. By permission, Macmillan & Co., Ltd.

have lived and made their living can be brought out. Religion can take its legitimate place. The student can get much needed training in looking objectively at facts rather than being carried away by the emotional connotations of words. Perhaps he can be brought to understand how often he is himself influenced by emotion-laden and question-begging words used by others with the conscious or unconscious objective of leading him away from the critical examination of facts toward conclusions he would not reach if his critical faculties were alert. Literature from Plato on has numerous examples of great books by great men dealing with one or another aspect of the problem which he can read, not as the high school boy reads Shakespeare so that he can pass entrance examinations, but because they have a direct bearing on questions of present-day importance which he sees around him. But he must not take an exclusively logical point of view or he will forget the human beings he is studying.

In spite of the complexities, an informed public opinion about this problem of balance between State and Society at home and abroad is essential. The problems are difficult and vary from place to place but the stark fact is that unless we have better understanding we shall make many mistakes in international relations, while at home we can readily lose by default the essentials of democracy to attain which our ancestors struggled against the power of the State for many generations. Sadly enough the principal exponents of action leading us in this direction think of their activities toward state control as modes of perfecting democracy.

Walter Lippmann has stated the case far better than I can.

> Although the partisans who are now fighting for the mastery of the modern world wear shirts of different colors, their weapons are drawn from the same armory, their doctrines are variations of the same theme, and they go forth to battle singing the same tune with

slightly different words. Their weapons are the coercive direction of the life and labor of mankind. Their doctrine is that disorder and misery can be overcome only by more and more compulsory organization. Their promise is that through the power of the state men can be made happy.

Throughout the world, in the name of progress, men who call themselves communists, socialists, fascists, nationalists, progressives, and even liberals, are unanimous in holding that government with its instruments of coercion must, by commanding the people how they shall live, direct the course of civilization and fix the shape of things to come. They believe in what Mr. Stuart Chase accurately describes as "the overhead planning and control of economic activity." This is the dogma which all the prevailing dogmas presuppose. This is the mold in which are cast the thought and action of the epoch. No other approach to the regulation of human affairs is seriously considered, or is even conceived as possible. The recently enfranchised masses and the leaders of thought who supply their ideas are almost completely under the spell of this dogma. Only a handful here and there, groups without influence, isolated and disregarded thinkers, continue to challenge it. For the premises of authoritarian collectivism have become the working beliefs, the self-evident assumptions, the unquestioned axioms, not only of all the revolutionary regimes, but of nearly every effort which lays claim to being enlightened, humane, and progressive.

So universal is the dominion of this dogma over the minds of contemporary men that no one is taken seriously as a statesman or a theorist who does not come forward with proposals to magnify the power of public officials and to extend and multiply their intervention in human affairs. Unless he is authoritarian and collectivist, he is a mossback, a reactionary, at best an amiable eccentric swimming hopelessly against the tide. It is a strong tide. Though despotism is no novelty in human affairs, it is probably true that at no time in twenty-five hundred years has any western government claimed for itself a jurisdiction over men's lives comparable with that which is officially attempted in the totalitarian states. No doubt there have been despotisms which were more cruel than those of Russia, Italy, and Germany. There has been none which was more inclusive. In these ancient centres of civilization, several hundred millions of persons live under what is theoretically the absolute dominion of the dogma that public officials are their masters and that only under official orders may they live, work, and seek their salvation.

But it is even more significant that in other lands where men shrink from the ruthless policy of these regimes, it is commonly assumed that the movement of events must be in the same general direction. Nearly everywhere the mark of a progressive is that he relies at last upon the increased power of officials to improve the condition of men. Though the progressives prefer to move gradually and with consideration, by persuading majorities to consent, the only instrument of progress in which they have faith is the coercive agency of government. They can, it would seem, imagine no alternative, nor can they remember how much of what they cherish as progressive has come by emancipation from political dominion, by the limitation of power, by the release of personal energy from authority and collective coercion. For virtually all that now passes for progressivism in countries like England and the United States calls for the increasing ascendancy of the state: always the cry is for more officials with more power over more and more of the activities of men.[2]

[2] Walter Lippmann, *The Good Society* (Boston: Little, Brown & Co., 1937), p. 3.

"But," as George Unwin says, "it is worthy of remark that, whilst the main feature of British history since the seventeenth century has been the remoulding of a State by a powerful Society, the main feature of German history in the same period has been the remoulding of a Society by a powerful State."[3]

History so taught would not fit into the subdivisions we arbitrarily make of the social sciences, nor if it were well taught, could student or teacher avoid the constant struggle with wide and varying relationships which arise out of shifting circumstances. Value judgments of the sort men must make throughout life could not be kept out. I hope the student would also come to realize the need for objectivity as a basis for the understanding he needs in making such judgments. Would such history, taught in ways that evoke student initiative and imagination rather than spongelike qualities, be easy?

Human Relations

Organized attention to human relations is clearly needed in the curriculum of general education if the college is to take an effective part in seeing that graduates have a useful understanding of men and their emotional as well as their intellectual behavior. They should have at least an intellectual grasp of the basis upon which skills in securing understanding of men and in handling them may rest, and as much practice leading to the development of the skills as possible. I know by direct experience that such things can be taught. When they are well taught, they will, for many men, hasten substantially the process of acquiring an intuitive grasp of human problems and how to approach them. I do not mean courses in laboratory psychology. These generally study the individual too much in isolation. The prime need is for un-

[3] George Unwin, *Studies in Economic History* (1927), p. 28. By permission, The Macmillan Company, Ltd.

derstanding and skills related to individual and group behavior, including the importance of group emotions, and for ways of finding and dealing with conditions which affect individual and group morale.

Many students wholly lack both effective individual adjustment to other men and the social skills out of which comes the ability to coöperate in the activities of social groups. Somewhere in our college training, men need to develop skills—practical skills in handling men, skills in working together, skills in reaching agreements with other human beings. At the Business School, we have made real progress toward such ideals. To maintain normality and to attain effectiveness, human beings need contact with men and things. Questions involving the individual student's adjustment to the group must in most aspects be dealt with by individual interviews, although group instruction is in some measure possible. It is a great timesaver. Methods of securing group coöperation and working out group problems lend themselves well to group work and to discussion in the classroom. Nevertheless, the individual and the group aspects of the subject are closely related.

Since problems of individual adjustment to college life require personal attention, they are best handled by college officers who are closely tied in with the dean's office and with the college physician. Many such problems are, in my experience, wisely handled by men who are separate in functions from the officials who have disciplinary or other authority. Ideally, all the information the college has about the individual student should be instantly available from detailed records. These should cover not only the formal facts about the student but a full description of contacts between the student and the dean's office. Of course most students can handle problems of individual adjustment themselves but a surprising number, including many sensitive men with fine minds, need help. Much help of this nature is given by all deans and college physicians but in many institutions it needs systematizing. Every effort should be made to sort out the men who have difficulties at the earliest possible moment. We have learned in the Business School that a sudden drop in the quality of intellectual work either in comparison with entrance records, or in comparison with earlier work in the School usually means either bad health, bad adjustment to social surroundings, or a serious emotional upset. I understand that similar conditions affect college work. Often such upsets originate outside the college, but they affect men both in the quality of their work and in their relations with other men. Each type of difficulty may bring on serious maladjustments and misuse of college freedom. The first problem is diagnosis. Here a skilled interviewer as the responsible officer can usually get at the source of the difficulty by using methods which lead the student to talk freely and by listening intelligently not only to what he says but also for what he avoids, and for the things he would like to talk about but cannot without skilled help. In this way the interviewer can often secure the understanding necessary to wise handling of the student's problem. Even more important, if the student can be led at his own initiative to talk freely about difficulties which he is bottling up and often not even recognizing explicitly, he will usually see them in truer perspective from the mere fact that he states them and faces them openly. In our experience, such interviewing is often uncanny in both its intellectual and its social results. We have had many instances of successful completion of work, with high grades, after it looked as though men would be dropped for poor scholarship. Sensitive men of ability are especially apt to have such difficulties.

Self-centered isolation can frequently be broken down in this way. Isolation is a serious college problem. Many men deliberately avoid coöperative effort and minimize social contacts. Most of them can be helped to overcome this point of view. But to help them skilled men are required. They need not be physicians, but if so, they should be physicians of the widest human experience and understanding who realize that they are usually dealing with personal, not with medical, problems. We cannot look to the medical profession to solve this problem of adjustment because it is too big, though it is quite as important a part of the physician's work as physical ailments. Such students are in most cases not abnormal. They are badly adjusted to life with themselves or with others. They need to see themselves in perspective, to face and overcome the attitudes which make them ill at ease and ineffective. When their tension disappears, they frequently seek advice and help which would have been resented without this process of blowing off steam. Such work is a fascinating full-time job for a levelheaded, well-trained, and experienced interviewer. It cannot be hurried. Often several or even regular interviews are necessary. Interviewing is now too often undertaken by inexperienced men as a side show to busy lives. If attention is not given to such individual problems, college life may easily give men a sense of failure and confirm their tendency to isolate themselves. The social confusion which surrounds men after leaving college lessens the chance of overcoming such tendencies later. The college has a great opportunity during its four years to help men become normal parts of social groups.

Closely allied with this work is the task of vocational guidance in the latter part of men's college careers. This requires both a knowledge of the lives men live in various types of careers and of the intellectual and human qualifications necessary for success. It also requires all the understanding of the individual student that can be attained from college records and from skilled interviewing. It should therefore be done primarily by members of the administrative staff of the college and whenever practicable as a follow-up on the other type of work. Most men have the basic intellectual and other qualities for a considerable variety of jobs, yet they would be happy in one task and not in another for which they seem equally fitted. Their emotional interests and their social surroundings often make part of the options distasteful. The task of the vocational adviser is sometimes to search out affirmative interests which should determine the choice of a career. Sometimes where there is no controlling specific interest his task is to search out the adverse reactions of the student to one career after another and help him to eliminate until he sees that instead of facing a haphazard choice from an indefinite number of careers, he is really choosing among a very limited number. I have found this approach very effective. Usually the student can readily make this final choice.

The wise vocational adviser in the present state of our understanding will in few cases affirmatively advise men to make particular choices. He will often, however, out of his knowledge of the individual take the responsibility of advising that he lacks the qualities needed for success in some of the careers which interest him. Like work with the individual student in relation to his undergraduate adjustments, vocational help skillfully given on the basis of known interests and abilities can do much to help men adjust themselves to life after graduation without taking away their initiative or ignoring their interests. Much time can be saved in vocational guidance by informatory orientation lectures and by questionnaires which sort out the men who have unsolved problems. Too many men now graduate from college with no specific basis for making their next elective choices. Of course when the student has chosen the field he wishes to enter, he will in many cases need advice on preparation for the career or intelligent aid in securing a job. If this advice is to be effective, it needs to be centralized so far as possible in advisers who possess both human skills and wide information.

In addition, men need training which fits them to deal with the problems they will face when after leaving college they take jobs and fit into their local communities. I have particular reference to their individual attitudes as they join groups of men engaged in common activities or seeking common objectives. Obviously such instruction must be in general terms for it is impossible to foresee the particular orientation of each individual. For this reason it can be given effectively in groups or in classroom. It will benefit greatly from realistic discussion of concrete problems. This phase of human relations can be elaborated in considerable detail by men of wide experience in breaking in young college men. They will know the handicap which many such men face from impatience, from their unwillingness to spend the necessary time getting the background needed for progress, from their failure to place themselves and their problems in scale with the importance of other problems of the organization they join. Many beginners, emotionally aware of the importance of the jobs to them, look at everything from a self-centered point of view. As a result they fail to turn things around and look at themselves and their jobs from the point of view of the boss or of men around them. He who would save his life must first lose it. This whole subject needs to be brought to the forefront of men's thinking. It can be done in ways which affect their behavior.

The most obvious facts about human interactions are left for the graduate to find out for himself. Yet a grasp of them is needed by all men who hope to attain positions of leadership where such interactions are important. For example, men are left to discover for themselves the importance of understanding the other fellow's point of view, the necessity of investigating and understanding the individual and group environment, both intellectual and emotional, which consciously or unconsciously influences the behavior of men with whom they are dealing. They need the understanding so gained in planning their own behavior. It took me fifteen years after leaving the University to see these things explicitly, yet they are basic in handling men. When I made this point of view explicit, my negotiating capacity improved greatly. Men are left to find out for themselves that they as well as other men are often wholly unconscious of the sentiments and emotions which control, not only their emotional, but their intellectual, reactions. Most men leave college assuming as a result of their over-rational training that men are controlled by their intellects. Few realize the extent to which all men are, in fact, controlled by their emotions, how universal it is for men to rationalize and explain even to themselves why they behave as they do. As a result they often think perfectly honorable men to be dishonest, and make other serious misappraisals. Except for what they gain from their social and athletic life, men leave college with, in effect, a vacuum so far as methods of understanding these facts are concerned. As a result they pay too much attention to words used and too little to the emotional urges behind the words. They have no techniques, skills, methods, or habits of searching out the human factors in different situations and using them as a basis for understanding the attitudes and behavior of men with whom they must live or, indeed, for understanding themselves. They may never find that behavior is in many cases not directly related to the verbal statements. They acquire no techniques of finding why the verbal statements are made and the underlying emotional urges which account for the behavior. These things can be taught effectively.

The student can be given some inkling at least of techniques of organization and methods of sizing up groups of men. Many groups have a formal management organization which may appear on an organization chart. This is customary and even necessary in groups of any considerable size. These charts give some crude idea of lines of authority but they do not disclose the importance of individual personality and the extent to which this modifies not the charts but the behavior of men in ways which are often inconsistent with the charts. Most industries have also an orderly technological basis which must be observed. Too often, however, the training of workers and junior executives is inadequate. Alongside these there is always in any well established group an informal spontaneous social organization of great significance. This is often ignored by managers and rarely recognized explicitly. As a result, they rely too much on authority and too little on human understanding.

Chester I. Barnard in *The Functions of the Executive* reaches the conclusion that authority always starts from the bottom rather than from the top of an organization. While from my point of view this is a rather strained use of language, I conceive that it is in most situations the only wise assumption which the possessor of authority can use in determining his own behavior. The parade of authority destroys human leadership and the capacity to secure enthusiastic coöperation. This is so well understood that in private life men are rarely given authority which they aggressively seek. Successful large industries with widely scattered plants are learning that regardless of the legal centralization of authority in a central office, this authority can be used only in general terms and on rare occasions if they wish to avoid stultifying the initiative and destroying the morale of local units. Where this is not recognized we are apt to find energetic smaller competitors running rings around the larger unit because they can secure more effective organization and a higher degree of collaboration.

The spontaneous organization and the attitudes it takes consciously or otherwise are oftener than not the key to the effectiveness or ineffectiveness of the group. To secure maximum collaboration, careful attention is required to all three of these types of organization and to the ways they fit together. Bad or undeveloped relationships between the formal corporate organization, the technical organization, and the informal organization of factory workers often leads, for example, to limitation of output which is unfortunate for both sides. If any one of the organizations is too weak, it is hard to strengthen the others and to bring about coöperation. These conclusions are based on concrete research.

There are ways of securing an understanding of such informal organizations and how they relate to the formal organization. Much can be picked up by talking with men and drawing the necessary inferences, i.e. by interviewing associates in much the same way that the college officer interviews students. The geography of the work places occupied by different individuals means much to the skilled observer with reference to the vital functioning of the informal organization. It may determine the efficiency of individuals as this is affected by their relations with others. The frequency and the nature of contacts between individuals as they go about their work is significant in relation to the way the group functions. Teamwork which is the key to group effectiveness comes out of this informal organization more than it does out of the formal organization. It is here that we find the spontaneous growth of mutual understanding and the unconscious sorting of men into natural layers of leadership and reliance on leaders. But the responsible formal leader can do a better job when he not only understands the informal situation, but, by getting himself accepted as part of the informal team, contributes to its effectiveness and influences its attitudes by his behavior. Of course time and habit are both important in the development of teamwork and rapid growth is a handicap. All these statements are backed up by research and experience. The weakness of the informal organization is largely responsible for the relative inefficiency of new and expanding industries. It accounts for many of the difficulties in war industries and for the confusion in the civilian agencies in Washington. It is a short step from understanding the group to recognizing the importance of sufficiently wide participation in decisions which affect the group. The natural leaders and their followers should feel that the leaders have their day in court. Out of this can come also an understanding of the importance of easy and natural two-way communication, up and down, in human organizations.

The organization of universities and colleges presents a special case. This is, however, so important to any change in the existing situation that I shall devote a separate chapter to it.[5] The necessity for explosive expansion of numbers in the Army and Navy and the nature of war risks with the resulting rapid changes in personnel make them also a special case. Each man's desk must always be ready for his successor. They account for the centralization of authority, as the compelling necessity to be ready for quick action accounts for the greater use of authority. In a world-wide war like this, the delegation of great authority to separate commands is also a necessary consequence of the nature of the risks and the necessity for quick action. Rapid growth compels the elaborate development of routines and rituals and both red tape and insistence on standardized channels of communication in such organizations. Without these there would be utter confusion, nothing to which effective organization or effective human relations could be tied. Of course the emergency which brings the expan-

[5] See Chapter XX.

sion predisposes such organizations to collaboration. Nevertheless the weakness of communication from the bottom up which results presents a real problem. The difference between a tried and seasoned army or naval crew and a well trained but inexperienced one is quite as much in the shaking down of human relations into mutual acquaintance and mutual confidence as it is in combat experience.

The greater effectiveness of our untried new troops in North Africa, Italy, and France as compared with similar untried troops in the last war is clearly in part the result of training in this country and in England, prolonged and thorough enough to allow mutual confidence and acquaintance to develop.

Fortunately our army recognizes these things. The *Basic Field Manual on Military Courtesy and Discipline* as revised in 1941 starts its statements on discipline as follows:

> Military discipline is intelligent, willing, and cheerful obedience to the will of the leader. *Its basis rests on the voluntary subordination of the individual to the welfare of the group.*
>
> Discipline establishes a state of mind which produces proper action and prompt coöperation under all circumstances regardless of obstacles. It creates in the individual a desire and determination to undertake and accomplish any mission assigned by the leader.
>
> Acceptance of the authority of a leader does not mean that the individual soldier surrenders all freedom of action or that he has no individual responsibility. *The American system of discipline calls for active coöperation from the subordinate.*

And again it says:

> Man is and always will be the vital element in war. As an individual, he is most valuable when he has

developed a strong moral fiber, self-respect, self-reliance, self-confidence, and confidence in his comrades. *A feeling of unity must be achieved if the group of individuals is to function as a unit instead of a mob.* Modern warfare requires self-reliance in every grade; individuals capable of independent thought and action, who are inspired by a distinct feeling that as an individual or as members of a unit they are competent to cope with any condition, situation, or adversary.

I quote also from its discussion of leadership:

Good leadership, based on personality and character, is essential to the attainment of military discipline. The key to effective leadership is the development of respect and mutual confidence. *It is gained when the leader shows in every possible way that he is a member of the unit,* and as the ranking member thereof he will leave nothing undone to promote the unit's comfort, welfare, and prestige. Similarly, loyalty and respect are developed through mutual understanding and consideration, through fairness and justice, and by sharing dangers and hardships as well as joys and sorrows.

and:

Mutual trust is essential for group unity. It stimulates and fosters that unity of purpose and spirit, which under such names as morale, élan, or esprit de corps, is the very heart of a unit's power.

In each case the italics are mine.

Similar conditions exist in the Navy. A recent *United States Naval Medical Bulletin* concerned with combat fatigue says:

Men need thorough training in all aspects of their work before engaging in actual combat. Any method of increasing training adequacy will greatly increase the effectiveness of the ship in combat on psychological grounds alone. The medical officer should assure himself that his own corpsmen are thoroughly drilled in the duties of their department, and, in addition, should see that the remainder of the crew are completely indoctrinated in the principles of first aid. Nowhere more than in the psychiatric casualties of war is it demonstrated that knowledge helps to banish fear.

No ship should attempt to meet combat conditions until the crew has been assembled for a reasonable length of time, and the men have come to know each other fairly well. To do so is to invite disaster. Wherever possible, crews should be assembled early in the fitting out of the ship, and kept together thereafter. As a matter of policy, shifting of men from one unit to another should be kept to an absolute, unavoidable minimum. . . . In dealing with the neuroses of war, we find that "morale" is not some ethereal myth, but a tangible problem composed chiefly of sound leadership, good training, familiarity with shipmates, and lack of fatigue.[6]

The same medical report lists, on the basis of interviews with what we used to call shell shocked men, four factors which "have occurred, singly or in groups, too frequently to be ignored":

(1) The patient entered combat without faith and confidence in his leader.
(2) The patient was insufficiently trained, did not know his job or his ship as thoroughly as he should.
(3) The patient entered combat surrounded by new shipmates, men who were comparative strangers to

[6] "Combat Fatigue and War Neurosis," reprinted from *United States Naval Medical Bulletin* (July and September, 1943).

him, and whose conduct under fire he had not had time to estimate.

(4) The patient experienced the combat situation when he was suffering with marked physical fatigue.

These research conclusions correspond closely with results obtained in our studies of absenteeism and labor turnover in war industries. These studies bring out the importance of leadership by men who handle their personnel with social skills, the stability of groups of men who have worked together for some time in comparison with new groups and new employees, particularly those who are finding difficulty with living conditions, and the growth of absenteeism and labor turnover when fatigue is excessive from too long hours. Of course American industry has suffered continuously during the war from the inevitable inadequacy in training of new employees and particularly from the necessity of almost improvising supervisors. All these things make effective teamwork hard to accomplish. They account for many labor difficulties, including wildcat strikes resulting from lack of coherence and weak teamwork within the unions.

No college can afford to neglect training which fits men to understand men with whom they will work. When they lack this ability, men are isolated and often unhappy in their jobs. They easily turn into troublemakers. Such men frequently build an individual intellectual life in the clouds wholly disassociated from real life. More emphasis on group activity and group work in college courses, especially if it results in spontaneous groupings of men with diverse backgrounds, would take many out of their shells and give effective practice in human relations. In the world of affairs, group work is the rule; isolated individual work, the rare exception. Yet drastic rules are evolved by the colleges to minimize or prevent group work in connection with courses.

The grading system is designed to prevent group work. Instead every feasible way to encourage such work should be adopted.

But in addition to encouraging group work, course instruction based on the discussion of actual human problems arising in social groups and reported as they arose can be used to great advantage. Because students can readily imagine themselves in similar positions, we have found their interest in such cases strong and their enthusiasm for what they get out of such studies high.

Further elaboration here of possible subject matter and methods for the study of human relations seems neither necessary nor desirable, but there is no part of a curriculum in general education which is likely to be more important, either to the individual graduate or to society, in meeting one of the most pressing problems our democracy faces—the necessity for a higher degree of coöperation. We have given far too little attention in our educational system to training men to coöperate with their fellows in the everyday work of the world. We have watched the gradual disintegration of the capacity for coöperation in the nation without finding out why it is happening and what can be done about it. Yet this is close to the heart of democratic problems. It is primarily an emotional problem. The intellectual job is to understand and guide it, not to get rid of its emotional basis.

We have fallen woefully short of any practical recognition that democracy presents the most difficult problem of social coöperation posed by any type of society. Historically, most democracies have been short-lived. We cannot follow the easy course of taking its perpetuation here for granted. The fact that a democratic form of government has in a few spots in the world offered the maximum of individual freedom and opportunity is by no means enough to assure the effective continuity of such forms or, more important, that widespread freedom will always exist under the forms. We know many countries where this is not the case. The very elements in our democracy which lend so much satisfaction to life through their emphasis on individual freedom and opportunity tend to break down the capacity to coöperate and, with this, the capacity of the nation to maintain effective equilibrium, except through centralized autocratic controls. Yet individual freedom for nearly all men finds its opportunity not through isolation but through coöperation.

Not only have the colleges failed to make students appreciate the importance of human collaboration and how to get it, but much of their instruction, particularly since the last World War, has in fact trained men, not to work together to some common end, but in dialectics. Overemphasis on purely intellectual points of view which ignore human limitations and unavoidable errors in judgment has led to debunking and narrow criticism of the past. Much of this is based on hindsight. It is generally destructive because it oversimplifies the difficulties men face and minimizes the good they accomplish by emphasizing only error. There is too often no effort to give balanced consideration to the situation as it was faced by men who were forced to act. This has led to skepticism—and even cynicism—about human beings as an end in itself, rather than to training in constructive coöperative effort. In thinking about the future, too, it is easy to avoid honest effort to understand situations which face us in their uncertainty and generality, and to demand that alleged wrongs be removed before serious over-all study is even considered. As a result, the remedy is often worse than the disease. The complexity of the concrete situation with all its social ramifications is ignored or dismissed in favor of an emotional reaction to some small point, often elaborated into a great logical structure or into a fixed principle. How often this happens when dinner-table conversation turns intellectual.

Through this overelaboration of logics and this failure to look at the facts in any rounded sense, college men tend to use their capacities for leadership in furthering programs of reform which wholly ignore the harm and the human disorganization which may result. How many college graduates in public or private life ever apply to social ills Hippocrates' motto—do no harm? Yet many academic people, as well as most politicians, act as if they were social physicians. Colleges have made significant contributions to national unrest by weakening faith, by discrediting tradition, and by training for coöperation in disillusionment only. Organized work in human relations is essential if more effective training for collaboration is to be attained.

Such work in human problems is necessary to make intellectual training effective in human and social situations. Men must learn either in the colleges and universities, or by slow experience in life, more about the emotional reactions of social groups, and how to use this knowledge in accomplishing the results they have determined upon intellectually. They must learn how to displace hostile sentiments by stronger friendly sentiments, or to assume the hostile emotional reactions of those they would influence, and fit their objectives to these sentiments.

Out of such stuff leaders are made. It is through such processes that other men may be brought happily in line with intellectually sound programs. Most college men lack a working grasp of them. Yet if such things are not learned in college, men who seek careers in the world of affairs will find the usefulness of their intellectual training seriously limited. Many will be unable to translate soundly reasoned conclusions into action, and many others who use authority to secure action will unconsciously create unnecessary emotional problems which may weaken or even prevent attaining results they seek. Even if through experience they come finally to realize the importance of adjusting their intellectual conclusions to the emotional attitudes of their organizations or of the society around them, the process will be unnecessarily slow and the road unnecessarily hard.[7]

In those colleges which have developed tutorial or preceptorial systems, tutors should be chosen in part because of their social capacity and understanding, and should be urged to develop such capacities in students by their personal relations with them. They should be expected to know their men as human beings. In my judgment group tutoring,

[7] On the general subject of human relations, reference is made to the following publications by men associated in research at the Harvard Business School: Elton Mayo, *The Human Problems of an Industrial Civilization* (New York: Macmillan, 1933); "Sin with a Capital 'S,'" *Harper's Magazine*, vol. 154 (1927); "What Every Village Knows," *Survey Graphic*, vol. XXVI, no. 12 (1937); "Frightened People," *Harvard Medical Alumni Bulletin*, vol. XIII, no. 2 (1939); "Routine Interaction and the Problem of Collaboration," *American Sociological Review*, vol. IV (1939); L. J. Henderson, "Physician and Patient as a Social System," *New England Journal of Medicine*, vol. 212 (1935); T. N. Whitehead, *Leadership in a Free Society* (Cambridge: Harvard University Press, 1936), *The Industrial Worker* (Cambridge: Harvard University Press, 1938); F. J. Roethlisberger and W. J. Dickson, *Management and the Worker* (Cambridge: Harvard University Press, 1939); F. J. Roethlisberger, *Management and Morale* (Cambridge: Harvard University Press, 1941); Report by George C. Homans, *Fatigue of Workers* (Committee on Work in Industry, National Research Council, 1941, Reinhold Publishing Corporation, New York); J. B. Fox and J. F. Scott, *Absenteeism: Management's Problem* (Harvard Graduate School of Business Administration, 1943); Elton Mayo and G. F. F. Lombard, "Teamwork, and Labor Turnover in the Aircraft Industry of Southern California" (in preparation; Harvard Graduate School of Business Administration). See also Chester I. Barnard, *The Functions of the Executive* (Cambridge: Harvard University Press, 1938); Kuo-Heng Shih, *China Enters the Machine Age*, edited and translated by Hsiao-tung Fei and Francis L. K. Hsu (Cambridge: Harvard University Press, 1944); Carl R. Rogers, *Counseling and Psychotherapy* (Boston: Houghton Mifflin, 1942).

with a considerable emphasis on group work, could be an important factor in humanizing college work. Obviously, on the intellectual side, the tutor who deals with men seeking a general education should emphasize the wide implications of problems. He should not approach tutoring as a specialist.

Economics

Instead of starting the study of social science with a sophomore course in economic principles as is now the general practice, such a course belongs, in my judgment, late in the curriculum when it will be taken by men who already realize the variety and changing nature of facts in their concrete reality. They will therefore know and appreciate that the valuable close reasoning required in such a course can reach no higher level for policy determination than its source in the assumptions and exclusions from which it gets the basis for its logics. Moreover, any well designed course in economic principles or economic theory will emphasize rather than destroy understanding of these limitations. To this end it is important that such a course be based on cases honestly reported to avoid excluding noneconomic factors. One of the hardest subjects which we ever undertook to develop in the Harvard Business School is business economics taught by the case system. The objective is to give students tools of economic analysis useful to business administrators. If the case reporting is honest, cases from life never stay economic. Noneconomic factors always intrude unless they are deliberately discarded. Yet for this very reason it is important and illuminating. The exclusions necessary to focus attention on the orderly development of economic analysis can be made in class. Then from time to time the instructor can point out how conclusions would be modified by bringing in other facts. Such a course in economics, though less orderly than present courses, could be excellent training in close reasoning. It would not lose touch with reality. It would be far more interesting.

Policy

The course in contemporary civilization, of the freshman year, should serve as an introduction not only to history but to a course dealing with general policy. This is an integrating subject. In our own professional field, it is most significant. In general education it is the point where things must be pulled together if our general direction is to improve. To make a maximum contribution to general policy, all areas interesting to men which are now studied and taught as specialized subjects in liberal arts colleges need to be taken into account and, so far as may be, focused on policy. Life is not in separate watertight compartments. But research and instruction will not be integrated and related to life problems as men meet them in their full variety unless it becomes the business of able groups of men to accomplish this. Training in policy is necessarily related to the over-all problems men must meet when uncertainty is dominant. Understanding of the impact of science should be included in such a course. With this emphasis on policy liberal-arts general education can perform as important a function as pure and applied sciences perform in fields dominated by certainty. Such training is what the largest group of men who enter liberal-arts colleges need as imaginative preparation for life. To serve its functional objective, it should itself be focused on the present. In its emphasis on concrete situations, policy is comparable in practice with the practice of medicine. It asks men to face contemporary problems and formulate responsible judgments about them. It expects them to use their knowledge of the past, but they will be engaged in deciding what should be done with reference to specific situations now or in the immediate future.

Since change and uncertainty are constants in many, if

not most, of the interdependent variables which make up each social situation, we must recognize that in general no integration, no basis for judgments, can exist unless the time under consideration is agreed upon. It is futile in analyzing a social problem in Rome, to define one factor as it existed in the best days of the Republic, another as it existed in the golden age of the empire under Augustus, and still a third as it was when the barbarians were at the gates. In studying the past, since there are many gaps in the record, this necessity of agreeing on a time presents a difficult problem. For most modern purposes the best focal point in time is the present. Indeed the present has the definite further advantage that responsible action can only be taken in the present.

> The only use of a knowledge of the past is to equip us for the present. No more deadly harm can be done to young minds than by depreciation of the present. The present contains all that there is. It is holy ground; for it is the past, and it is the future. At the same time it must be observed that an age is no less past if it existed two hundred years ago than if it existed two thousand years ago. Do not be deceived by the pedantry of dates. The ages of Shakespeare and of Molière are no less past than are the ages of Sophocles and of Virgil. The communion of saints is a great and inspiring assemblage, but it has only one possible hall of meeting, and that is, the present; and the mere lapse of time through which any particular group of saints must travel to reach that meeting-place, makes very little difference.[8]

Policy is, I believe, essential to a well organized and integrated general education. The work done should be designed to tie in the other work taken by the student and

[8] Alfred North Whitehead, *Aims of Education* (1929), p. 3. By permission, The Macmillan Co.

to give him essential practice in making decisions. It should train him to use the experience he acquires in other aspects of his work with a firm grasp, trained imagination, and sound judgment when he faces the novel conditions and problems not only of the present but also of his unpredictable future. In view of its difficulty and its importance, policy should be a required subject for the last three years. Skill and wisdom in determining policy is not easily acquired. Indeed, if our civilization breaks down, it will be mainly a breakdown of policy and administration, both private and public. Private and public administrators constantly make policy decisions and act in situations of the widest significance. Too often before they act they examine only some narrow and highly specialized segment of the concrete situation, and as a result create more serious troubles than those they cure. So we fix the price of cotton at a point which destroys export markets and stimulates foreign competition. Policy can be taught realistically and effectively in ways which create the habit of thinking of things in relationship.

Our universities and colleges have on their liberal-arts faculties social science specialists in great variety. Nowhere, however, is there a group of men whose interest is in the integration of these specialties. No group is stressing the implications of constant change and uncertainty, and of human and social behavior, in an effort to educate men for the lives they must lead. No group centers its attention on developing methods of training men to deal with current problems as they meet them later in life with understanding of their complexity and flux. No group is making students face responsibly the necessity of formulating policy judgments about present conditions in their novelty and complexity, or attempting to develop the habits, skills, and intuitions necessary to effective action. In fact, so far as I know, no liberal-arts faculty stresses the importance of wide background and well-established habits and skills as the basis for effective judgments in dealing imaginatively with the present, and contrasts it with the inadequacy of theories and principles. No group in liberal-arts faculties is considering the limits on foresight in a world of uncertainty, or the possibilities of developing social mechanisms of adjustment to the unforeseen contingencies which constantly face us.

Yet every physician, every administrator, public or private, every leader of public thought, and indeed every citizen with capacity for leadership needs training in policy. In one sense, of course, policy is part of administration, but the undergraduate college cannot within its time limits cover effectively the whole field of administration, nor if time allowed would it be well equipped to do so. Many details of wise action depend so much on intimate knowledge of the specific situation, and on careful attention to the exceedingly important subject of timing moves, that only a school giving professional education in some particular field of administration can give the necessary orientation effectively. The situation is similar to the relationship of pure to applied science. If the proper foundation in policy is laid in college, the aspects of administration involving action are better left to professional schools or to experience in life. The liberal-arts college should, however, make it clear to students that the end and aim of policy can only be realized through action.

In my judgment policy can best be taught by the case system. It should stress problems important to our leaders and to citizens. This is the natural way to teach policy for this is how policy problems come up. Students should be presented with cases carefully graded for difficulty and start simply and slowly. Patience in evoking imagination is necessary. Cases should constantly increase in scope and difficulty as skills and habits of seeing things in relationship grow. It is our experience with an older group that after a slow start in studying cases, the capacity to see facts in relationship and to use them as the foundation for judgments grows rapidly. More patience and more careful grading would obviously be necessary with undergraduates. But I am convinced that if such work were well taught, the subject matter would soon come to take a prominent part in the everyday discussions of both students and faculty. The cases should not be artificially simplified to fit them into the present arbitrary limitations of any single social science. They, and well selected collateral readings, should be used to evoke judgments about social problems in their full complexity. When, as is inevitable, the reporting of cases or problems has to stop, the stopping places should be determined by pedagogical necessity, not by squeezing out pertinent but unwelcome facts. Specialized social science points of view, e.g. the importance of economic or political aspects of cases taught, should be brought in and discussed because they illuminate parts of the problem. Men should not, however, be led to believe that by using these modes of attack they are released from the necessity of relating them to other facts and points of view. The background of understanding of the past could be brought in partly through other courses, partly through collateral reading. Students should be trained to use initiative in suggesting facts and factors drawn from their other work, from their experience with life, and from their human and social contacts. This process should be continuous through the last three years. Habits and skills can only be developed by practice.

I believe students could in this way be trained to the habit of constantly seeking new pertinences and using them. Discussions based on the responsible, imaginative handling of cases chosen because they are important to life would develop the essential powers of selection, and would train men to weigh by the use of intelligence the factors pertinent not only to present problems but also to future problems as they are met. Such methods work well with us. Out of such a process many students would get not only a new vision of liberal arts but an interest akin to a vocational urge. They would see that such work bore a direct functional relation to their lives. In our experience the process does equip men for their future. I believe general education would no longer stop on Commencement Day.

A simple conceptual scheme of policy starting in foresight, the importance of freedom of action in dealing with unforeseen contingencies, and the necessity of constant adjustment as conditions change should be drawn from actual cases which the student faces responsibly. Human behavior and relations should be stressed constantly. It is not necessary to await the development of a finished theory before using a conceptual scheme. Under the best of conditions men can never know all they need to know about the varied facts and forces at work as interdependent variables in our human and social environment. Indeed, if they did have such comprehensive knowledge, the variables are so numerous that it is beyond the capacity of the human mind to prophesy with assurance what the resultant of the forces would be. This limits the use of logics. Yet some logical basis is both important and possible.

Generally speaking, except in unusual conditions where mathematical methods are available, the interactions of interdependent variables cannot be prophesied with assurance when they pull in more than three directions. Obviously in most human affairs of any complexity many more than three forces are at work. In other words, the capacity for foresight is severely limited. On the other hand, the behavior of many of the individual forces at work can be forecast with assurance for longer or shorter periods. It is therefore frequently possible, by breaking problems down into their components and exercising judgment as to the length of time each may be expected to continue pulling in the same general direction, to sort the different forces at work into groups heterogeneous in most characteristics, but homogeneous for some period of time in their behavior in relation to the problem under discussion. If such groups can be reduced to not over three, effective judgments can often be made where without this process foresight would be a sheer gamble. A well-developed theory of foresight is much needed. It would not be elaborate logically, for at every point judgments would be involved, and at every point it would be subject practically to the intrusion of unknown or unexpected facts and forces which might upset conclusions. It would, however, serve to bring home to the policy maker the varying limits within which he can decide and act with assurance. And these limits vary from certainty, like the annual advent of the seasons, to great uncertainty, like the future of Industrial Europe or Asia, or the foreign trade policies of Soviet Russia.

But if general policy must be limited as assured foresight is limited, it can never solve the problems which need to be solved in the world of uncertainty where men live. A theory of adjustment must also be worked out. What can be done to keep human society in tune with its changing internal and external environment, with constant individual and social uncertainty, with the unknown and the unknowable? Curiously enough, there is more experience in the world which bears on this problem than there is on any other problem human beings face. Throughout the whole history of biological evolution nature has been working at it, so far as we can see, blindly—eons of trial and error. These trial-and-error experiments have determined, by the success or failure of adaptation and adjustment to environment, whether individuals and species, plant life and animal life, should survive or disappear. They have, through these eons of time, developed "the wisdom of the body" so interestingly described by Cannon, and made individual men the most adaptable creatures of the animal kingdom. At no stage of this history, until civilized man appeared, was the thought of the individual or the purposeful action of a species a factor in successful evolution. Unfortunately social organization in large units is so recent, and change has come on the human race so fast as a result of the conquest of mind over matter in science, that there has been too little time to work out the problems involved in the adaptation of modern societies to their environment. The slow working out of experiments through trial and error—nature's methods—takes too long to meet the social need.

Moreover men gifted with minds as well as emotions wish to use their minds in working out their own social destiny. Fortunately the record of nature's successes and failures is preserved in sufficient variety to point out many directions in which by copying her successes we may improve our social capacity for adaptation to change and therefore our basic social stability. The very limitations on human capacity for intelligent foresight, coupled as foresight must be in the nature of things with substantial chances of error in all complex problems, make the development of a practical theory of social adjustment the more necessary.

The history of biological evolution should be seriously studied to see how we can profit from nature's experience in dealing with similar problems in ways which lead to the extinction or to the survival of individuals and species. Indeed, if we are ever to attain a scientific foundation for social science, it will almost surely be found in human biology in its broadest sense, in human behavior, individual and social, that is, in the areas now typically subsumed arbitrarily.

Required Work vs. Elective Work

The required work I have outlined, plus other work which turns out to be basic as a rounded curriculum is evolved, should, I think, take something like four-fifths of the students' time for the first two years and three-fifths for the last two. In the first two years of general training I see little place for elective work except in the humanities. Freshman and sophomore electives, like fields of concentration chosen at the end of the freshman year, are in most cases gambles. Of course, they may be passed down from class to class as ways of avoiding difficulties. This is one way of loading the dice. I conceive it to be the job of these early years to lay something of a foundation for later intelligent electives, just as I conceive it to be a basic task of all general education to lay a foundation for intelligent judgments and elections in life.

At the beginning of the third year of the four-year course, it would be possible and probably wise to cut the required work down from four-fifths to three-fifths of the year's work, but in the three-fifths still required, space must be found for instruction in human relations. Indeed, to fit the needs of men who will start specialization in their third year, such instruction might well start in the second year. By increasing the electives to two-fifths of the total, the opportunity of the student to make further explorations in subjects interesting him may be expanded. In general, except in mathematics and certain sciences where these are necessary as a foundation for later careers, such elective work should be designed as part of general education and not as a stage in specialization. Such work should seek to give understanding or skills useful to the man who does not intend to seek a specialized career in the field, rather than to the man who intends to specialize vocationally.

Yet there will be necessary exceptions to this statement. I have mentioned the need for special consideration of mathematics and some of the sciences. Men whose interest in these fields is aroused by the introductory courses which I am advocating will in many cases wish to get a better grasp of the fields. Some will wish after finishing their general education to specialize in science in the graduate school, or to enter fields like medicine or engineering, where they are necessary basic training. Such men will need more of the sort of specialized work now customary in such subjects. In mathematics they will need more study and practice in handling important mathematical concepts and abstractions. In science they will need the intensive laboratory work which is an essential basis of the skills required for their later work. If they plan later to enter some field of industrial management, they will benefit by being exposed to a severe course in practical mechanics or industrial chemistry where they become acquainted with types of knowledge needed in many industries, for example, with the basic types of machinery and the ways chemical processes are controlled in industry.

I would, therefore, in premedical work and in some other fields, offer the necessary specialized training, scientific or otherwise, through electives. While it is of great importance that doctors have an effective general education, medical training is already a long process, and medical schools are forced to require a substantial amount of scientific work before entrance. The student who wishes to follow his four-year general education with an engineering training should be able to work out some combination of electives which would save him a year on the combined course.

A small part of the elective work of many students for

whom college ends formal education may well be directed toward vocational ends. Such men need a toehold to help them start in life. In our work, we rate high the importance of such toeholds. In a world where economic motives with all their limitations are so significant, students who cannot take graduate work are justified in wishing some preparation for making their living. Of course, it will be a poor makeshift compared with organized professional training, but their general education will be the more effective for it. Accounting, for example, is one of the great languages—not a subdivision of mathematics, but one of the most widespread languages in Western civilization. Because it betters one's capacity to understand many aspects of the world around him, it is an important liberal-arts subject. Statistics have a similar status. Because the two are the principal languages other than English used in the world of affairs, they have special vocational importance. Men are seriously handicapped unless they have some understanding of both languages. Similarly, men who wish, without intense specialization, to enter a field of work which depends on particular science, such as geology or chemistry, should be allowed to carry the subject far enough to talk the language of the appropriate science. The special problems faced by women should have similar attention through available electives.

I am aware that in always assuming five courses or their equivalent in hours as a minimum, I am suggesting more than some colleges now think wise. If proper attention is paid to arousing student initiative and interest, this does not bother me. Nor do I think it requires reduced standards. Men will work far harder under the spur of interest than they can be forced to work by college requirements. College men do not overwork. They are underinterested. If, as I think may be necessary for a time, the colleges have to meet postwar conditions with a three-year course or its equivalent,

I hope they will do so without reduction in requirements or standards. Rather they should adopt methods which arouse greater interest so that they can ask for more work each year, and they should make more effective use of part of the summers. It is to be hoped that the financial problems of students now met by summer earnings will to a larger extent than in the past be met by scholarship aid and by reduced living costs. I have become convinced that continuous operation of liberal-arts colleges offering general education is unwise, though the school year might be lengthened.

Suggestions for Immediate Action in Reorganizing General Education

Obviously, the content and balance in any such coördinated liberal-arts curriculum for general training as I hope to see could only be worked out slowly. Even if such a plan meets with active approval, it must stand as an objective unattainable by the college in any brief period. To reduce such ideas to a specific well-balanced and coördinated curriculum would require experimentation and hard coöperative work at every stage.

Immediately practical first steps must be devised. Suppose in the first year men were obliged to study courses so selected that they open a few great areas of human experience. Then suppose a teacher, selected because of the breadth and range of his understanding, and aided when he asked help by others on the faculty, gave a coördinating course in which he sought to differentiate the modes of attack on problems with their several limitations and consequences, and to relate all the courses to contemporary life. This integrating course might be given by lectures, but the lectures should always be concrete and specific as well as imaginative. They should try constantly to answer the question why these things are studied by showing how they bear on the life around men; i.e. on the present. Such a course might be taught alongside a course in contemporary civilization.

Beginning in the second year and continuing to the end of the four years, courses in policy might be required, similar to those suggested earlier. In these courses current problems could be posed and the students be asked out of their organized and unorganized educational background to suggest facts and factors pertinent to the kind of responsible opinion on concrete policy an educated democrat should possess. What can they draw from History I, American History, Mathematics, Economics and Government, Physics, Chemistry and Biology, plus human behavior so far as family life and college life has given them any understanding or basis for understanding it; i.e. from the liberal arts and life so far as they have gone? There should always be insistence on the responsible formulation of opinions and judgments.

As rapidly as possible, realistically reported cases, starting with the present social situation and its background, should be used as the basis of instruction. To begin with cases should be simple, for men must learn by easy steps in this difficult field, but while simple they should not be restricted to any one special field.

This integrating course in policy should be stiff or it would fail. Men must be induced to stretch themselves. In spite of this fact, I think there are almost no college curricula to which such a course could not be added every year without dropping out any course. The college would be asking men to use their other courses. To a heavy extent the necessary time could come and (if the course was well done) would come from time now devoted to trivial bull sessions. I don't believe there is a college in the country where the men have anything like a full load—a remark based on reactions of many graduates of many colleges. After a few weeks in the Business School, men often lament the waste of time in college. In my opinion the reason is that the colleges have relied on requirements and minimum standards to enforce work, the value of which is rarely clear to the student, rather than on interest and demonstrated utility to inspire work.

Such a solution is temporary and far from perfect. It still leaves most courses in their old specialized form, but it makes a start and gives time to convert specialist courses into liberal-arts courses. I suspect that student reactions would quickly induce specialized teachers to pay more attention to the relationship of their work to other factors and to the present, if for no other reason than the fact that the new coördinating courses would be doing this. The teacher would want to have a hand in the interpretation.

Even to approach the ideal, each individual course should be so taught that its importance, its limitations, and its general relationships to contemporary problems are constantly impressed on the student. This should be done in ways which arouse his initiative and give practice in formulating judgments. The many pedagogical and substantive problems involved in such an approach would require constant experimentation. By so doing they would vitalize teaching and give a new persistent interest to teachers. Work so conceived could be kept alive by the constant feeding in of new case material. Cases newly gathered or phrased would include new contemporary material, requiring reappraisal of the significance of old facts. Greek history could not be a dead subject because each shift in the contemporary scene would bring new meanings out of ancient experience. So we find that a change in the date line of a case in business often radically changes the case.

I am convinced that real progress could be made in such ways from the beginning, but necessarily in any ideal sense the process of conversion will be slow. The first steps suggested would give the necessary time to develop new points of view, new coöperative effort, and the faculty interest which is essential to any radical improvement. Nor would the student suffer from the imperfection of the process. I have seen a faculty go through such a conversion. The very process infected the students with interest.

I suspect that the only practical way for a large university or college to try any such approach to general education as I am advocating would be to start with an experimental and development group. Admission to the group might be restricted to students who intend to use the whole four years in getting a general education without the intrusion for vocational reasons of specialization in any one field. A big group of students in the first years would be undesirable. I would exclude men who intend to start specialization in college with the intention of finishing it in the Graduate School of Arts and Sciences or the Medical School. I would not exclude men who intend to specialize after graduating from college. When the work was thoroughly organized, I would as rapidly as possible require all men not specializing vocationally in college to take the general course. Later I would require men using substantial parts of the college course for vocational specialization to take the first two years of such training. All this of course if the experiment succeeded.

Such a gradual procedure would slow down the effect of the plan in redistributing the demand for other courses and give time for teachers to broaden their viewpoint. In the long run I think such redistribution of courses would be substantial. So far as general education is concerned, fewer liberal-arts courses would be needed, though most of them would be radically changed. Many old specialized courses would of course have to be continued as part of the training of specialists, but even here there would be a substantial change in the kind of instruction required and in the early stages of specialization a real reduction in the number of students in the old specialized courses.

CHAPTER XIII

The Individual — The Unit of Education

NOTHING could be more unrealistic than the old wheeze about the ideal college: Mark Hopkins on one end of a log and the student on the other. There is evidence in plenty of the damage done men when their educational process is individual and isolated. Education should be a group undertaking, with normal social contacts. This is as important as its intellectual side. Nevertheless, each individual differs from his fellows in background, capacity, and interests. For this reason it was assumed that the elective system, plus the development of many specialized fields of concentration, would enable each student to get from college what he needed and desired. These assumptions have not been justified by results. Indeed, both developments have added to the confusion and ineptitude of the training taken by nearly all students who do not choose to become interested vocationally in some one specialized field. More could be accomplished to fit education to the individual than is now done, but it requires much closer knowledge of students, rather than a long *à la carte* menu of courses. Too often, now, individual experience in living is lost sight of in quantity production.

In spite of the importance of group work, the individual should be the unit of education; and his educational process should be considered as a whole, irrespective of the subdivisions of our institutions for higher education. Existing college rules in many cases prevent proper coördination with graduate work. This I know from experience. Except when it starts men on specialization which is finished in a graduate school of arts and sciences or in a medical school, the college too often thinks of its course as an end in itself and pays little attention to coördination with other faculties or with professional schools even in the same university. As a result, insufficient thought is given to the kinds of undergraduate education needed by men entering professional schools and, particularly, to the general education they need most. Under the guise of better preparation for professional work, there is often undesirable duplication resulting from early specialization in college.

The problems involved in fitting education to the individual, start, so far as the liberal-arts college is concerned, with the admission of students. Indeed, one additional source of weakness in the liberal-arts college and in general education arises from the admission of students who should not be in the college. Many forces bring about the admission of badly prepared students, and, far more important, of students incapable of doing reasonably high-grade college work because of limitations on mental capacity, interest, or self-discipline. Among these forces are external political conditions, the social prestige of college, internal financial problems in the college, competition for students among colleges, and great variations in standards and accomplishments among the high schools. These problems are in most cases insoluble in any short run. Unfortunately, the high-school situation, while it adds to the number of weak students admitted, results also in the exclusion of many able and fine youths from colleges which rely on examinations as the basis for admission. To some extent the restrictions imposed on competent men graduating from the poorer schools, or from schools which do not fit the pattern set by college-board examinations, can be alleviated by giving more weight in selection to scholastic aptitude tests, followed by skilled personal interviews. I am told that the combination is very effective. Relative standing in high school can to advantage count for more, and the absolute results of school records and college-board examinations for less. This is a device for selection which has been effective in the experience at Harvard College.

More efforts should be made to check and to rate the character, social capacity, adjustment to life in an all-round sense, and potential capacity for leadership displayed by men selected. I note that Harvard College, even though it does not effectively rate its men after entrance except by intellectual standards, goes to great lengths in selecting men for its national scholarships to supplement intellectual tests by appraisals of such qualities. Such bases of appraisal, because they are difficult and expensive to administer, are likely to be ignored in selection, as they are now ignored in our college curricula.

It is not anti-intellectualism to point out the crying need for considering men who apply for admission from a balanced viewpoint. Men of the high intellectual capacity so important to leadership in affairs surely need character, responsibility, and loyalty; and, more than any others, it is important that they have a sensitive appreciation of human and social behavior and a trained capacity to handle human problems. Nor, in spite of its superficial appearance, do I think that the present startling preference to sheer intellectualism in contrast with other qualities would be democratic, even if we knew how to test intellectual capacity and accomplishment adequately. We do not. These problems are difficult. I hope their difficulty will not result in their being neglected. An aristocracy of intellectuals badly adjusted to social life would present serious dangers.

I am not impressed by the decision of Chicago University, St. John's College, and perhaps other institutions to admit selected men to college when they are part way through high school. True, a century and a half ago our ancestors frequently finished college at about the age men now enter, and some such men attained distinction in life. But other things are also true. The colleges then were at a level not far away from good high schools today, and fortunately even now many men who finish their formal education with high school attain distinction in life. Then, too, the nation had hardly more than started on its vast experiment in mass education. In the last fifty years this experiment has brought many more men to the college. In addition, the environment in which educated men lived was in many ways simpler and changed more slowly then than now. Typically, I suspect, the men of that time who by their works impress us with their breadth of viewpoint and accomplishments owe this success to forces in their environment and within themselves which are only vaguely related to their education in college and hardly at all to present conditions.

I am convinced that it would, in many cases, be desirable if men entered college a year younger, but I do not believe the shortening process should be accomplished by lopping off the top of the secondary school structure. The process could be speeded up if school standards could be raised. This is slow business. Under existing conditions, the immaturity of college freshmen constitutes a real handicap in most fields other than languages. Clearly the college would to some extent be compelled to pick up subject matter that is now given by the high schools. Of course, the colleges, not being oppressed by compelling numbers and possessing abler faculties, should be able to do a better job in subjects now taught in high school than the average high school, but I question whether this is the way to use its teachers. Moreover, I question whether, in fields where they now overlap, any college ever has done or is likely to do as good an educational job as the best preparatory schools—for example, Exeter and Andover.

But I should not expect even consequences from such a policy in all subjects. I anticipate that subjects dependent mainly on certainty and logics would suffer less than subjects dependent on experience and on judgments about shifting facts. Social science and many of the humanities may be expected to suffer more than mathematics and natural science. The understanding of human interactions would be harder for men to acquire. The increased danger of freedom in college, which is one of the great ways of broadening human contacts, is so obvious that it is proposed to duplicate in part boarding-school modes of control. General education at the level which I conceive to be possible would, in my judgment, be far more difficult to attain. It could probably go little further than is now possible for men who use their last two college years to start specialization. Indeed, long before this effort to reach back and take away part of the high-school job, President Hutchins, as I understand him, reached the conclusion that the last two years of college should be turned over to the graduate schools. This of course, in most cases, means to vocational specialization. I should not expect college men to contribute more to our general direction as a result of such a combined process.

In general, however, better training of men by the schools and more selective ways of admission to college are outside the scope of my thesis; the educational implications of the present situation when men have been admitted to college are not. The forces at work cannot be easily or quickly changed. Information about men of high-school age is difficult to get and at best unreliable as a basis for prognosis. Mistakes are inevitable. Men with a wide range of ability, personal quality, and uneven training will continue to enter college. A large part of the selective process necessary to attain even reasonably high standards must be undertaken after men enter.

In view of the fact that the college admits many students who are badly prepared and lack essential qualities of mind or self-discipline, it has a responsibility in handling such men so far as possible to do them no harm. One of the curses of our present system is that men who find themselves out of place after a fair trial—two years or its equivalent would be such a trial—can stop only with lost self-respect. So long as they get passing grades, neither the college nor the individual can do anything without creating this sense of failure in the student. A respectable two-year stopping place, with a lower degree or certificate of accomplishment, should be offered. Since false starts on intellectual tasks, such as men meet in college, can rapidly unfit men for other types of work which are within their powers and of importance to society, the selective processes should start as early as possible. There is grave danger in preparing men for careers which they are incapable of handling or which they cannot attain under existing social conditions. The selective process should not, in cases where men meet carefully fixed minimum requirements, involve separation from college.

If the necessary basis for adverse appraisals can be obtained during the freshmen year, such men should be urged to transfer into some job or into vocational work adapted to their interests and powers. Preferably, as a way of avoiding damage to self-respect, such vocational training should lead to the lower degree or certificate of accomplishment. It should also lead to a way of making a living. Where conclusions on the adaptability of men to liberal-arts training cannot be reached in one year, men who meet the minimum standards should be allowed to continue their liberal-arts work for a second year. Again, if they meet such minimum standards, they and all their fellows—high-standing men included—should be offered the new degree or certificate. Since a large fraction of those who attained this first degree would be unable to pursue graduate work effectively and just as clearly unlikely to attain in life positions involving wide responsibility in which a liberal-arts background could help them, such men should be sorted out at this stage. It can then be done without the stigma of failure. Some should be advised to take jobs at once. Some should be urged to prepare for narrower vocational pursuits requiring skills and intelligence, but not involving capacity to deal with abstractions or with complex problems, or to formulate wide judgments. Special short courses, well adapted to this objective, which train in various techniques, are now offered in many city schools of business and in state universities in a variety of subjects. Shop courses are given in engineering schools and in specialized technical schools. Trade schools could be used in many instances. The universities and colleges can do much by their attitudes and policies to dignify the work of the artisan. If they meet minimum standards, men whom these options fit should be urged to consider them.

Under such circumstances, admission to the later stages of liberal-arts training, general or special, and to the regular curriculum of undergraduate professional schools, could and should be restricted to students who stand in some defined upper fraction of the whole student group involved and have given promise of possessing the human qualities needed. There would be fewer men who were educated misfits if this were done. There is also incentive value in such a plan. A self-respecting stopping place at the end of two years is essential to its effectiveness. The social pressures to complete college, regardless of the wisdom of such a course, are now very compelling. It should not be necessary in peace times for a man who has passed in his work, but who is doing, nevertheless, the wise thing when he leaves college, to include in his informal wedding announcements a statement that he "attended" some college.

From my standpoint, therefore, the length of time spent in particular colleges should vary from student to student. For some it should be two years. For some who pursue a vocational or professional course after the second year, it should be adjusted to the need of the chosen profession. Many narrow skills will be attainable in one additional year. Professional training, if started after two years, and if prewar conditions are restored, will take two years in undergraduate business schools, three in undergraduate law schools, and four to six in medicine. Though it is unfortunate, men headed for academic careers must, I think, be allowed, if they choose, to *start* specialization after two years of general education in college. For men seeking, as many men should, a full college general education, either as a preliminary to professional or graduate training or for a life in affairs, four years should be the customary length of the college course.

I am convinced, however, that no academic standards covering periods of time as long as four years can be designed and enforced for whole college classes which cannot be hurdled easily in less time by exceptional men—provided only they are judged by a rounded appraisal of their accomplishments, intellectual and social, and not forced in form or substance to meet arbitrary time requirements. I should like therefore to see arrangements under which such men, particularly those intending to do graduate work of any sort, may, when they have demonstrated their capacity, be allowed to meet the full course requirements of the four-year curriculum—without additional annual charges for instruction—in three or three and a half years. I feel strongly about this because, without the opportunity to finish Harvard College in three years then given men willing to take an overload, I would have been unable to take my professional training in law. Moreover, my college life and work did not suffer. The senior year in college is generally a happy year, but so is the first year in a professional school. A successful graduate year in any approved school should be accepted as compliance with general examination requirements where these exist. In my judgment, rules of concentration should be relaxed in the same way. Men attempting to shorten their course should be allowed limited use of summer-school courses; preferably, to avoid the dangers of continuous intellectual work, not more than two half-summer terms. Satisfactory quality in performance of full-course requirements should be expected of them in spite of the overload. This might well include higher quality requirements than usual. Men who have the intellectual quality should use this method of shortening their total training, rather than early specialization.

Such procedures would require high-minded efforts on the part of the colleges to know their students and to think of their interests as controlling. Most colleges lack the resources, the facilities, and for good reasons lack the desire or willingness, to expand their instruction into many vocational fields which should be open to students. A policy of advising transfers whenever they are wise for the students would result in smaller upper classes in college and in more effective teaching. These classes would be made up of men of higher quality. In some institutions the problem of total numbers necessary to support budgets could be met by increasing the size of the freshman and sophomore classes. If the upper-class work in such colleges was sufficiently effective, they could also expect transfers of selected students from junior colleges after the sophomore year. Many colleges which are relatively weak financially might drop their last two years and become junior colleges or combine with similar colleges. By becoming junior colleges, they would be able to cut out the most expensive part of their work and do a more satisfying and better-quality job. By combining, they could make one stronger college. The principal difficulties working against such changes are vested interests inside and alumni sentiment outside the college. Nevertheless, if the human assets, limitations, and interests of students have first attention, much can be accomplished.

Because of the greater difficulties faced by students seeking a general education and the unsatisfactory results already shown from the attempt to give four years of liberal-arts training to poor-quality students, the development of real selective processes is peculiarly important in this field. The college should no longer offer four years or its equivalent of liberal education to men incompetent to take it. Certainly, general education, such as I am advocating, will be so difficult that it will be beyond the capacity of many. Where this is true, students may be damaged by the confusion resulting from their own limitations. I have observed cases where I believe the second year in the Business School harmed men of limited capacity.

The able college undergraduate who is taking a four-year general education course should be advised that graduate training directly related to the career he chooses after graduation is sometimes necessary and, if well organized, usually desirable. It is a timesaver and will be a source of effective power in his special orientation in life. He should, of course, think of such training as the further implementation of his general education and directly related to it. If he is to plan his whole work wisely as a unit, he needs better advice than is now generally available.

I have intentionally omitted discussion of returning veterans, because the situation has not clarified. I hazard the opinion, however, that most such men will be looking for quick and immediately useful results, and that relatively few will seek a four-year college course. If this is the situation, these facts will affect admission policies and course offerings everywhere. But long-time problems should not be settled by short-time policies adapted to war veterans.

CHAPTER XIV

Continuous Operation

MOST of our universities, colleges, and engineering schools are now operating on a continuous basis. As one of the early advocates of this method of operation, I still think it was wise. Indeed, as it turned out, it was the only way to operate under wartime conditions. Nevertheless, as a long-time policy I think the whole problem of the academic year and the length of the college course needs reconsideration from the standpoint of both students and faculties. I no longer think continuous operation wise for either.

I feel that, if education of students were the only consideration, the typical summer vacations are too long. In many cases the time, or part of it, can be used more effectively. But I have become convinced by observation that students who are in college eleven months out of the twelve, with the other month split up into several short breaks, cannot as a maximum work hard and effectively for more than one calendar year. The quality of the work suffers. I suspect that the conclusion would be different if the usual summer break for the student was approximately six weeks instead of twice that or longer. This would give many men an opportunity to shorten their college course, when necessary, by picking up in six-week summer courses electives involving a distinct change of subject matter. They would still get a summer break of adequate length. Older men free from physical disabilities and from too severe nervous tension, who are working at least as hard as students, find a month or six weeks an adequate summer vacation, both for physical and mental refreshment and for the complete break and fallow period which starts the sorting and digesting process so necessary psychologically to effective work. For young men a similar result may be attained by a change in the subject matter studied or by a new environment such as summer jobs give them when they use their summer vacations to earn money. Continuous operation ignores and, I am convinced, suffers by ignoring the process of intellectual digestion as a part of the educational process. When students work hard and systematically through the regular academic year, I have frequently observed the increase in power which comes between the end of the spring term and the opening of the fall term, and I have personally noted how similar breaks clarify my own thinking. The sorting process is peculiarly necessary and effective where the interrelations of many facts and forces are involved. I believe it would be wise if our war leaders, public and private, paid more attention to the need for rest and recreation. It is worth observing, however, that this sorting process does not, in my experience, operate well unless the intellectual hopper has been filled by hard work in some field.

But student effectiveness is only part of the problem. Similar conditions exist now in our college and university faculties. Many of these faculties are tired and stale as a result of continuous operation. Of course, if it had been possible to expand the faculties to correspond with the increased load, as universities on the quarter system can in theory, this would not be the case. But for financial reasons affecting both the college and individual teachers, and because of manpower shortages, this was typically out of the question. When manpower is again available, financial difficulties will still be a factor. Except where this problem can be met effectively, no college interested in the welfare of its faculty, or its students, can safely operate continuously.

Both teachers now working the year round and teachers on leave for war service will need time for physical and mental rehabilitation and for readjustment after the war. When normal conditions return, all teachers will need uninterrupted time for their own research. Many will need opportunities for direct contact with practice in their fields, or for consulting work which gives them a chance to combine theory and practice and to break down the isolation so typical of academic life. They will need time for rest and recreation and for the same digestive process from which hard-working students benefit so much. Even teaching in a six-week summer course in addition to regular academic-year loads involves too much pressure to enable these things to be accomplished. I have observed this fact from experience. Nevertheless, summer-school teaching will continue because the schools meet a need and teachers need the money.

Some of these considerations are, I think, especially important to general education. Such education can only be developed effectively by faculty teamwork, and in social fields at least, where neither laboratories nor books do the trick, by breaking down the fences between theory and practice. Teamwork is a slow growth. If the personal contacts on which it must be based are constantly interrupted by the absence of faculty members for whole terms—some in summer, some in the fall, and some in the spring—the difficulties of attaining effective teamwork will be intensified. Teachers when they return from such absences will resent the shifts in policy which have in the meantime come out of coöperative effort. They will feel that their interests were affected without their being consulted. Feeling this they will, after the manner of human beings, be less inclined to carry out such policies. If I am right in thinking many changes in policy are required for effective general education, this objection to continuous operation in the independent liberal arts college is conclusive. It forms another obstacle to revision of the college curriculum in universities which operate the year round on either the quarter system or the three-term system.

As for the fence-breaking job of combining theory and practice, some men in almost every college and in all universities have, through war jobs, taken long steps toward this. The progress so made should continue in peace times. This will require, particularly in social fields, much greater provision than is now customary for secretarial help and fact-gathering assistants free from obligations in connection with teaching. But even these will not serve the purpose unless the professor himself can get and keep sufficient firsthand acquaintance with the life and behavior of men as they practice in the field where he teaches, and with its surrounding complexities. This is hard to accomplish in between teaching appointments. Free time in summer as well as travel money is exceedingly important. It is hard to exaggerate the need.

CHAPTER XV

Vocational Training and General Education

I HOPE I have made it sufficiently clear that I am not opposing specialization in college provided it is related logically and functionally to life's activities and provided it does not displace or too much weaken general education. Moreover, under the same limitations I do not object to the existence in college of vocational training, either of the traditional sort or of the newer varieties. These newer developments do, however, involve serious questions of educational policy. Indeed, the rapid extension of vocational training in our universities and colleges presents real dangers to general education.

One objection is the increasing complexity and confusion which results from offering multitudes of courses. All our universities, state and privately supported alike, when they offer hundreds and hundreds of courses to undergraduates, covering many subjects in great detail, should take note that the results have about the same relationship to coordinated general education that a grocery store has to a well-planned dinner. There is food in great variety. But the storekeeper does not know the tastes and desires of the family and, as so often happens now, there is no cook to make the essential combinations. It is unfortunate, too, that the meat is lacking. Our university colleges even more than our independent colleges need to work out a well-coördinated core of general education. They should not let the most important things suffer and become confused under the pressure of immediate vocational objectives, or in the interest of making it possible for undergraduates to specialize anywhere they choose within the scope of the traditional liberal arts. The need is greater in the big universities than in the good small college because the variety of offerings is greater. The difficulties, too, are greater because more and more varied men have vested interests. Nevertheless, even in the university colleges, many courses could to advantage be dropped out of undergraduate work and a better organization and coördination of general education substituted. The colleges need a careful appraisal of vocational training in its relationship to general education.

The state universities have developed out of the ideals, aspirations, and ambitions of whole communities, and are supported by the sweat of men's brows. They have an obligation to give in return a great variety of services to their communities. Accordingly, they not only inevitably but wisely stress vocational objectives more than many of the privately supported universities and colleges. A large proportion of undergraduates leave such universities after four years with concrete preparation for some career in life. Many others start professional training after two years. Vocational interests are strong in the students, and the careers for which they prepare include many which the privately supported universities would not consider. The city universities tend to follow a similar pattern, with heavy emphasis on night schools. But the effective coördination of general education is neglected. We need quality in education more than we need variety.

Unquestionably, moreover, many state and city universities offer vocational instruction in too many fields. There is danger that emphasis on the more important social and individual opportunities which will be open after graduation may in this way be lessened. There is danger when men are offered training for narrowly specialized vocations. Students may easily be confused by a multitude of offerings and be led down blind alleys. Now before normal relations return is a good time to re-study the subjects taught and eliminate the unimportant ones. Careful tests should be worked out. I suggest three which seem important. The work given should be in fields which need a body of knowledge and a background not easily acquired systematically in practice, or it should depend on laboratories, libraries, or experimental work neither within the power of individuals nor of commercial trade schools. Finally, all vocational work given should pass the test that it is important to socially significant groups in the community served. I believe many subjects now taught would not pass such tests. Indeed a glance at the offerings in some of the great universities reminded me of a River-and-Harbor Bill in the palmiest days of logrolling. The range is from muddy creeks to great harbors. Some city universities give the impression that they add almost any subject which any group is prepared to finance.

The colleges which have no university connection and are in this sense independent fall into two groups. The first group, like many of our privately supported universities, completely avoids offering opportunities for men to prepare for careers—except, of course, as they can either start or finish such preparation in traditional fields of concentration. True, a large part of the specialized work is in fact taken by students with vocational objectives. Specialized graduate work in arts and sciences is often integrated completely with undergraduate vocational specialization, in one continuous process. In addition, a few of the customary fields of concentration give toe-holds on jobs. These fields are not, however, in most cases consciously offered for any vocational reason other than the training of teachers or as premedical work. Rather they are given because it is customary to think of them as liberal-arts subjects. Science had a long struggle to get its place in the sun of liberal arts, engineering subjects are still taboo in many liberal-arts colleges, business administration is questioned even as a subject for professional-school study. Yet I know from direct observation the important cultural growth of liberal-arts graduates when they struggle with administrative problems. The definition of liberal-arts subjects accepted by many scholars secure in the inclusion of their own fields depends on tradition more than it does on present function or on actual cultural values.

Those independent colleges and university colleges which pride themselves on avoiding new vocational subjects may fail to study seriously enough the real needs of many of their students. They make too little effort to see what might be taught vocationally and still serve purposes allied to general education. Some of the privately supported universities and colleges are too easily horrified at the thought of adding new vocational subjects to the curriculum. They are scared away if someone inadvertently suggests that a subject might have practical value. Colleges and universities which concentrate their vocational efforts on the education of research men, teachers, and premedical students, and otherwise offer students only nonvocational liberal-arts education, are not really justified in looking down their noses at all instruction which is narrowly and immediately useful to graduates who must seek jobs. The educational problem should always be to balance the student's whole training, including his graduate training, according to his talents; so that it meets effectively and wisely his legitimate needs and objectives, and—even more important—enables him to make the maximum social contribution. Socially sound and important student objectives should not be ignored. An important objective for most students is to start earning a living as soon as the college course is finished. Of course, on the other hand, the educational policies necessary to achieve their chosen ends should not be left for students to determine. Their essential ignorance of the life around them prevents appraisals which have any perspective. But student ignorance is no more serious an obstacle than the faculty neglect of critical student problems which arises from ritualistic adherence to precedent.

The second group of independent colleges includes many colleges which have added a few or even many vocational subjects to reduce the loss of students to state universities at the end of two years. Other colleges in this group add vocational subjects because they, like the state universities, feel they can serve the needs of their local communities better by so doing. I have no quarrel with these conclusions except when a weak college, which already finds it hard to make both ends meet and attain quality, spreads itself still thinner and lowers quality still further; or when a college so relates the new subjects to its earlier curriculum that it sells its birthright of general education for a mess of vocational pottage. State universities emphasize, and many independent colleges are developing, vocational training. It does not follow that general education should be either crowded out or left in its present diffuse and chaotic condition.

With our present diversity of collegiate institutions, it is neither expedient nor desirable that all colleges attempt to meet all legitimate student objectives. There should be division of labor among collegiate institutions. The advantages of such division of labor should be passed on to students by transfer.

Since state universities have in the natural process of their evolution become functionally related to many vocational aspects of life, other types of institutions should avoid unnecessary duplications. This applies to state educational institutions like agricultural schools. They should not try to become second state universities as they have in some states. So in extension work given throughout a state, the state universities should avoid unnecessary duplication of work with city universities. Division of labor is *prima facie* better than duplication of effort. Few privately supported institutions have or could get the resources necessary to duplicate the diversified services given by state universities, and almost no liberal-arts college has a large enough student body to justify much vocational expansion. Vocational courses should, therefore, be scrutinized with care before they are added to the undergraduate curriculum. When such subjects are added, instead of setting up several courses and making catalogue claims which cannot be met with quality instruction, colleges should stick close to minimum essentials in their vocational instruction and maintain quality. The vocational work will benefit. Colleges that cannot compete on this basis should become junior colleges. Vocational work should not interfere with effective general education.

In the last analysis, the most significant contribution any liberal-arts college can make to its able students will be a thoroughly coördinated general education. Such education should be functionally related to the overwhelming need for better general direction and leadership in our society. Nor should it ignore the fact that many less able students will, as citizens and as leaders in smaller ways, need general education up to the limit of their capacities. Failing this, they can hardly be effective to the maximum in their vocations and in their local communities.

Balance between the amount of general education and the amount of vocational training taken by an individual student should be struck with reference to that student and his interests and capacities. In general, the abler the man, the more he will benefit from prolonged general education of the sort I am advocating and the more important it becomes socially. His very abilities increase the dangers which may result from narrowness. Yet our present processes all tempt men to early specialization, and indeed typically require a large measure of specialization in the last two years. My impression is that many able men in state universities cut short their nonvocational education too soon. I doubt if they would do this so often if general education were effectively organized. On the other hand, men of less than the average ability of college groups will often be confused and damaged if their general education is prolonged beyond their ability to handle it and beyond their capacity to tie their education into life as it must be lived. The less able men need more help through vocational training than the able men if they are to bridge the gap between college and life without real difficulty. The state universities and some of the independent colleges are well organized to give such help. In contrast, many other independent colleges and some of our great universities, in their desire to avoid vocational expansion, do nothing to help such men adjust themselves to the necessities of their later life. I am convinced by observation that they actually harm many students in this way. I have watched too many men drift for years before finding themselves. I have in too many cases seen high hopes, often unrealistically high hopes, turn to discontent and despair. Sometimes our educational objectives are imposed on men without enough attention to their inherent inability to benefit from what we decide to insist on.

CHAPTER XVI

Languages and International Understanding

PERHAPS one of the most conspicuous failures in American education is in English. The situation is complex. The trouble starts in the home and in the community. One clear consequence of our melting-pot has been a decline in large numbers of homes and in nearly all segments of the country in the standards of spoken English which children pick up from their environment. Yet this is the way habits of speech are developed. Under our social and political conditions, the very size of our experiment in mass education prevents us from having enough competent teachers of either spoken or written English in the schools. As a result they do not do their part while students are young and malleable. There is widespread lessening of pride in good English, not excluding favored groups. The nation has not sufficiently coalesced to bring about a new and stable American subdivision of English with its own new standards. Perhaps this will come. In the meantime the colleges find it a hard task to convince the run-of-mine college student that it is worth his while to speak and write good English, and that he should take pride in so doing. They can hardly get satisfactory results without doing both these things. It is my belief that any attempt to do either will fail until students have learned to think and have something which they wish to say or write in ways which accomplish results useful to them. I am not underestimating the importance of both written and spoken English, but I am emphasizing the difficulty of overcoming bad habits formed in childhood and adolescence, except at an appropriate time and by methods which have a strong appeal. Since it takes real effort to break bad and substitute good habits, satisfactory results will be difficult to accomplish until there is a strong emotional desire in the student to achieve them. If we start by really interesting men in their college work and present spoken and written English to them as a means and a necessary tool for getting effective results, I believe more can be done.

It is frequently stated that foreign language study gives command of English. It might, but judged by results it does not. Perhaps the study of Latin and Greek did, but we cannot reëstablish these. Many students do not learn to write English in this or any other way. Some part of the college time which is so often shockingly wasted on studying foreign languages could be used in training men to read English with understanding, either rapidly or slowly according to the objective of the reading. Students would understand the value of this. Now, too many can read only at a fixed rate, while many are unable to read with understanding at any pace. I would like to see more attention given to English composition—not, as now, in the freshman year, when most boys have few ideas they want to express, but in the later years of college and mainly in connection with other work. Then, if the college has done its job, men will have something on their minds and an urge to express it. They can be made to realize more easily the importance of being able to put factual statements and ideas on paper clearly, concisely, and logically. I am afraid we try to teach boys to write before they learn to think and before the college has had any opportunity to broaden their vision. One result is that up to one-third of college and engineering-school graduates entering the Harvard Business School each year before the war from a shifting group of one hundred or more American collegiate institutions had to be given elementary instruction in English composition. This was always given in connection with other work in the School. Yet all these men had spent a large amount of time studying both English and foreign languages in high school and college.

For generations, college students have wasted large amounts of time which could have been spent on other vital subjects in almost wholly ineffective study of modern foreign languages. A small minority have, of course, benefited permanently from such study, but the present rituals compel all other students to waste their time.

In the interest of saving such wastes, reconsideration should be given to the place of foreign languages in the college. The natural time to learn languages is in youth. The natural way is by use either in preparing to accomplish something that the student desires or in accomplishing it. The child is avid to learn any languages used in his environment. By the time men reach college, the period of youth, in the sense that my first statement is true, is already past. In most parts of this country the environment offers little opportunity to imitate and no opportunity to use spoken foreign languages. For many men, tonal discriminations have weakened by the time they reach college. For others, visual memory is weak. Of course, in numerous cases neither of these statements is true. The task of learning foreign languages too often becomes a dead chore, unilluminated by any form of necessity except college requirements. Where the necessity is great enough, the Army language training has demonstrated that a working knowledge can be quickly acquired by apt pupils. There will be vocational and other reasons of controlling importance why more civilians than ever before should learn specific languages. Nevertheless, the prospective environment of the vast majority of educated men in this country will continue to offer little opportunity to use, and thus keep alive their ability to use, foreign languages. Sound educational policy requires that as soon as the things known about a student seeking general training disclose a lack of interest in and aptitude for learning languages, and the improbability of his needing them for his objectives in life, compulsion be taken off their study in college. I would not, of course, hesitate to require languages where they are necessary; nor would I prevent men who wish to do so from taking such subjects. We need many such students. Our foreign-language requirements should be selective. I would not only recognize that languages are now to many students a stupid chore quite unrelated to life, but I would stress the vast array of vitally interesting subjects that crowd around young men as they seek a general education.

Today, in view of the changing international situation, many take it for granted that much more emphasis must be placed on foreign languages. Indeed, such languages have a clear functional relationship to a great need in international relations. Obviously, if we are ever to secure an understanding of other peoples, we need many more men with real command of their languages. Students should get as much international understanding as time permits. I do not, however, believe they will get this from language studies. We might as well face facts: our young men are not in great numbers going to study Russian, Chinese, or Japanese—to give a few examples—nor are any considerable proportion of them going to carry their study of Greek and Latin, or of Italian, German, French, or Spanish to the point where they get a command of these languages which will last through the indifference of their environment after leaving college. Unfortunately, they do not now get any understanding of other peoples from the large amount of time they spend on language studies. The approach through human relations and studies of other cultures is far more promising.

Much of the time now spent by uninterested men ineffectively studying foreign languages could be spent in studying foreign civilizations, so that we may have some sympathetic understanding of their economic necessities and their human and cultural behavior. Should we not realize that our only hope of widespread understanding of our neighbors in the world lies in bringing students to realize human and social differences sympathetically through interpretations by competent experts and through the use of translations backed up by an intuitive grasp of human relations? Even for men who show an aptitude for and elect to study languages, the texts used should in some measure be interpretative of the civilizations using the languages. In addition, such students will still need to acquire through interpretations and translations an understanding of other great civilizations whose languages they are not studying. The emphasis should be on parts of the world that are obviously important to us and can therefore be made interesting to youth. Now, for historic reasons, our universities and colleges almost completely neglect areas which are becoming most important—Russia, the Far East, and even South America.

In this respect, Chinese universities give a more rounded training to students than we do. Their liberal-arts students study the Far East, but they also study Europe and America. The future of the world will be jeopardized if we continue, without careful examination of the facts, to ignore or make easy generalizations about India, China, and Japan. We shall continue at our peril and at peril to the peace of the world to act in international affairs with our present almost complete ignorance of the social situations which our activities affect. How little we know of Russia! Nevertheless, I submit that no effort to found an understanding of Asia or of the Mohammedan world on the widespread study of Asiatic languages or of Arabic can succeed. These views are, of course, wholly apart from the need for many American scholars and travelers who have command of these languages, both spoken and written, and know the countries in question well enough to have a real grasp of their social structure, human problems, and controlling sentiments. Without such the problems of translation and interpretation are alike insoluble.

Now, without understanding, we tend to apply our own cultural standards to the attitudes and problems of other peoples. A striking illustration of the reaction this point of view evokes is given by Henry J. Taylor in his report of an interview with Hadj Thami El Glaoui, the pasha of Marrakech, which appeared in the Boston *Herald*, January 13, 1944.

> The palace is in the restricted Medina section of the beautiful mountain-rimmed city of Marrakech. I was escorted to El Glaoui who, as is customary, stood with his retinue in full Arab raiment and fingered a large bunch of keys. Following the salutations, he directed the chamberlain to open a huge mosaic door to the reception apartments. I was motioned to enter along, and the pasha himself locked the door from the inside.
> We went into a sunlit garden like something out of the Arabian Nights, with rows of beautiful fruit-bearing trees shading a brilliantly tiled pool. Next we entered the potentate's personal apartments, removed our shoes and reclined on magnificent low divans beside a table laden with sweet mint tea and honey cakes. My host now was ready to talk.

At the time of the American landing in North Africa, El Glaoui had wholeheartedly urged French and Arab coöperation with us, and I now asked why he had done this. Speaking in low, musical Eastern tones, in perfect French and with some English, El Glaoui told me that his impressions had been thoroughly bad of earlier visits paid him by Dr. Fritz Grobba, the "Colonel Lawrence" of Germany, and by George Werner von Hentig, chief of the Arab bureau of the German Foreign Office.

"Superficially, the Germans' contact with the Moslem world have been excellent," he explained. "But basically, the Germans never have understood the Moslem world in its roots any more than they have understood America.

"The Germans are provincial Europeans. That is why they always make bad guesses, proceed half-way, then fail. Notice the parallel between their traditional expectations that America will stay out of war, and their traditional expectations that the Arabs will revolt. Both are hopeful major policies of Germany, one pre-dating Hitler and consistently followed by him—for Hitler is the complete German traditionalist in foreign policy. And notice that both of these hopes still fail, at vast cost to the Germans."

For contrast, I asked the Pasha about Moslem reaction to America's current policies overseas. He answered: "I am sorry to say it is already plain that, while America's policies are completely different in spirit and intention than Germany's, America must proceed with great caution—a caution not evidenced so far—or she will fall heir to the same deep-rooted antagonism and unending conflicts which the Germans would have encountered if their plans had prevailed.

"For example, Americans want to do everything quickly so they are likely to do it badly. This mistaken speed will embroil your country in the same suspicions, resistances and resentments as though her purposes were bad. Strange as it may seem to far-off American policy-makers, the fact is that the Moslem world does not want the wondrous American world or the incredible American way of life. We want the world of the Koran. There are devotional fragments in the Koran which represent sustained theological, social and political doctrines for the Islamic areas, and nothing can be done peacefully in matters of individual freedom or prosperity which does not remain within the limits of the faith expressed by the Mohammedan Bible."

Referring to American radio campaigns suggesting a new day everywhere and undertaking to implant American concepts globally, El Glaoui said: "If it does not sound impertinent, coming from what I realize you regard as a backward people, my view is that in these current, worldwide guarantees, America either must omit the Moslem world, which is the largest bloc, or else it must take over the responsibility for French, Belgian, British, Portuguese and Spanish positions throughout the Moslem world.

"The radio talk from distant America is contrary to the actual performance of America's allies, and such a position is obviously untenable if not dangerous in the extreme. America either must assume the bewildering economic, social and military responsibilities inherent in her dramatic words or else permit others to do the best they can on the spot—including the French here and the British elsewhere.

"American policy today stirs up everything and settles nothing. The result is that it creates a void opening the way to new tyrannies instead of new freedoms. At the bottom of America's attitude is the assumption that all the world wishes to be American. And this assumption is false."

Any effective coöperation among contrasting and therefore potentially clashing cultures must depend primarily on sympathetic recognition of deep-seated differences in individual and social reactions as men unconsciously adapt themselves to their differing surroundings. In any well-integrated society such adaptations are essential to the individual's sense of belonging to his social group and a source of security and satisfaction to him. In a rapidly changing and disintegrated society like our own, this type of subconscious adjustment out of which comes a sense of belonging is hard to accomplish. As a result, many individuals turn to material objectives and things for their satisfactions. They take great pride in our material accomplishments and realize the limits of such satisfactions only slowly. Their typical reaction to other cultures less advanced materially is therefore that other peoples should copy us. The Pasha of Marrakech has different ideas about his people. Are we sure our ways are best not only for us but for them? It must be recognized that even widespread knowledge of many foreign languages would fail to solve such problems of mutual adjustment.

We shall not, however, give enough attention to Far Eastern civilizations, Russia, or even South America, unless our universities and colleges are able to obtain large new funds for the purpose or unless in the alternative they radically readjust their present budgets. Our national roots and consequently our educational efforts, both in research and instruction, are deeply imbedded in Near East and European cultures. We are badly equipped both in resources and in faculties to perform the essential task of furthering understanding of Russia, India, the Orient, and South America. Yet the center of gravity in the areas of importance to the future of our own civilization is shifting rapidly toward these fields. Under the economic conditions which appear likely to exist after the war, great private gifts for these new purposes seem likely to be few and far between. If this turns out to be true, both boards of trustees and faculties should in my judgment collaborate to work out a thoroughgoing redistribution of their present resources, so that the use of funds bears some relationship to the present and prospective importance of subjects studied and taught. The present relative use of funds is shockingly disproportionate to conditions as they exist in the world. Fewer courses should be centered on Europe and more on the neglected fields. Economies resulting from dropping old courses or combining several into one, and from less futile teaching of foreign languages to uninterested students, should enable some of our institutions to expand realistic research and many to expand instruction into new fields. The process cannot be rapid, because we have so few equipped to do the necessary research or teaching. There is, however, little to be proud of in the present situation. Already Russia, Japan, China, and India are vital factors in a world war which strains us to gigantic efforts. As something like three quarters of the population of the globe awakes from sleep, we are neglecting efforts to know and understand them and to follow their cultural development.

CHAPTER XVII

Superficiality and General Education

WE NEED NOT be disturbed too much that the student busily engaged in acquiring a broad background and in forming imaginative habits and skills in understanding the relationships of novel facts, will necessarily fail to push his studies in any field of human knowledge to the point where he gets a real mastery of the field. In the first place, this cannot be done by an undergraduate anyway. He has neither enough time nor enough maturity. As in the engineering schools, knowledge has expanded beyond his time-limits and his capacities. In the second place, after he finishes college he will inevitably specialize if he amounts to anything, either by graduate work or in a life job. In the third place, when he specializes he will be a better and more imaginative specialist—not necessarily a better pedant or a more faithful worker in the vineyard—if he can light up his specialty out of a wealth of general viewpoints. Finally, he needs, and can use through life, breadth of imaginative habits and skills.

Professor Whitehead once said to me, "When I made up my mind to begin to think, I gave up all hope of ever being a truly learned man." The hope of the wisdom essential to the general direction of men's affairs lies not so much in wealth of specialized knowledge as in the habits and skills required to handle problems involving very diverse viewpoints which must be related to new concrete situations. Wisdom is based on broad understanding of relationships and on skill in utilizing this understanding in perspective. It is common sense on a large canvas. It is never the product of scientific, technological, or other specializations, though men so trained may, of course, acquire it.

Necessarily, since men cannot have specialized understanding of many fields of knowledge affecting human affairs, what general training gains in scope of understanding it must lose in narrowly conceived depth. This need not and must not mean substituting superficiality for thoroughness. For all individuals, time is crowded and capacities are finite. Superficiality in most areas is inevitable. The physicist, for example, is necessarily superficial, not only in biology but in chemistry. Narrow specialization is as superficial as shallower breadth. Different habits, disciplines, and skills must be developed to meet different urgent needs. The generally educated man will need experts to overcome his limitations, but general thinking will be his form of specialization. To be effective as he faces novel situations he must possess both habits and skills useful in apprehending novel relationships imaginatively. The specialist or expert who studies partial facts deeply is of great importance, and his aid is essential if the general thinker is to offset the shallowness inherent in efforts to acquire the variety of background necessary when men must deal imaginatively with complex situations. Of course, the student seeking a general education should understand the limitations he is accepting. Just as schools of technology should stress for their students the narrow limits on engineering training, the liberal-arts college should acquaint students seeking a general education with the self-imposed limits which result from their choice of breadth rather than specialized grasp as an objective. But students should also understand the limits on the use and usefulness of specialists and experts, and the importance of correlating with their specialized viewpoints many general ideas which the expert leaves out.

This does not mean that the habits and skills needed to

think about the relationships of things in flux will be easily gained by shallow methods or undisciplined minds. On the contrary, the problems presented are most difficult. They require severe intellectual discipline. They can be attained only by much practice and by hard and thorough work. A college program effectively designed and taught to reach such ends would stretch the capacity of the best without losing its value for men of considerably less ability. It should not be designed for dullards.

At the present time, admittedly, most men in college who ramble over a considerable variety of subject matters are less serious in their work than men who for vocational reasons specialize in college, or than men who take engineering training. Responsibility for this failure should be assumed by the college rather than blamed on the student. Students with vocational objectives see a reason for what they do. On the other hand, students seeking a general education usually fail to see convincing values in their miscellaneous courses. So far as they can see, they are adding apples, tapioca, and sugar. The heat which turns these to puddings is missing. Nothing is done to show them such values or how to use them. No effort is made to tie the work together and bring about significant cross-fertilization of the various special subjects they study. As a result, the vital interest out of which comes the stretching process so important in education is lacking. Yet the job could, regardless of its difficulty, be made fascinating to most men. And it is difficult. It is far harder to acquire the skills, habits, background, experience and trained imagination needed if the student is to meet with sound judgment the shifting circumstances of his future than it is to overcome the complexities involved in securing an effective background for work in a natural science or in meeting the requirements of any other narrowly defined specialty.

Some will say imagination does not lend itself to training. On the basis of my experience I disbelieve this utterly. You cannot make silk purses out of sows' ears, but imaginative capacities can be stimulated, their use turned into habits, the habits turned to skills. Unfortunately, imagination can also be stultified by bad training and restricted in scope by narrow training. Habits of generalizing from facts can be developed. Skills can be attained by practice under guidance. Breadth of imagination is possible only to those who one way or another have touched and *can call up from the depths of their minds* those things superficially impertinent which once grasped may be the fundamental pertinences. Failure to bring them into social decisions may end in efforts to reduce the fever without treating the source of infection. Now this unimaginative habit is widespread. For example, a study of any great city at the present time is likely to concentrate heavily on economic and engineering questions, with only back-handed and number-3-on-the-list attention to the fact that the most important problems go back to social disintegration and the breakdown of community living. The economic problems and often the engineering problems, like fever, are largely symptoms. Of course, the fever is part of the disease and may need treatment as well as the fundamental social problems. Sometimes such treatment is an essential first step, but it is disturbing when a start is made by applying the tests and remedies of economics or of engineering while great human problems are ignored. Even when social problems stick out so clearly that they cannot be overlooked, it is too often assumed that the situation can be cured by material or economic remedies. So it is generally assumed that slum rehabilitation can be accomplished by housing projects, with little or no attention to social organization. Yet in one city we found that slum-like disintegration exists in the same kind of houses as those occupied by the well-integrated part of the population. In a shocking percentage of cases the total situation is never even looked at. The imagination can be trained to look beyond the obvious and to some degree at least outside the blinders of ways of thinking customary in one's immediate social environment. What constitutes superficiality?

I may be challenged on my statement as to the relative difficulties of scientific and general training. Of course, if so-called general training is in fact made up of diffuse attacks on the elementary stages of many subjects tempered by some and often too much concentration in one field, if no thought is given to finding relationships among the subjects taken, if no effort is made to relate them to life as men will meet it and no effort is made to develop effective skills or habits in solving novel problems, the challenge is well made. And yet the evidence as to the relative difficulties of the subjects is clear. Men with mathematical minds can and do accomplish outstanding work in their early twenties. Many if not most of the vital advances in the recent revolution in physics were made by men under thirty. Our scientific research institutions have been much disturbed by the apparent decision as I write that young men under twenty-six now engaged in radar research will be called to active service. A distinguished chemist like President Conant, in discussing the organization of scientific research, emphasizes the importance of youth [1] and even suggests periodic liquidation of scientific research organizations to give the fresh point of view of young men a better opportunity. In contrast to this, men who are working in areas where human problems are involved, where uncertainty is the dominant note, and where judgments rather than logics are the goal, almost never reach real

[1] James B. Conant, "Science and Society in the Postwar World," *The Technology Review*, May, 1943.

maturity or do outstanding work either in university life or in the world of affairs before they are thirty-five or forty years of age. Yet, even at that, these men in most cases arbitrarily simplify their work by making assumptions which exclude many problems.

Why is this so? To me it seems clear. Youth loves and is adept at logics. Conversely its knowledge of and acquaintance with concrete facts in their changing complexity are slight. Youth not only lacks acquaintance with facts, but is impatient with the slow process of acquiring experience and wants to get on with its logics. The college abets the young in this attitude by making little of the search for current facts in their full and changing complexity. Easy assumptions give a foundation for logics and make the work done satisfactorily intellectual. Many mature men will testify from conversations with their sons that men in their twenties are keener in their logics than they will be later, as they will also testify that such men are impatient not only of the process of getting experience but with experience itself. Science emphasizes logics and certainties, and its basic experience is acquired largely in the laboratory. Able young scientists, particularly physicists, with their background and training in looking at material facts, skillfully evolve logical theories about such facts and devise experiments to prove or disprove these theories. They pick out of their own or other scientists' experiments facts which existing theories do not account for, and integrate such facts logically with, or modify, existing theories. Frequently they can devise experiments to check these theories which so far as possible exclude all irrelevant facts. The facts studied are relatively few and certain. The logical structure is imposing. The main tool is mathematics. Mathematics is, of course, pure abstraction. Theoretical physics applies mathematics to phenomena which can be isolated and subjected to experimentation In such fields men are free from the constant struggle with disorderly shifting circumstance which is necessary whenever human and social situations, with their uncertain surroundings and their complex emotional content, must be studied; in such fields men are free from the slow processes involved in attaining experience and judgment in life. Since mathematics is the only language we have which can express thought with approximate accuracy, scientists are relatively free from the perils which afflict other thinkers through the inadequacies of ordinary language. As a result, men of apt intellectual equipment can attain important results in these fields early in life. Indeed it is probable that, for many scientists, early successes, by the limitations they impose on the areas and the subject matter explored, prevent equally fresh and imaginative work later in life.

On the other hand, as we get away from abstractions based on assured fact and face the problems of applying intelligence to uncertain and changing human events and characteristics, it becomes more and more difficult to keep a continuing grasp of facts, and both mathematics and logics become less useful. The facts are more numerous and less certain; the logical structure necessarily slight. Experience counts for more, and is hard to get. The college does little to accelerate the process of acquiring such experience. In the social sciences and in the humanities (other than languages), prolonged experience with life and therefore greater age become progressively more important as an essential to distinguished performance. Judgments rather than theories become the true objective. New facts constantly change old judgments. Real maturity is correspondingly delayed. The problem is intensified by the failure of liberal-arts colleges to acquaint students, by directed attention or by responsible study of concrete problems, with the shifting nature of the process involved in social facts and human relations. Teachers prefer to evolve principles, and to this end prefer to fix facts by artificial exclusions and by assumption.

All these things confirm my belief that social fields are more difficult than natural science. This is to be expected, for one field searches out certainties or overwhelming statistical probabilities while the other fields must struggle with uncertainty and change. If this were not true, our general direction would compare more favorably with our scientific accomplishments. Too much should not be expected under such conditions.

CHAPTER XVIII

Training Men to Handle Problems Responsibly

LARGE PARTS of my thesis depend on a change not only in the emphasis but in the objectives of liberal education from training in unrelated specialties to training for an interrelated grasp of things. It involves thinking of general education as having unity. It requires a shift, particularly in all fields where uncertainty and human interactions are dominant, from the search for controlling principles or laws to an approach through problems in their concrete but shifting complexity. It recognizes the importance of changeless law in the material world and the successes of science in describing these laws. But it recognizes also the effect of these material laws in adding to the uncertainty in human environment when men act by using these laws. Science in consequence of its success is brought into direct relationship with social science and with the humanities, both of which must deal with uncertainties and with human problems. Science and its impact on life become essential factors in understanding the behavior of men as they succeed or fail in adapting themselves to their changing environment. But this is only part of the problem. Scientific methods are inapplicable even in studying the consequences of science.

The physician treating a patient seeks aid from pertinent science through the scientific specialist but he is nevertheless dominated in his treatment by his over-all look at the problem which the sick man presents. So the generally educated man approaching life's successive novel problems should be dominated in his thinking and action by an over-all look at the problems he and his society face. To this end he needs the help of specialists whether they be from science, the social sciences, or the humanities. But in the last analysis he must go back to his over-all look if he is to understand his concrete present problem and its implications. Unfortunately, he is himself specialized by his environment. In the largest sense from the point of view of the perfectionist, his problem is therefore insoluble, but from this point of view everything becomes impossible, for life is never perfect.

This does not mean that nothing can be accomplished. The contrary is true. This kind of correlated thinking can be coupled with watchfulness for change in facts and for new facts as they develop. It can combine foresight with efforts to maintain the kind of elasticity in dealing with alternative future developments which gives the maximum of freedom of action in making necessary changes of plan and adjustments when foresight proves mistaken. This kind of judgment and action is the hope of intelligence in an uncertain world. But education to this end must make the student come as close as possible to "the practice of deciding and acting under the burden of the responsibility for the consequences." Of course, one of the assets of training in the university or college lies in the fact that the student can learn by practice without facing the penalties for mistakes which come in practical life. In spite of this freedom to make mistakes painlessly, the great professional schools create a real sense of responsibility for the consequences of decision and action. The liberal arts college can do more in this direction than it now does.

A sense of responsibility in formulating judgments which relate policy to the world around us should be created.

These judgments should take into account both short-time necessities and distant ideals. The sense of responsibility in human affairs inculcated through general education must so far as possible be comparable in strength with the sense of responsibility to the material world so effectively inculcated by science. Because of the greater difficulties, we must be content with lesser results. Nevertheless, a real sense of responsibility and a greatly improved capacity in formulating judgments, coupled with greater tolerance toward mistakes in judgment made by others and less cynicism in imputing motives, seem within our power. The humanities should be drawn on heavily. Men of general education need breadth of background which will illuminate many facets of the long human struggle. Otherwise their imagination will be in chains, not only the chains of inevitable ignorance, but the far more ignominious chains which result from having no sense of direction as to the areas which should be brought into the imaginative process. General education should lead the student to bring into his thinking constantly, and so far as possible on his own initiative, points of view of wide variety and analogies to the past with its likes and differences.

As part of this broad background the student needs as much intimate concrete knowledge of human beings and their individual and social behavior as can in the present state of our knowledge be given to him. In addition, he needs to learn from studying many situations that superficial generalizations about human behavior not based on open-minded study of specific human situations usually deal with symptoms without even recognizing the disease. Human behavior as men adapt themselves to changing environments can be understood only by examining the specific situation with an open and receptive mind. Few broad generalizations are possible and these can be left until he has acquired a sufficient background of experience, so that he develops a beginning at least of skills in understanding human behavior. Even then the generalizations will be more useful as working hypotheses to suggest concrete things for exploration than as conclusions. Nevertheless, skills useful in understanding and handling men which will serve in many situations can be developed. Most important of all, modes of attack on human problems can be demonstrated.

Both in dealing with uncertain human behavior and with the uncertainties inherent in the changing world, he should have much practice in facing facts responsibly for thus only, as I believe, can he acquire the skill which is an essential to imaginative breadth, to insight, and to wise judgments. Breadth of background is not enough. In spite of the fact that the problems he will meet in the future are almost wholly unpredictable in a narrow sense and wholly unpredictable in their complex detail, and indeed because of this fact, much of his education must be focused on the present. He will, in his future, need experience and background, an alert trained imagination, habits and skills which he can use in the present which he then faces. True, we cannot equip him with conclusions which he can use to settle his problems any more than West Point or even the War College could years ago have told General Eisenhower how to invade Europe, or than Annapolis could years ago have told Admiral Nimitz how to clean up the Pacific and reach the coast of China. This does not mean that, because the problems they are now meeting are different from any past situation or from any situation previously assumed, the background, the habits of thought, and the skills which these institutions seek to develop are useless. The only realistic basis for attaining such habits and skills is by practice in studying problems and seeking responsibility to formulate judgments about them. The training will require dealing with many different situations, for only in this way can habits and skills in formulating sound judgments be developed. Specific judgments are at best currently useful rather than as guides to future conduct.

I emphasize the need, therefore, for training in responsible thinking leading to judgments and decisions—what to do about many present problems seen in their generality and factual complexity. But I also emphasize the danger of leading students to form judgments which are based on logical conclusions drawn from specialized abstractions of facts and from assumptions like those dear to the economist, the engineer, or the businessman. I stress the danger of economic and engineering abstractions because of the widespread and false assumption, too frequently shared by businessmen and politicians, that most great problems can be settled by direct application of economic principles or remedies or by technological changes. The facts which students deal with should be selected because they are pertinent to the concrete total situation which is under consideration. Some will be economic, some engineering, but many very important facts will be neither. Businessmen and other men of affairs suffer now not only from their own narrow background but from overreliance on economics and engineering. Almost surely, human factors receive far too little attention from all three groups. The only productive approach to life's problems is to select by the use of intelligence those facts and forces which should be taken into account because they are important for the specific situation. Facts which cannot be known must be considered because they present alternative possibilities. At best the facts selected for examination will be abstracted from the whole situation, and many significant things will be missed or misweighed, but no specialized viewpoint should control the selection. Economic, engineering, and business points of view can illuminate parts of the problem. Breadth of background and trained imagination will still be needed to supply overlooked factors. Then all the facts and forces chosen can be laid under the scalpel. Otherwise many vital facts will be implicitly or explicitly ignored because they are not economic or not engineering or not business; i.e. because Charles F. Dunbar's point of view of looking at all the circumstances does not yet dominate the thinking of economists or engineers or businessmen as they define and approach problems.

Unfortunately, the academic environment tends to insulate men from the facts of human behavior and social life in their concrete and changing complexity. Detached intellectually and practically from everyday life, many are forced to depend on books for their experience. No matter how important books may be, life cannot be reduced to books. Academic human contacts are mainly with men of similar environment. Under such conditions, it is hard to keep one's feet on the ground of shifting everyday fact and uncertain human behavior. This, too, throws the emphasis on logical theories, away from concrete facts and the problems they present. Teachers, like students, enjoy playing with logics.

I feel confident that the college both can and must, if it is to perform its function of general training effectively, adopt methods which break down this isolation, give more opportunity for direct experience, and develop effective supplements to direct experience. Professors cannot imagine direct experience without some start. Once, however, they are at home in a realistic environment through firsthand experience, once they understand how men practicing in a particular field approach problems, teachers can, consistently with their college obligations, keep a concrete grasp of similar situations. For example, a combination of direct contacts, made possible in the summer vacations through a fund for travel expenses, with realistically reported cases brought to the teacher, makes just this possible. Sabbatical leaves can be used in this way. A teacher who from time to time renews his direct contacts and experience can use concrete cases effectively to expand his own and his students' grasp. The fact that he has a direct knowledge of acquaintance with his field will make his teaching more vital and his judgments more assured. It will give him a basis for realistic judgments on novel sets of facts. These things I know from experience. Teachers need direct contacts as the basis for skills which they can use effectively in novel situations involving uncertainty and human behavior. It is hard to convince students that the teacher has a grasp of contemporary problems near at hand unless he can think of himself as acting responsibly in solving them.

There are aspects of this problem which have important implications on the ever vital subject of academic freedom of speech. The arguments for freedom of speech, thought, and research in colleges and universities are final and conclusive. But just as the institutions have a responsibility to protect men in their search for and expression of the truth as they see it, so, too, they and the men on their faculties have a responsibility, not to preserve the status quo—God forbid—but to do their part in preserving the essential moving equilibrium in our democratic society without which the ordered freedom for which we now fight can be so easily lost. Otherwise, we, too, shall turn to some form of totalitarianism as the only alternative to intolerable social chaos. Our form of totalitarianism will, of course, be phrased as an extension of our democratic American way of life, as our recent extensions of government control are phrased. Freedom in universities and colleges untempered by intimate responsible and rounded understanding of present difficulties and problems, by understanding which is based on interrelated consideration of many points of view and on firsthand knowledge of acquaintance with the ways in which problems arise, may be destructive in its influence. Lacking such understanding, our institutions of learning in the coming peace may again develop cynicism and materialism in students as they did in the peace after the first World War, and may again stress shortcuts to social reforms. Clearly, however, this problem is one to be solved by faculties rather than by trustees or overseers, except as trustees can make available the resources for contact with and resulting understanding of immediate social and administrative problems.

Changes in and supplements to the academic environment which bring many faculty men in closer touch with current realities and their complexities are necessary if short-range problems are to secure the intimate attention they require from university men, and if programs of reform based on general ideas and ideals are to be constructive rather than destructive. Nothing should be done to control thought, but just as clearly something should be done to give men attempting to appraise current conditions closer contact with the things they are appraising. Now our universities and colleges furnish scientists adequate laboratories and materials and often adequate resources for research. They furnish historians and humanitarians, libraries, works of art, and museums necessary to the study of the past. Unfortunately, the funds for travel, assistants free from teaching obligations, and secretarial work, which are essential if men are to explore facts currently surrounding them and become habituated to the life they are studying, are almost never forthcoming on the scale necessary to break down the isolation so fatal to realistic understanding of contemporary social situations. Men are forced to rely far too much on published material and far too little on a direct acquaintance. I have observed over many years the growth in balance and judgment which comes when teachers of business administration have support of this nature, and I have observed further that it does not lessen their critical faculties to get in close touch with the difficulties men in public and private life must face. Nevertheless, their criticisms being based on wider understanding of difficulties are rarely cynical. College undergraduates and even many college teachers, as I observed them through the period between the two wars, carried their cynicism far beyond its level in the society around them. I am not disturbed by radicalism in youth. It is often the product of idealism, inexperience, and the natural impatience of youth. Cynicism, on the other hand, is unnatural to youth. Its widespread existence among college men disturbed many observers.

It is on this background, backed up by experience in essentially similar problems, that I urge as at least one approach to the problem, experiments with the case system in substantial parts of the curriculum in general education. I do not mean exclusive reliance on cases. A large amount of reading must be required if students are to get the necessary background in a great variety of fields. But cases both point up problems as they come to the man who must determine policy and act responsibly, and vitalize background material by compelling men to use it. They develop essential habits, skills, and capacity to form judgments on diverse factual situations. They stimulate student initiative.

Originally, at the Harvard Business School, we borrowed the method experimentally from the law school and used it in one course. We hoped that with us, as in the teaching of law, it would stimulate both student initiative and student interest. From the beginning it accomplished these results so satisfactorily that its use spread rapidly. Many adaptations of law-school practice were of course necessary to meet new conditions. There were no court precedents, no opportunities to buy finished cases from law-book sellers as law teachers can. Changes in emphasis were essential. The facts as they are reported in law cases are simplified in several ways to include only facts of legal significance in the particular situation. As the case is printed after decision by the appellate court, two sets of attorneys have excluded facts which seem of great importance to the layman whose interests are involved. The difficult problem of establishing facts essential to the decision is settled by the lower court, by a jury or by agreement of the parties. In the final report of a law case we end up, therefore, not with a realistically reported segment of life as it occurred but with a situation from which everything not pertinent to the specialized viewpoint of the law has been excluded. Essentially the facts included in such a case are comparable with the condition which exists when a social situation is defined and looked at only from the specialized angle of a single social science. For obvious reasons it became apparent that cases so reported would not serve our purposes. Business administrators must, so far as possible, act with reference to all the circumstances surrounding their problems. The business administrator faced by the necessity of deciding and acting in a concrete situation excludes from his consideration at his peril any important facts including unknown or unknowable facts. The analogy of cases in the medical schools displaced the analogy of law cases because the clinical physician like the administrator must face all the facts. Few realistic reports of business problems come into existence naturally. So for our purposes, it was necessary to do our own reporting, to send men out and collect facts. At first, since many of the faculty had been trained as economists, much of the reporting was unrealistic as a result of the natural belief that if the economic facts were reported, they would cover the situation adequately. While this error is unquestionably still made in some instances, we soon became aware that cases so reported are partial and unrealistic. Even now, of course, for pedagogical reasons, we exclude many factors from cases which are collected as the basis of specialized instruction in a single field, for example, in marketing. But when this is done, the instructor is always aware of it and students are reminded frequently that the case as it stands does not give the basis for decisions of general policy—decisions which would of necessity be be based in part on other relevant but unreported material.

As we made progress, two significant things happened. We soon came to realize that most generalizations which we thought of as established principles would not stand the tests imposed by changing facts, while most concepts thought of as established theories would not stand the tests of practice. Out of this experience we came to realize that factual situations realistically reported are more than a basis for improved pedagogy. Far more important, they pointed the way to a definition of our job as a school of administration, oriented of course in the field of business. They gave us a foundation for developing the simple conceptual schemes which have become the intellectual basis of our work. Policy became more important. As we studied our experience, the concept of action became recognized as the core of the administrator's job as it must be faced in life. This focused attention on the present as the time when policy must be determined and action taken. We came to realize that all administrative action is taken through people, and secures its significance through its impact on human beings and their society. From this realization in part, and in part because much of the existing literature in labor relations—the only field where the academic world had done much exploratory work in human relations twenty years ago—showed a lack of direct knowledge of actual problems, the whole subject of human relations gradually assumed its proper place.

For financial reasons most of our case reporting was done

by young graduates of the School on beginners' salaries. These men found the process excellent as part of their education, whether they intended ultimately to go into business or were looking forward to teaching business administration. For this reason we could for limited times get the services of men of ability. Necessarily such men needed considerable supervision from the professors under whom they worked and for whom they were reporting cases. It soon became apparent that the quality of the supervision was improved if the professors had been through the process themselves. In this way and through consulting work on administrative problems the members of the faculty came in direct personal contact with men practicing in their fields. Several results followed from this direct contact. Their teaching became more realistic and satisfactory to students. Because they could conceive themselves in the surroundings of the case with sufficient accuracy without actually visiting the industry, this realistic touch spread to their teaching of cases collected by their assistants. More important, and indeed almost essential to success in handling cases in business administration, these direct contacts gave them assurance in formulating judgments about problems in classroom. They were freed from the feeling that they were amateurs looking on from the outside. Not only their classroom experience but the constantly repeated experience of discovering that they could hold their own in business conferences where business problems were discussed realistically and policy decided, confirmed this. The fence between theory and practice was broken down.

I know from experience that background, habits, and skills important to the administrator can, by this method, be acquired through practice by the teacher and through practice under guidance by competent students. The quality of judgments improves with such practice. In this way imagination can be trained and its scope widened. I know that habits and skills so attained are an effective basis for meeting novel situations posed by changing conditions.

I observe also that many students who are competent in important but relatively narrow fields cannot handle more complex problems which bring in wider ranges of experience and require the integration of superficially contradictory or even actually opposing facts and forces. Many men who would have done well if they had stuck to narrow fields are damaged by being asked persistently to handle work which is beyond their capacity. Too much should not be expected from the poorer men.

It is well understood in business that there is danger in expanding men's responsibilities beyond their capacities. For example, Chester I. Barnard says,

> . . . neither men of weak responsibility nor those of limited capability can endure or carry the burden of many simultaneous obligations of different types. If they are "overloaded," either ability, responsibility, or morality, or all three, will be destroyed. Conversely, a condition of complex morality, great activity, and high responsibility cannot continue without commensurate ability. I do not hesitate to affirm that those whom I believe to be the better and more able executives regard it as a major malefaction to induce or push men of fine character and great sense of responsibility into active positions greatly exceeding their technical capacities. Unless the process can be reversed in time, the result is destruction. In the doubtful cases, which are quite frequent, the risk of such results, I think, is commonly regarded by such executives as among the most important hazards of their decisions.[1]

[1] Chester I. Barnard, *The Functions of the Executive* (Harvard University Press, 1938), p. 272.

In education a stretching process is essential to the best results but if carried too far such a process can only lead to confusion and deterioration. It frequently has the result of making men believe they have capacities which in fact they do not possess and of making them discontented with the things which lie within their power. Such considerations should be taken into account if wise advice is to be given students concerning the direction and even the duration of their academic work, the choice of careers, or of jobs in life. Yet this is too rarely done.

I emphasize the case system because I know that it is well adapted to accomplish the objectives of general education. Moreover, I have never experienced any other method until the very small group seminar is reached which secures similar striking results in student interest and initiative. It is the ideal vehicle for training in relationships because case material drawn from life necessitates consideration of the whole related situation. That is the way of life.

Some evidence as to probable student reaction to the case method can be found in the frequency with which college and technical school graduates in the Business School express regret that their undergraduate work was not presented in this manner, and the contrasts they draw between the initiative and interest aroused by such methods compared with those used in most of their undergraduate work.

One initial handicap to be overcome is the lack of cases to use as teaching material. It costs time and money for supervision, travel, assistants, and secretarial help to get such teaching material. I am convinced, however, that funds could be obtained if the academic world really wanted them and organized to get them. Another and perhaps quite as serious an obstacle arises out of the sense of insecurity which afflicts many teachers when, with their background as specialists, they themselves face the necessity of formulating policy judgments on complex shifting facts. We are frequently told by teachers of business administration, who are unable to establish direct contacts with business because of lack of funds or because of heavy teaching loads, that they find it difficult to use cases. Often their reasons are explicitly stated in terms similar to those I have given. Once, however, this is conquered, teaching becomes more fun. It can be conquered by a combination of direct experience, group effort, and realistic cases as it has been conquered in the experience of the Business School. I used to assume as Dean that it would take a new instructor with a specialized background about three years to make the transition to his own satisfaction and I made deliberate plans to subject such men to a considerable variety of experience. A third obstacle to the use of case material is heavy teaching loads. Preparation for handling case discussion requires much more work than going through last year's lecture notes. The additional work leads to fresh insight and without it the instructor is too often tripped by students.

I have heard fears expressed that the case method would reduce everything to a dead level of uniformity. The exact reverse is true. In our experience the two uniformities which run through instruction by the case method and the only two are, first, the very much greater reliance on discussion in which students take full part, and second, the fact that every discussion starts, as the student knows, from some honestly reported segment of concrete reality which calls for a decision or a judgment. There are no other fixed formulas. Descriptive material and extracts from books showing diverse opinions of experts can be useful as background and as aids in interpreting facts on which the student must make up his own mind. In my judgment they should often be so used and when used the student should be held responsible for them. Teachers experiment constantly with varying modes of presenting material for different purposes and with variations in ways of handling cases in class. Some men always lecture part of each hour to summarize discussion; some never lecture. One former member of our Faculty uses freely texts pertinent to various aspects of coming cases as background required reading in undergraduate work. He is enthusiastic over his results. Some summarize at the end of each section of a course. The cardinal sinner is the teacher who sees things as absolutes. Believing that only one correct judgment is possible, he tries to cram that one down his students' throats. The best teacher is always seeking to evoke currently useful generalizations as well as to develop habits and skills in interpreting facts. Case teaching takes far more varied forms than lectures.

Written work, where men are assigned a case such as might be used in class at that time and are required to formulate and present their judgments about it in writing, is an exceedingly important part of case instruction. It can be, and with us is, used effectively in teaching English.

The case system is radically different from the project method used in the extreme progressive schools and from the use of problems as isolated bits of student research. The emphasis is always on systematic development of a subject, and the choice of things important for study is always the teacher's choice. There is nothing haphazard about it and no possibility of the student's avoiding intellectual discipline and systematic rounded experience under the guise of developing his disassociated ego. It involves group work as life involves group work. Men are encouraged to work together. Nevertheless, because its relationship to concrete reality is explicit and because the student sees the importance of the things he studies, it does result in hard work. Without the risk of making the student think his own interests are the only guide to education, it develops his individual interest and capacities because he sees its clear functional relationship to life.

One of the most interesting facts that has come out of our experience is the discovery that a far larger percentage of men who use the case method are not merely acceptable but good teachers than is true of men who use the lecture method or the quiz system. Whatever may be the case in graduate schools, pedagogy is of high importance in the college. I think it is important everywhere. I believe a wide adoption of the case approach would lead rapidly to greater interest in teaching and to more successful results, as it has in professional training.

Nevertheless, whether or not the case system is used, the vital necessity in any reorganization of general education is men and methods that prevent the repetition year after year to unwilling students of mere disassociated unused facts, inert knowledge, or ideas, and substitute what Whitehead calls "understanding of an insistent present." By some method instruction must tie itself into life and develop the habits and skills required to form imaginative judgments. In so far as we keep constantly in mind this insistence on the present, and lead students always to think in terms of that present which happens to be with us at the moment a subject is being taught and how they would handle its problems, courses cannot go stale from repetition. Last year's lecture notes no longer fit this year's problems. An old problem modified to bring in new facts or a past experience with its similarities and with differences from the present emphasized becomes the foundation for driving home the flux of events with resulting shifts in the balance of judgments. Under such conditions I have observed that teaching ceases to be an unwelcome interlude interrupting "productive" scholarship and becomes a perennially fascinating thing in itself; not a task turning to boredom for both student and teacher because it is stale, but as new as the present.

CHAPTER XIX

Science, Social Science, Human Relations, and the Humanities—Their Interdependence

THE DRIFT of modern higher education toward specialization has long troubled me. This is not because I wish specialized progress to stop, but because inadequate attention has been given to balancing specialized progress by attention to an over-all point of view. President Conant has recently emphasized the mutual dependence, the relationship of symbiosis between different aspects of human knowledge and affairs. Such relationships are needed not only between science, the social sciences, and the humanities, but between specialized and general thinking, between the expert and the policymaker. Too often they do not exist in any effective sense. The roads to the development of mutual dependence do not end in disassociated specialties. Dr. Conant has also emphasized the serious dangers which follow when one aspect of such interdependent situations dominates. To this I agree. Indeed science is now in this dangerous position and society suffers from it. As one result science is seriously threatened. But the relationship of mutual dependence involves not only division of labor and methods appropriate to each field, but complex mutual adjustments. Where these adjustments are the result of a well-developed evolutionary process they have involved eons of trial and error, never consciously planned. President Conant, in emphasizing his point of view, illustrates biological symbiosis, living together, by the lichen.

At the root of the relation between science and society in the post-war world must lie a proper educational concept of the interconnection of our new scientific knowledge and our older humanistic studies. Teachers of the social sciences and the humanities can hardly relate their teaching to the present if they are ignorant of one of the forces which has reshaped our world. Those skilled in the natural sciences and their application, on the other hand, must be educated to understand not only how inanimate materials can be shaped to human usage, but how men and women can work together for the maintenance of a nation that is truly free.

It is not only the false antithesis between science and human values which we must hope to overcome; we must likewise have a clearer understanding of the past relations between economic and political forces and the technological changes of the past century. Not long ago a distinguished philosopher stated that "by and large, the economic changes of recent centuries have been parasitic upon the advances made in natural science." I humbly suggest that he chose the wrong biological metaphor. If we view the history of science in relation to the history of society, we are led to characterize the relation of industry to pure science by the word "symbiosis," which means living together, not by the word "parasitism," which implies a host and a devouring parasite. I trust I am not insulting either your intelligence or your scientific training by reminding you that the common lichens on the rocks afford an example of symbiosis. A colorless plant akin to a fungus lives together with a minute green unicellular organism, an alga. The green plant manufactures the food for both by photosynthesis from the air; the colorless plant lives on this ultimate source of energy, but thanks to its tough tissue, protects and stabilizes the manufacturing unit. Without both you do not have a lichen. Which is more important, the fungus or the unicellular green organism? A meaningless question, if you will. But if you were either an alga or a fungus, you would feel differently about it. And from the implications of this fact arises perhaps the major problem in successfully operating a human order.[1]

Obviously this illustration is a beautiful example of the amazing results accomplished not only in mutual dependence but in mutual adjustment by nature working through limitless time. Unfortunately we are interested in preserving our civilization now. If we are to do this, we have no such time elements within which mutual dependence and mutual adjustments can be worked out. Moreover, no specific answer to our problems will last in face of constant environmental change. The human intellect working in free science introduces vast changes in human surroundings in each generation. We must learn to deal not with one change but with change itself. If the essential symbiosis is to be attained in time to preserve the related parts of the whole situation, the necessary mutual adjustments can only be worked out by continuous conscious coöperative effort involving both scientists and workers in other fields. We cannot wait for the slow processes of evolution with time elements measurable in units of hundreds of thousands of years. We can study the known facts about evolution and sort out the unplanned methods of dealing with change which have worked out to the survival of individuals and species. The question is whether intelligence can shorten the time elements which nature uses in its evolutionary processes. The best chance is by copying nature's successes. Science can help us to read the record.

[1] Address before the New York Academy of Public Education, Feb. 18, 1943.

Right now the relationship between science and the liberal arts, between science and social problems, and between specialized and general thinking are all dangerously one-sided and the adjustments are badly worked out. Our Western civilization is critically unstable. The war has momentarily reversed the trend in this country by its unifying influence, but at heavy cost in strains on our social and political structure. After the war, the restoration of freedom through orderly processes will require our highest capacities. Failure will bring confusion approaching social chaos, and social chaos inevitably brings authoritarian government of some type. If human intelligence can influence human future, now is the time to demonstrate this fact.

The adjustments required for an effective symbiosis of all these fields are left to chance. Most university research is conducted in watertight compartments. Little or no thoughtful attention is paid to the problem of mutual adjustment and few concerted attempts are made to obtain effective coöperation among the great areas of human thought which will better their impact on each other. The men working in each field are at fault.

Science, particularly, has long been in a watertight compartment. Yet free science depends, as clearly as the colorless fungus depends on the green alga for its food, on a persistent social climate in which intellectual freedom is encouraged, free universities provided and lavishly supported, great laboratories furnished both in the universities and by business. Self-supporting careers for many men reasonably free from distracting hazards and insecurity are essential. In return science gives a curious mixture of good and bad: power, useful material things, constant change in environment, widespread social disorganization, and consequent unhappiness. It creates, for men working in nearly all fields which have to do with ordinary men living their lives as social animals, more problems than it solves. It brings material values rather than happy lives. Yet it goes on its way in the universities and in the industrial laboratories heedless of these consequences and, in using its freedom, makes little effort to find out from students of social situations or humanitarians what it might do to alleviate the problems which oppress them. It takes a war to enlist the wholehearted support of science and focus it on socially necessary problems. Yet wars are incubated in peace. It is accepted that we lost the last peace. When this war is over, the problems of peacetime may well be more serious than the problems we now face.

Many scientists are contemptuous of results in other fields —a bad basis for coöperation. Too often they assume that social science also could, if it would, progress by building brick on brick and ask for the use of their methods in other fields. The quicksand of uncertainty in the world of social relationships is forgotten. There is little realization that scientific logics, developed under conditions which allow isolation and control of individual variables, furnish no foundation for social sciences. There is no general understanding of the logical and practical limits within which we must approach deep sentiments and emotions. The failure of science to take into account deep-seated emotions, indeed, its habit of brushing them aside as on a lower level of activity; its failure, in the phrase used by the late L. J. Henderson, to understand the value and importance of nonsense is amazing lack of perspective. The hopes and fears, the joys and sorrows, the things which make life worth living or make it intolerable for human beings, almost all have their roots in sentiments and emotions rather than in the intellect. They never make logical sense. There is no other field so important to study, for there is none so important to understand. Continued intellectual progress in the natural sciences is simplicity itself compared with the complex problem of understanding and controlling wisely the novel social forces, stresses, and strains, loosed on a world of sentiment and emotion by the progress already attained in the sciences.

When scholars and practical men face such difficulties, it is no excuse for science that others are responsible for making good use of knowledge. Rather under such circumstances, it is the responsibility of science to minimize the difficulties it imposes on social science and administration. The direction which increase of knowledge shall take is of first importance, and a large part of that problem of direction is within the control of science. Workers in natural science have almost unlimited fields from which they may choose where to direct their abilities. At best they will add new social stresses, but at best also they may relieve great social problems and simplify the tasks both of students of society and of practical administrators.

The direction of scientific effort in times of peace should not be left to the chance untutored choice of individuals or through industry to the specialized profit opportunities of the moment. If science continues to adopt this attitude, it will almost of necessity bring government control on itself. It is no longer necessary to grope experimentally in complete darkness. Considered scientific objectives can be defined which offer hope of socially constructive progress.

Except for the war we have little or no social direction of effort by scientists. Worse still, industry gives much direction to science through great industrial laboratories. This direction by industry is not toward the conscious attainment of wide social objectives other than the creation of useful things. Its main urge is toward the making of profits. Such commercialization of science disturbs many university scientists. As a consequence, but wholly illogically, they neither consider nor tolerate any direction except their own scientific interests.

My objection to great industrial laboratories does not lie in their inefficiency. They are often peculiarly efficient. It does not lie in limitations on the freedom of thought of their staffs. Industry often leaves great freedom. It does not even lie in the emphasis on practical commercial problems. Much of our progress is the result of profit motives. It lies rather in the exclusive emphasis given the thought of many of our ablest scientists wholly without regard to the great need for social stability.

Scientists have an obligation to society, and to the continuity of the search for knowledge even in their own fields, to make a serious effort to discover and select lines of attack in science which will lessen or help solve social problems. They cannot do this alone. It is part of the coöperative adjustment needed to bring about an effective symbiosis with the social sciences and the humanities. In defining ends they need the help of social scientists and humanists. Thereby they may alleviate rather than increase strains. In the emergency which will follow the war we shall need the same kind of devotion to public service we now have from administrators and scientists alike. This time, however, it can happily be free from concentration on destruction.

Whitehead says that the great ages have been unstable ages, but he recognizes that instability may attain proportions inconsistent with civilization.[2] We now approach that degree of instability. I can agree enthusiastically with him that it is the business of the future to be dangerous, for progress always involves ventures into uncertainty. I distrust security as an ultimate objective and believe its attainment must rest on adventure. I can agree that science equips the future for its task of being dangerous. So far I find no evidence that natural science, by its methodologies or the direc-

[2] *Science and the Modern World* (New York, 1925), p. 299. By permission, The Macmillan Company.

tion of its effort, equips the future for that part of its duty which involves preserving enough social stability and security to make continued civilization possible. If the future be not so equipped and quickly, we may well face a dark age with no monks to carry on the torch of knowledge and no basis for order except force.

Nor is the problem of mutual dependence soluble if science alone helps. I have emphasized the need that scientists take a proper and active part because so much of our social disorganization has roots in science, pure and applied. But the other two fields into which we are accustomed to divide the indivisible field of human activity must share the burden. I add also the neglected field of human relations. So far as social science is concerned, I have discussed some things which seem necessary—rethinking their logical basis, integrating their subject matter into a unity, and transferring the emphasis from theories to facts and from principles to problems. Social science needs both a better understanding of science and closer relations with it in mutual efforts to solve social problems. It needs also a better grasp of human behavior. It needs help from the humanities in defining both its short-time and its long-time objectives and in attaining a better balance between the material, the spiritual, and the aesthetic sides of life. Today social science emphasizes the materialistic side of life in its analyses and in its remedies, almost as exclusively as science emphasizes materialism by its results.

In discussing the humanities, I have emphasized that they should be less aloof from the arena of our national life and environment in the world and take a more explicit interest in relating their work to the critical problems around us. The ability of educated men to aid in the great task of defining and helping to implement practically the ideals, aspirations, and purposes of human life is more important to, and the process of acquiring it would be more interesting for, students than the increased joy of living which comes from training in aesthetic appreciation which can be exercised only from the side lines of the arena. Somehow out of the great arts, the great literatures, and the great religions, many men and many social groups should come closer to a useful purpose in life than they do. I believe the humanities can do much in coöperation with science and social science to offset materialism, the most obvious result of which converts knowledge into gadgets but in so doing destroys the significance of life for many. Education can contribute to a better balance between knowledge and understanding through greater coöperation among its component parts.

To secure an effective and better balanced mutual adjustment in the universities and colleges between the natural sciences, the social sciences, the humanities, and human relations, we need, particularly in our great research universities, social mechanisms for accomplishing these and similar results. Even in the natural sciences, logics rarely work out to progress except through loyalties and sentiments. Because this is so, logics, before they can be effective, require organized social organizations to bridge the gap between logic and sentiments. Mechanisms of coöperation in and out of the universities, once started, might grow organically as common interest among men of diverse specialties became apparent. Proper organization would make contacts natural and lead to mutual understanding of the interdependence of fields. But such coöperation should not become a great undertaking planned in advance as a grand project. Those who are brought together must be held together by common interests, common aims, common interest in concrete problems, and in the long run because they find the association valuable through the exchange of ideas and through mutual aid. It is not enough to say "Here are funds. Let us co-operate." The vital thing is recognition of mutual interest. Mechanisms of coöperation, social organisms, will help disclose mutual interests. In our experience a faculty lunch club so designed that men meet informally in the living room on their way to the dining room is a great aid in bringing about spontaneous collaboration. Such processes would make it natural for men of diverse backgrounds to coöperate in assuming the responsibilities of which I am speaking. If each group attempts to work alone, it will fail as the lichen would fail if the fungus attempted to get along without the green alga. It is only in such ways, so far as I can see, that President Conant's symbiosis can be developed in our universities and colleges. Even such collaboration will not carry the subject matter into undergraduate education and thereby create groups of men who as citizens and as men of affairs have a grasp of the situation. But general education could do so. If we could get such a spirit of coöperation in our universities and colleges, it would help in the reorganization of our educational work and aid us to attain better understanding, in Elton Mayo's phrase, of the Human Problems of an Industrial Civilization.

If I am vague as to the concrete research problems which might be studied in collaboration, it is because few precedents exist. Nevertheless it is incumbent on anyone suggesting the assumption of important responsibilities by others that he offer samples of the categories he has in mind and suggest promising lines of approach to the questions involved. I outline two research areas involving diverse specialties which might assist in solving great social problems and stimulate the interest of thoughtful men in coöperative effort.

First and most important is the study of human behavior. We shall never get all the results we need in this study, but we shall neither attain the necessary emphasis on the subject nor discover sufficiently effective modes of attack except as men in many divisions of human effort, both separately and coöperatively, join their efforts in realistic research. There is no more significant area for work. Unless we can secure a better basis for understanding and for the leadership of men, the chance that human intelligence can do anything important to control the future, even at the level of survival of nations, is slight indeed.

The second example involves, primarily, coöperation between science and the social sciences, though it should be of interest to the humanities because of its impact on our national ways of life.

For many years the growth in numbers and size of great corporations and the constantly increasing percentage of the total industrial production and other business of the country done by such corporations has been a threat to our national stability. Aside from types of business which in the public interest are necessarily monopolies, like railroads and utilities, several factors have brought this about. Large size may be essential. A small steel mill or a small automobile manufacturer is still a very large company. With this qualification, large size is in my opinion generally a handicap in production. Small companies, given adequate resources, can change and adapt themselves faster. Small labor groups are, I believe, typically happier and more efficient than large groups. Overhead costs are much lower, and management is frequently better for its purposes. Big plants, if they do not, in order to get labor, start in cities whose size already presents difficult if not insoluble social problems, inevitably become the nucleuses of large communities. Small plants can be in small towns or cities. Yet in spite of these handicaps, all of which increase production costs, big companies increase in size and number. One reason lies in finance, which is affected by modern technology. More and more investment per worker is required constantly as more and more effective machinery and chemical processes are evolved. We have not found out how to supply capital to small companies on a scale necessary to meet this situation or on terms anything like as favorable as the terms available to even badly managed big companies. A second force is marketing. Our great almost free national market is open only to big companies, for the costs of national distribution are beyond all small companies. Yet in spite of these handicaps a large percentage of the nation's business was, up to the outbreak of the war, done in small units. I believe the prewar situation would have been even more favorable to small companies but for a third fact which is of particular interest to universities and engineering schools because they are directly involved. Scientific and technological research is too expensive to benefit small companies under the present unified attack by universities and engineering schools, by professors doing consulting work, and by industrial laboratories. As a result, progress in applied science and technology tends more and more to become a monopoly of big corporations—far more serious as a threat to small business than any of the aspects of so-called monopoly and monopolistic competition which fill our economic journals and reverberate in Congress and in the courts.

The war intensifies these problems enormously. Inevitably the only way to fight Germany and Japan was to mobilize at once all the big companies which could contribute. On no other basis could the essential volume be quickly attained. Small business has been less successfully mobilized. Many small businesses could not in the nature of things contribute to the war effort. As a result, their financial structure is weaker, their markets in great segments gone, and their organizations, in many cases both management and labor, weakened or dissipated. They are further out of step with scientific progress in comparison with big companies than ever before. Hit hard in their weak spots, they are prevented in a vast number of cases and often, in my judgment, unnecessarily from making what they can best produce. The share of the total business done by them is seriously reduced. The problem of reconstruction is correspondingly difficult.

Here is a problem which affects more than the small entrepreneur. It threatens whole sections which are built up on small business. Its solution requires wisdom in government, state and federal, in the transition back to peace. It deserves the effective attention and aid of big business, financial wisdom, perhaps new financial and marketing agencies. It will require a different attitude on the part of universities and engineering schools and their professors if small business is to be kept in touch with scientific progress. Some socially sound way must be found to place applied science more effectively at the disposition of small companies and to get the universities and engineering schools out of their present position where, without design and without their ever having consciously intended the result, they are, in fact, through a weakness in the functional relationship between science and the social situation, helping to build up big business and tear down small business. The method adopted should not take the form of a Federal W.P.A., nor should it weaken or destroy industrial laboratories. Either of these solutions, in the long run, could hardly fail to injure small business.

And the stakes are high. The question whether we regain some new effective equilibrium after this war under a democratic organization of society, or descend into chaos so complete that the only way out is totalitarian control by government, depends in my belief as much on our ability to preserve, strengthen, and propagate small companies in effective touch with technological progress as it does on any other factor, except our capacity to employ willing workers. An early step toward totalitarianism would almost surely be taking over the big companies and the labor unions. Moreover, I do not believe the employment problem can be solved without a solution of the small business problem.

In the last analysis, my observation of the life around us and of the impact, particularly in the last quarter of a century, of collegiate education on that life leads me to a plea for coöperative effort in our liberal-arts colleges and our universities to break away from the present almost exclusive emphasis on specialties, to see individual and social life as a unity. It is further a plea that these institutions which exist because we believe they are beneficial to man pay more attention to understanding him and his behavior and making his education useful in his struggle with present uncertainty and his unknown future. If these can be established as objectives, our colleges can devise methods and content which will, on the one hand, lessen the dangers of narrowness for specialists who start their specialization in college and, on the other hand and even more important, enable men seeking a general education to get something which may properly be called general. Then there will be some chance of harnessing the forces of practical common sense, wise idealism, and farsighted self-interest in a joint effort to offset the disintegrating effects of specialization and rebuild our national unity through coöperation on a higher level of general direction.

CHAPTER XX

Academic Authority, Leadership, and Responsibility

SOME OF OUR educational leaders, conscious of the flux in social problems and struggling against the inertia of educational institutions, conclude that the necessary adaptations in these institutions can only be accomplished by the direct use of authority, i.e. by changes forced from the top. I do not reach this conclusion.[1] Admittedly, the difficulties are great. Fortunately education is one field involving human beings where experimentation is possible. Can we attain the necessary experimental attitudes?

Regardless of how radical professors may be within their own fields, when it comes to substantial revision of college curricula they are often more influenced by their vested interests than the most conservative businessmen. Indeed, some of the most radical movements going on in American educational institutions before the war were directed at increasing the strength and number of academic vested interests. The college, when its own structure is in question, is one of the most conservative of institutions. Education which should lead tends to follow. That is why the opportunity offered by the weakened vested interests resulting from the war must not be lost. Curricula are now in new and temporary forms, and many courses are discontinued. But it will

[1] For a more general discussion of the place and limitations of authority and the basis for leadership, illustrated from business administration, civilian agencies in Washington and the Army and Navy, see pp. 186–197.

require high-grade leadership by college administrators and the coöperative effort of many faculty members to accomplish the needed reforms. It would be foolish to underestimate the strength of the movement "back to normalcy" which will come in liberal arts colleges after the war. We can expect nothing but disastrous results for general education and from the leadership of educated men if such efforts succeed.

Almost universally in this country the legal control of universities and colleges is in boards of trustees, of which the presidents are usually members. So far as authority is based on law, they are the source of authority. But either by explicit delegation or by controlling custom much of the real authority is vested in the presidents or the deans and even more in the faculties. Trustees properly exercise their authority directly or through the president when budgetary considerations require, when problems arise which are beyond the scope and power of any faculty, or to strengthen the hand of the president without jogging his elbow as he carries out his great responsibility of working with and through his deans and faculties to secure or retain first-rate men in teaching and research groups. Under normal conditions the authority of boards of trustees should rarely be used otherwise. The fact that authority exists is important, particularly if it is used only rarely and with restraint, but in general a board of trustees will contribute more to the institution if its major attention is devoted to aiding the president in building up and using his influence as a coördinating and creative force than it can accomplish by exercising its legal powers. The existence of authority is of importance mainly because it gives a base on which influence can be built. If the board often relies on authority, it inevitably weakens influence by arousing resentment rather than stimulating willing coöperation. Occasionally, however, its exercise is of high importance to the life of the institution. Problems affecting the general structure of a university can only be solved through the decision and action of the trustees. The same applies where for some reason a whole school gets in unsatisfactory condition and must be drastically reorganized. Of course, too, when an old faculty must be discontinued or a new one established, the authority of the board acting through the president must of necessity be used. In all such cases there are grave risks to be weighed unless there is widespread recognition in the university community of the wisdom or necessity of the proposed action. The decision may easily be made with too narrow and partial grasp of the problems involved. Similarly, the general policy and attitude of the institution toward such emergencies as those created by the war or those which will face us in the transition back to peace will of necessity be defined by the president acting under the authority of the board of trustees. Here, too, however, the active participation of the dean or the deans and, through them, a sympathetic and understanding public opinion in the several faculties will be of great importance. In all such emergency problems there is, in my experience, little difficulty in getting men to realize the necessity of decisive administrative action. In most cases, provided human relations are sound, faculty backing can be assumed. Such decisions will be less likely to be acceptable if over a period of time the unwise or unnecessary reliance on authority has built up an atmosphere of suspicion and resentment.

The authority of the president derives in a legal sense from the board of trustees. Just as the board of trustees cannot safely exercise authority except rarely or within narrow ranges fixed by necessity or custom, so the president cannot safely rely on authority delegated by the board which the board could not wisely use itself. Actually in most problems of interest to the faculties, the president's use of authority as such is dangerous if it goes beyond the point where through his abilities, vision, and personal relations, he secures and keeps the support of important faculties over which he presides. These faculties are the heart of the institution. From the very nature of the problems which the institution exists to solve, no lay board of trustees and no president who relies on authority delegated by such a board can often substitute their or his judgment for the judgment of a faculty on its educational and research policies and hope to maintain the virility and prestige of the faculty or to make membership in it continuously attractive to able men.

When it comes to educational problems and processes which are customarily within the scope of particular faculties, the use of authority by boards of trustees or by the president is dangerous, for both involve centralized control by men who are detached from the concrete complexity of the particular problems and who lack the necessary specialized grasp and knowledge. As a result they too easily cause friction and discontent and too often reduce the sense of responsibility and the pride of accomplishment of both the faculty and its dean. The net result is that the president succeeds or fails according to his capacity or lack of capacity for wise educational and human leadership, not according to the extent of his technical authority.

I believe this situation is far more hopeful for the future of American education than a suggestion recently made by President Hutchins and subsequently withdrawn for lack of faculty support. His sound objective was to improve the methods by which universities adjust themselves to changing social conditions. His specific proposal was to "make authority commensurate with responsibility" by electing the president for a short term and giving him power "as long as he retained the confidence of the faculty" to "make educational decisions with the advice of the Faculty. . . . While he held office he could decide and he could take the consequences."[2] Unfortunately, not the president but the institution would take the most significant consequences both of educational errors he might make and of the inevitable human discontent which would result in the society of scholars. The capacity for accomplishment in such a society depends not only on the individual intellectual capacity of its members but on independent initiative and high group morale. These would inevitably suffer. Instead, he should rely on the slower process of securing results through patient attention to human relations, the skilled use of influence he can exercise through his general grasp of university or college problems, the prestige of his position, and his own social and educational vision. Nevertheless, President Hutchins states clearly and forcefully one of the great difficulties confronting universities and colleges when he states explicitly how important it is that any such institution be capable of "rapid and decisive action which will enable the university to remold itself to meet changed conditions. . . . The problem is how to reconcile the necessity for responsible decisions with recognition of the fact that a university is a community of scholars and that the community must move as a community."

The vested interests of particular professors or departments or sometimes even of special faculties cannot be allowed to hamper and control the whole institution as it adjusts itself to changing social and intellectual conditions. Neither good organization nor the possession of authority can create good leadership, but unwise use of authority, confusion of purpose, and unwieldy organization can make it harder to attain and limit its extent. Is there no way to solve

[2] *The Organization and Purpose of the University.* An address by President Robert M. Hutchins, July 20, 1944. Published by the University of Chicago.

this problem except by the president's assuming the handicaps which accompany centralized and overriding authority?

The limitations inherent in authority do not mean that either the trustees or the president can have no influence. Far from it. The road to maximum influence is only occasionally and for short periods coincident with the way of authority. The influence of trustees should be based not on authority but on grasp of community problems and public relations. It should be exercised through the president. The president will have the greatest influence if in each faculty he so handles his personal relations directly and through the dean that he is accepted not for his authority but because through his wisdom, his social vision, and his general grasp of educational problems he, as one member of the faculty, gives important aid in the statement and solution of its problems. He is in the best possible position if he is accepted as a full-fledged member of the faculty team. Except where there is no other way out, authority centralized in the president, as Dr. Hutchins suggested, would be the enemy both of the president's influence and of the faculty's effectiveness.

Since the president's ordinary medium of communication with any faculty in a large institution must of necessity be with and through the dean, he needs as dean in each faculty a man who can combine effectively the functions of loyal but independent thinking and frank assistant to him with that of leader of the faculty. "Yes" men will not do. Neither presidents nor deans should expect to have their way always. Leadership does not mean constant domination. Indeed it suffers from such domination. They should, wherever practicable, avoid raising issues which turn on authority in the minds of the faculties.

Because of the inherent limitations on authority as the mode by which the essential unity of purpose and capacity to act in ways which keep the institution adjusted to change can be attained, human capacity for leadership should be given great weight in choosing presidents and deans. Ability to size up men as individuals and to stimulate their best efforts, the capacity to work coöperatively with others and to secure their enthusiastic coöperation in the joint enterprise even when coöperation involves sacrificing special interests and desires to the larger objectives of the group, are all parts of the leadership capacities which are called for. This kind of leadership in a university or college is harder to attain than similar leadership in most human organizations. When it is attained the results far transcend those which could be brought about through the exercise of authority.

The president must have personal confidence in the man he chooses as dean and must weigh heavily not only the known or expected capacity of the candidate to secure influence with the faculty and to exercise it wisely but his ability and willingness to interpret and reflect faculty attitudes accurately and sympathetically. Intellectual ability and scholarly attainments are not enough. Administrative tenure for deans is objectionable. They should hold office only at the will of the president. He should have the power after discussion with the trustees to remove deans from office as deans and he should be alert to exercise this power whenever in his judgment men are not successful.

Deans will succeed best if they recognize that their effective administrative authority, even in operating matters, comes from the willing consent of their faculties and as a necessary subdivision of work within the faculty team comparable with the specialized job of the teacher rather than through the delegation of authority from either trustees or president. In dealing with the faculty they should operate as if their authority came from the faculty. There is one exception. The dean should be responsible to the president and through him to the board for the careful preparation and carrying out of the budget which should of course be approved by the president and the board. There is no other way in which the president and the dean can meet their practical and educational responsibilities. The dean should have power to make transfers from item to item in the budget as these may be necessary to meet changing conditions. Any other policy, and especially the policy of fixed appropriations placed at the disposition of particular departments within a faculty, hamstrings both administration and education.

In many instances in American higher education the dean is prevented from carrying out effectively his function as assistant to the president or from attaining the position of influence he should have as leader of the faculty because of the existence of powerful departments with formal organizations under chairmen chosen for their prestige. These organized departments combine administrative and educational functions. They meet in what amounts to star-chamber sessions without representation of either the president or the dean. The spokesman and point of contact is the chairman who is almost forced to magnify his own prestige by fighting for the special interests of the department, often as these interests are defined by votes of the department. Separate budgets for departments within the faculty intensify the danger. In each faculty it is the faculty, not a series of semi-independent departmental units, which should possess authority over educational problems. Powerful departments may destroy the ability of the faculty to act effectively. By separating the faculty into groups, they accentuate the evils of specialization. They lead to logrolling for special interests and prevent an over-all look at faculty problems. Thus they weaken the faculty in its most significant functions and emphasize disunity. Necessary departmental administrative work should, in my opinion, be handled by a secretary chosen because he can keep things going smoothly rather than because he is the educational leader of the group. He would of course call conferences of the special group but he would not deal with the president, dean, or faculty as official spokesman for a unit in the faculty. When important differences of opinion developed, these should be brought up with the dean or faculty as differences of opinion, not as something settled because the department had voted on it. As I have said elsewhere, the way to strengthen the faculty and its leadership and make it more efficient lies in part through weakening the organized coherence of departments.

Standing faculty committees with administrative functions are also devices leading to administrative delays and futility. Moreover, they consume a vast amount of time and energies of teachers and research professors which would be better spent on their regular work. It is a serious matter when scholarly activities are interfered with in this way. Yet it frequently happens.

I distinguish clearly *ad hoc* committees for the study of educational problems. These are a necessary condition to the effective working of the team. They should be appointed by the president with the advice of the dean with a view to carrying weight with the faculty. They should be dissolved when their tasks are completed. The dean should be chairman of specially significant committees of this nature. Detailed arrangements will vary with the size and complexity of faculties. There will be a general agreement as to the necessity for considered but firm decisions culminating in action, and for changes in methods to meet changed conditions. This necessity is as clear in educational institutions as it is in the community which the institutions serve.

Inevitably, securing new funds is one of the important necessities of privately supported institutions. This function should so far as possible, in my judgment, be decentralized. Some degree of control is obviously needed to prevent willing horses from being ridden to death through appeals from varied directions. It is surprising how the same names show up on everybody's lists. Nevertheless, since a university or college when it raises money is selling satisfaction and the chance for social service to men whose imagination has been aroused to the importance of particular opportunities, the necessary stimulus to imagination and the satisfaction earned by a donor can rarely be given except by those who are themselves vitally interested. Boards of trustees, presidents, deans, and professors all have opportunities which are unique because their positions and interests are unique. Any process which centralizes the money-raising function and prevents realization of these opportunities by anyone except the group which is given authority is intrinsically objectionable because it arouses a sense of frustration. It is costly to the institution. The necessary controls should therefore be kept at a minimum and the machinery should function both rapidly and sympathetically. The losses will otherwise far outrun any gains. But skilled advice and aid should be available.

The president will secure a large part of his leadership because he is better situated to see the educational problems and public relations of the institution in perspective. So the dean of a faculty will owe much to the fact that by the nature of his position he is best situated to see in perspective the problems of the particular faculty. Because they see things in perspective, the president and the dean will stimulate many but not all educational innovations needed to keep the faculties adapted to new social surroundings. To keep this perspective, however, they must keep close touch with the changing community situation within which the faculty must operate. The dean must also understand the student body and the special problems of graduates of his division of the university. This is often thought of as his major function. I dissent. It is more important that he develop close personal relations with many members of his faculty and understand not only their difficulties and limitations, but their hopes, aspirations, and personal qualities. By so doing he can add to their achievements.

Large numbers and confusion of purpose are both handicaps to the administrative and educational efficiency of a faculty. These can often be avoided in part by adequate administrative assistance to the dean so that he can delegate part of his functions and selectively control his own time and its use. The dean's job in a faculty of size and importance should be a full-time job if he is to have a real chance to develop and exercise the requisite leadership. He will almost necessarily accept serious limitations on the work he can do in his former specialty. Regular teaching or research by the dean both use time needed for imaginative administrative leadership and give a one-sided slant to his thinking which diverts attention from over-all problems. In compensation he may have the satisfaction of helping the members of the faculty by improving their facilities for work and by serving them. Prohibitive size and confusion of purpose in individual faculties can in many cases be avoided by separating the college faculty from all graduate faculties including the graduate school of arts and sciences.[3] The difficulties faced by the president and the dean in developing the highest type of leadership of which they are capable will be greatly reduced.

The realistic view is that the authority of a leader can never be commensurate with his responsibility. Indeed, the true responsibility can almost never be met by the use of authority. The exceptions are not in universities and colleges.

[3] Cf. p. 50 and pp. 303–304. See also Chapter IV.

The most important task of the board of trustees as it faces the choice of a new president is to find a man whose native abilities, experience, human understanding, and social vision will enable them and him to acquire and exercise leadership commensurate with their and his responsibilities. If final authority were delegated to the president, this fact would surely make the type of leadership and influence which makes a president great almost if not quite impossible to attain. It is a sound development in the life of university and college faculties that president and deans have only one vote each.

In all types of organization, wise human leadership accomplishes more than authority. In an academic community with the high rating it gives to independence, freedom, and originality and with the great range of specialties represented, the difficulties of securing the essential leadership are great but reliance on authority is even more of a handicap than it is in most other groups. An elastic tradition, readily adapting itself to different circumstances and different personal qualities, is a better guide to the distribution of authority than tidy legalistic definitions. In colleges and universities not the authority but the leadership of the president must be commensurate with responsibility.

CHAPTER XXI

Is General Education Possible?

AM I SETTING UP impossible ideals of general education? Of course all educational ideals are unattainable, and by this test all education fails. But within human limits I do not believe the task is impossible. Except within certain professional schools which occupy extensive fields, integrated general education has had little trial since the world became so complex and changeable and since the intellectual world became so highly differentiated into specialties. If I approach being right in appraising the present state of general education in the liberal-arts college and its potential importance, it is clear that such education should become a real center of experimentation directed toward attaining more effective results with students and of research directed toward relating such education more specifically to the constantly changing problems of the modern world. Many false starts are inevitable. We need a nice balance between the instruction necessary as background and the use of this background as part of the basis for judgments.

The problems faced by educated men in efforts to contribute to better general direction of our body politic or even of their private lives have much basic similarity in spite of great differences in environment. Physicians, public and private administrators, and statesmen all face problems of similar nature and similar intricacy. All are subject to the same logical limitations and face the same logical difficulties. All must seek constantly to draw effective conclusions from insufficient and shifting premises. All, if they know what they are about, must when they act do the best thing they can under all the circumstances. Many things are for all unknown and often unknowable. Each is forced to prophesy constantly in a fog of uncertainty and change. The impact of science with its certain premises and uncertain processes varies from one to another, but affects each. All must deal with situations containing a large measure of human and emotional elements. In general, certainty appears only when discretion disappears. Common sense judgments about men and shifting facts are primary objectives. Breadth of background and experience and skills in interpreting relationships are the necessary foundation for such judgments. Yet in spite of the difficulties and limitations many men succeed in accomplishing outstanding results.

Nevertheless there is great unevenness in the results attained in different orientations where men of equal ability work. Perhaps medicine is most successful. In spite of the fact that the best of them realize they can never know more than a minute fraction of what there is to know about the human body, many able physicians attain great skill in general diagnosis and treatment. A larger proportion of men of medicine seem to be intelligently successful in using a diversified background than is the case in any other field of similar breadth and complexity. We know that many businessmen acquire great competence in using their experience, particularly their technological experience. But we know that many such men are seriously limited by the narrowness of that experience. The same statements apply to public administrators, and we know that real statesmen are rare. Again we know that one important factor which prevents most public administrators in positions of great moment from doing a job wisely and which stands in the way of their becoming statesmen is the narrowness of their experience and background. Yet all these occupations, like medicine, have been preferred occupations which attracted a large proportion of our ablest youth. Why then are the results so strikingly different?

One reason is obvious. Science causes few diseases and cures many. The basic assumptions of science work within very wide ranges of medicine. The general impact of science on medicine is therefore favorable. By comparison, in its impact on industry it has mixed results. It makes great direct contributions to the national life, but, at the same time through its indirect social impact, it brings social disorganization comparable with diseases more often than it alleviates social disorder. This is an important difference. As a result, with few if any logical differences in the relation of science to the different fields where men work, science is apt to complicate all social problems while typically it aids medicine. The difficulties of making progress in the world of affairs are correspondingly greater. Again the contrast between the parts of human experience where practical certainty is attainable and the parts where uncertainty is controlling become important.

But there is another significant contrast which bears directly on the college problem. The effectiveness of education varies greatly from field to field, though the problems faced by clinical physicians, administrators, and public leaders have many similarities. Medicine is taught in great schools where many on the clinical faculties are in active practice and in hospitals. During the basic course, general medicine has not been sacrificed to specialized science. The objective of instruction is to train men to take all aspects of the case into consideration. This is true, in general, even though the medical schools often neglect to think of the human being as a whole, only part of which is on the hospital bed, and though men who enter medical specialties after graduation may never get experience in understanding human relations equal to that which their predecessors got through general practice.

The best medical schools do the most finished job of training which is done in the whole field of education. It is general education with a very broad base. Its feet are on the ground of fact. Its theories and generalizations are drawn from and constantly checked with facts. It can bring together the student and the patient on a cot. The habits and skills it succeeds in imparting, the ability it develops in able youth to cut through the complex maze of material which must be appraised, and to marshal those things which bear on the particular case are the envy of all thoughtful educators. Even the less able graduates attain a real capacity to do this.

Education in business administration, a field of similar complexity and generality, started a century after medical education. It is relatively handicapped because it can never bring a business into the classroom, but by bringing teachers into direct contact with business and by emphasizing problems and cases drawn realistically from life it can do much to simulate direct contact for the student. Professional education for business administration, like medical education, is developing its own conceptual schemes clustering around administrative problems and its own methodologies clustering around training men to formulate responsible judgments designed to eventuate in action. It must, if it is to succeed properly, avoid the danger of thinking of business as an aggregation of disassociated specialties, and keep a large and interrelated view of its function. It needs to give more explicit attention to problems of foresight, elasticity, and adjustment, and to human problems. It must stimulate imagination and train men to bring many diverse social factors effectively into business decisions. It must constantly fight the narrowness of the immediate moment. It takes time to find ways of doing these things. Nevertheless, while it still suffers in many respects from the defects of youth, as training in any new field must, it has already demonstrated that it can develop in its students habits and skills in formulating business judgments which are comparable in nature with the habits and skills of medical students.

Since change is a constant in human affairs, habits and skills in formulating judgments are stressed in medical and business education. The scientific laboratory effectively develops the habits and skills necessary for the scientist's work. Why not equal attention to the habits and skills needed as a basis for judgments about other human affairs? Such habits and skills can be acquired only by doing over and over again, not by accumulating inert knowledge through lectures and reading. To be the basis for understanding, knowledge must be used actively. It is not necessary to explore all problems to acquire habits and skills. The selection of subject matter and its reselection, as the significance of facts used as the basis for practice changes, is an imaginative task which faces the teacher not once but constantly. So far as possible, factual information should be acquired by the student as an incident to intellectual processes and responsible judgments, because the student wishes to use it for his own well-understood purposes, rather than as disassociated information. The world is too full of a number of things to make the uncoordinated accumulation of facts, most of which will change either actually or in their current significance, a proper primary objective of education. Yet factual knowledge will be an important and lasting by-product of training designed to give skill in handling facts in their relationships. By contrast with medical education, training for public administration was even later in starting and lags behind training for private administration. As for training in statesmanship, there is none so far as I know which really fits the need.

Certainly there is little evidence of human understanding in those who deal with international affairs, and there is a great lack of it even in domestic affairs.

The professional schools have typically had a breadth of viewpoint within their fields which liberal-arts general education lacks. A good deal of successful experience exists in such schools directed at giving students an over-all and related grasp of large areas of human experience. It is a curious phenomenon that methods and approaches widely successful in professional training have had so little influence on the college. This is the more remarkable since the logical problems of training in clinical medicine, as of training for all fields of administration, are essentially identical with the logics of general education.

Education in all these fields suffers from the lack of good general training in the colleges. They are the only places where it is possible to survey the problems from a base line of sufficient length. Special professional training could go further if it could assume a good background of general training in college.

Any experiment directed toward the improvement of general education in a liberal-arts college must start with the present human organization of the college faculty, its assets and limitations. The principal handicaps will come not only from the narrow specialization of nearly all courses customarily offered, but from the narrow training and specialized interests of nearly all teachers. Any effort to bring out the relationships among subjects studied will require substantial modification of courses, methods, and teacher attitudes, inevitably a slow process. Very few men on the ordinary faculty are equipped by their academic training to deal with such relationships. College teachers, whose primary job should be to contribute to general education, attain their professorial appointments almost exclusively because they have tackled some narrow field intelligently. To some extent the small college faculty is better equipped for general education than the university college group. Fewer courses are offered and fewer men are available to offer them. Each therefore has to broaden the scope of his work. The result is less atomistic. Pedagogy receives more attention because the pressures for research and publication are less in the nature of categorical imperatives than they have come to be in many universities, and contacts with students are closer. I suspect, moreover, that the closer personal relations of faculty men in many small colleges produce a larger fraction of men with broad points of view and less interest in becoming authorities in narrow fields than is true in the central university faculties which place strong emphasis on research and publication. I believe there are more men relatively in the small colleges whose primary interest is in teaching rather than research than there are in many similar university faculties.

Teaching is emphasized now in universities which mainly stress their undergraduate work. It would be given more weight in the universities which stress their graduate schools if they set up independent college faculties whose primary job was undergraduate education rather than the training of specialists and research and the writing of books in special fields. Indeed I doubt whether any university college associated with a great graduate school can make the necessary adjustments unless it is reorganized with an independent and responsible faculty under its own dean whose sole objective is the college. Certainly this will be true unless the graduate schools develop powerful departments whose field is general education, including human individual and social behavior, departments whose doctoral degrees are based on constantly widening the scope of things studied in relationship rather than on narrower and narrower specialization as men progress. For candidates for such doctorates, secondary material would generally be more useful than primary sources. It would be no part of their objective to do research in narrow fields. Chicago's new field of social studies is a step in the right direction.

I do not suggest that the universities should stop their efforts to deepen our knowledge of special fields through research. Obviously research should continue and expand. It will contribute much to general education, as well as to the college function of starting the training of specialists. It is not in itself, however, general education, nor does it in any field now blocked out train the kind of teacher needed as the foundation for the general education curriculum.

In urging a separate independent faculty for university colleges associated with powerful graduate schools of liberal arts, I do not mean that men whose main interest is in graduate work should be prevented from teaching in the college or belonging to the college faculty if they teach there. But I would have them function as college faculty men and not as emissaries of the graduate school. The college faculty should be made up mainly but not exclusively of men interested primarily in the college. The college faculty should have the responsibility of defining its dual objectives in general education and in starting men on specialties. It should differentiate and develop courses and pedagogical methods adapted to each objective, and arrange its own dual curricula. In its curriculum of general education it should free itself from controlling tradition arising out of specialization. I would let it settle what general education it would require as a preliminary to all specialization and in all four years, and how it would integrate the program of each student into effective unity. I would let it work out its own restricted electives and the methods of relating those electives to the required subjects. General education is not accomplished in either two or four years by aggregating bits of specialized studies any more than a successful football team is eleven individuals. Each member of the team must combine specialized training with a grasp of the whole play. For college graduates who take a general education, detailed specialization should come later either through professional training or in life. In its function of starting the training of specialists, I would leave it to the college faculty to find the most effective balance between required general education and specialization. I would have only one prohibition—that is against organized departments. I believe the college would gain immensely. Small independent colleges could do these things.

Group action as well as wise leadership is a necessary condition to such a change. Speaking generally, no one individual in a well-organized college can break new ground except in his own field. Each specialty tends to be approached by courses organized in a standardized succession of steps. Sometimes these steps have a logical foundation. More often, however, they have little more basis than custom, the intellectual hierarchy established by textbooks designed to fit these customs, or the desire of specialists to train specialists. Unfortunately, both the customs and the successions of textbooks have taken their present form as a resultant of forces all working against general education. Perhaps the most important element is pure historic accident. The hierarchies of courses in many specialized subjects are arranged as they are because they were arranged that way. When a basis either in logic or chronology exists it usually results from an analysis of the specialized subject to meet the needs of specialists rather than of students seeking general education. The specialist authors thought of their books as steps toward specialization rather than as steps toward the kind of understanding needed by the generally trained men. The publishers of new textbooks generally wish books which fit competitively into the established customs of colleges. Imaginative rearrangements within a particular specialized subdivision of a major subject customarily taught in a fixed order are a business asset to a textbook, but an unusual approach to a large field requiring a rearrangement of several courses taught in the field meets sales resistance because it forces teachers to scrap old divisions of labor and take on the arduous task of rethinking and reorganizing. Usually this process involves the coöperation of several teachers.

I know it will be said that research on the border lines where subjects are advancing is essential to effective teaching. At the level of specialized graduate students this may well be true, but the job of starting youth at the college level toward those adventures in understanding which constitute general education requires a different type of research. It requires research and experimentation in teaching material and pedagogy directed toward vitalizing subject matter so that it is recognized as exciting and important by the student —as something in which he can participate by use, which contributes to effectiveness in life. There are few gaps in our understanding more serious than our inability through general education to make the experience of the race live effectively in the present and to inculcate habits and skills which will make it live effectively for our students in their future. What we don't know about bringing youth to a useful general understanding is almost all there is to know. This gap will not be bridged until many able men see its importance as a field for research. It is an open field offering great satisfaction. The university in the nature of things preëmpts the research job of advancing knowledge in specialties. The college has an opportunity to make its own the research job of stimulating young men and women to a more effective understanding of life present and past. Thus it can give them a better equipment for responsible living.

There is no danger that men attacking this problem of general education will be afflicted with dry rot oftener than specialists who are doing research in their several fields. Nor will men of poorer quality gravitate into such tasks because of their simplicity. The intellectual and pedagogical problems involved present great difficulties.

I have seen a faculty go through just such a transformation in point of view, and as the process developed I have seen the interest in work and teaching increase in man after man. I have seen student interest and initiative grow as faculty interest grew. Student interest reached a high peak even in the earlier stages of this change when in many aspects of their work both faculty and students were breaking into new but obviously fertile ground. I observed that the transformation was difficult for some of the older men but that the young men attacked the new problems with avidity. It took about eight years to break the backbone of the problem, but much of this time was spent in working out a sense of direction and in discovering ways of training men to handle problems. I have seen specialists join such a faculty after the transition was well under way and observed that it took about three years for them to make the necessary adaptation. I am confident that a college faculty can make the same kind of change and enjoy doing it. It will require not only wise and skilled administration but real faculty interest to get the process started and to carry it through early days of trial and error. If we can work out effective general education at the college level, we may by so doing find a way to keep our whole adult education movement, clearly an important educational development, out of the slough of despond of narrow vocational training into which it is so rapidly falling.

Some such process as I advocate is, I believe, essential

if the liberal-arts colleges of a democratic country are to take the critically needed part which is open to them in the national life.

We were deeply disturbed when Germany after a long period of educational leadership converted her education into a mechanism used by the State to cement its control over the thought and behavior of her people, and skillfully related educational methods to this objective of concentrating all control and all major policies in a small group. Force as well as subtle forces of leadership, youth movements and the like, were used as well as education. Responsibility for action and for the judgments on which it was based became highly centralized. We can observe in contemporary history both the strength and the weakness of the process. Even where it succeeds temporarily we know from history the insidious and destructive effects on the leaders which so frequently follow the possession of arbitrary power and the difficulties involved in succession.

Our problem is the exact reverse. The very emphasis we put on individual freedom and initiative requires a widespread sense of responsibility in the use of freedom. This must rest on an effective capacity for and habit of coöperative effort rather than on the habit of obedience to fiat. Force is inconsistent with freedom and therefore under our conditions properly used only against the anti-social. To make our system work, many men must possess trained and skilled capacity to formulate socially sound judgments and to bring about coöperation in carrying them into effect. In our colleges we take pride when we develop the individuality of students and free them to think as they will. Have we in other respects related our methods and objectives to the basic needs of democracy and the necessity for coöperation as skillfully as the Nazis have related their education to totalitarian objectives?

Seventy-five years ago it looked as though liberal democracy would dominate the Western world. Today liberal democracy has almost disappeared in Europe. Before the war it was in retreat and government activities were increasing in both England and America. In the nature of things total war necessarily turned this retreat into a much greater acceptance of unprecedented government control. It is doubtful how far we can regain lost ground and reverse the old trend radically in the peace which will follow victory. After a more or less complete withdrawal of wartime controls we might easily resume the trend which has for years in all parts of the world expanded the power of the state and curtailed the freedom and initiative of the individual. The last seventy-five years have been characterized by the explosive changes generated by science. It is also the period where our universities, colleges, and engineering schools made their most spectacular growth. Is there any connection between our drift toward totalitarianism, the weakness of democratic loyalties and ideals, and the kinds of education given our selected youth in these institutions? I believe there is. In emphasizing freedom of thought we have neglected the responsibility of free men. In stressing the intellect we have ignored human behavior and coöperation and the habits, skills, and background necessary to effective judgments. Yet these are as important to an orderly free society as unquestioning obedience is to a totalitarian society. They are far more difficult to accomplish. Certainly we shall not do a more effective job without appropriate and systematic help from education. The success of science both intensifies the problem and accentuates the risks of continued failure. Neither individually nor socially are men well prepared to do those things which are necessary to strengthen or even preserve our democracy. This is the challenge to the colleges: if we do not learn to live responsibly we shall not live at all.